The Congregation
of
The Dead

A novel

By

Richard Cox

ISBN: 1-4107-3743-8 (Electronic)
ISBN: 1-4107-4295-4 (Paperback)

This book is printed on acid free paper.

1stBooks – rev. 04/14/03

To my wife Latonya Cox
and my children
Bud, Ladonna, and Rachael
With all my love!

Prologue

"Mail's in, Bud," said Gynna, as she handed him a large padded manila envelope sloppily marked for Fourth Class Book Rate.

Bud looked curiously at the return address.

"Good...good...I've been expecting this. I hope it is accurate. A lot of people spent a lot of time getting this story out." He opened the envelope, and removed the book. It was brand new, fresh off the press. He opened it, and glanced at the title page:

The Congregation of the Dead

By

Richard Cox

He smiled dryly, and began to read:

Everybody for miles around called Raymond Politnitroff *Grampy*.
Few people in or around Nohartinit knew his real first name, and
only a handful knew his full name. He had been known as Grampy for
so long, some of the younger people of Nohartinit sometimes wondered
if he even had another name.

Although he was not especially old, just touching fifty when his only
grandson was born, people started calling him Grampy, and now,
twenty-four years later, the nickname still stuck. It stuck among his
friends, his business associates, and his colleagues...everybody.

In the beginning, back in the days when he was in private practice
as a psychologist, the nickname made him feel good, but as the years
rolled by and he knew it was going to stick for the duration his feelings
for the nickname shifted from good to acceptance.

Now, at seventy-four, Grampy seemed to fit and fit all too well; with
his saggy jowls, his thin gray hair, his bony-looking frame and the slight
tremor in his movements, he fit the part. Continual aches and pains
affirmed the appropriateness of the tag. He had consoled himself in
time, reminding himself that they could have called him *Grumpy*, so
Grampy it was.

This day Grampy Politnitroff, former psychologist and now a
retired philosophy professor, and the old man's grandson, Richard,
were fishing from a skiff on a tree-rimmed lake. Grampy had lived by
the lake for many years. The lake was twenty miles outside of
Nohartinit, a small city that most folks referred to simply as the town.
This day he wore a gauze patch over a huge scar on his right forearm, a
scar the grandson understood to be a war wound; it protected the skin
from the sun. He didn't need that nasty-looking thing sunburned on top
of all his other aches and pains.

Nohartinit was a city with a poorly diversified economic base, a
hack school they called a university, and a high employment rate, but
very little in the way of prosperity. A chemical plant in the center of

town kept most of the townspeople employed. Few, if any, of the other legitimate businesses could survive without the chemical plant's payroll continually pumping money into the local economy. Few people in Nohartinit made enough money to do much more than get by from day to day or support their habits; they often had to choose between the two.

The citizens of Nohartinit pretended to be, for the most part, content. Nohartinit was not unlike any other stagnant, go-nowhere city; it had a fair share of old buildings and a couple of newer ones, meaning less than twenty years old. It had a low-rent district and it had a few middle class clusters of cheap and weatherworn modular homes that few could afford to rent or own. It had liquor stores, a pawnshop, two well-known crack houses and a fag bar tucked away in the boiler room of an old building on the backside of Main Street. It had a small hospital, which was, in reality, a three-day-a-week clinic. A rail line bisected the town. It linked up with the chemical plant. It was not unusual to have what seemed like a mile of ugly black tanker cars lined up through town, stretching, it seemed, literally, from one end of town to the other.

The University, however, was the pride and joy of the community having been a central feature on the landscape for decades. The University was Nohartinit's claim to fame, such as it was. It was, in actuality, just a six-room outreach and distance-learning center with a few post-graduate classes available, but nobody cared any more. They called it a 'University' because the word sounded impressive. In reality, it was not even a full-time operation, but nobody cared. It had degenerated from a legitimate college over the years from lack of interest.

The town, as they called it, was large enough if one listened to police and fire scanners they would probably not sleep too well at night. Most people were content to live without discussing the true nature of their town. They chose not to advertise that drugs were freely available, that whores, male and female, peddled their wares in the downtown area, that spousal and child abuse calls were becoming more and more frequent, that gang wannabes were roaming the streets after dark, and that kids were running wild.

There had been only two out-of-the-ordinary events in recent months of sufficient interest to keep people reading the local paper; there had been a nasty single car crash out by the Interstate that killed one of Nohartinit's least prominent citizens and someone stole a case of dynamite and some blasting caps from a construction site ten miles out of town.

Generally the big news in Nohartinit involved nothing but divorces, funerals and occasionally, drunken brawls. The lowlife stuff, the real stuff, seldom got into print.

But most people of Nohartinit did not want to advertise the real side of town. To them Nohartinit was simply a place to live. In reality it was an ugly, unplanned, nasty place...dusty, dirty, noisy, smelly, and given freely to every vice known to man. It had grown up around the chemical plant, but had been founded around saloons and brothels.

The most well known denizen was not the Mayor, who took up a lot of newspaper space, but an unaffiliated, persistent preacher who called himself Father. He used the title because it seemed to work in gaining people's confidence and trust. Father Wyman made it a habit to mingle with the people; he knew just about every man, woman, or child in Nohartinit who resided, by choice or happenstance, in the city's underworld.

He had no church building, although he had twice established the church in buildings in Nohartinit, and both times they had been burned to the ground. He simply changed his methods and kept such a high profile those days that he figured he was reasonably un-attackable, taking his church to the people. Only two other people in Nohartinit preached and they had a tiny building, a very small congregation; Pastors Link and Grayborn evidently posed no real threat to anyone and had been left unmolested for several years now.

Father Wyman was a huge man, gruff-sounding, but affable. He knew the real town as few other people did, and he was one of the few who acknowledged Nohartinit for what it really was...a grimy, smelly, sinful, nowhere spot in the larger order of things...the perfect home for his ever-expanding nomadic congregation of weak, spiritless meanderers.

Father Wyman knew in his bones that someday fire would rain from the sky and cleanse the town. He knew the demographics, and he knew from them Nohartinit was on borrowed time. Against all his instincts, he kept going, fighting the losing battle for souls, and he was getting tired...very tired. He knew, in his heart, the only real hope for Nohartinit's people was Divine intervention.

For all most people chose to know about their town it was a quiet, prosperous, university town with a bright future, all of which was untrue. They were content to live with the illusions. Father Wyman preferred the truth, and the truth was Nohartinit was poor in spirit, and the people, as a rule, were poor in every other way as well.

Father Wyman faced his people day in and day out, hoping someday things might turn around. There were more broken homes than traditional homes, marriage was almost unheard of any more, and birthing, inside the bonds of marriage, was a rare exception rather than the rule.

Alcoholism and drug addiction was commonplace. Sexually immoral or amoral activities were also commonplace, along with Syphilis, Gonorrhea, and genital Herpes. Father Wyman was one of the few in town who knew AIDS was festering among the back street whores, and the disease had already claimed a few students at the High School and one at the Junior High School. It did not shock him to find these diseases in Nohartinit, for he knew the city's people had, from several generations back, lost contact with standards for right conduct. At best guess he expected to see AIDS take a few dozen more lives in the next year or so.

Some people thought of Nohartinit as a safe place to live, but that was because they went to work, went home, locked their doors, and shut out things surrounding them. But Father Wyman knew what went on behind some of those closed doors, and at times it sickened him. He had never, in all his years, come to terms with wife beating, incest, adultery, mate swapping or homosexuality. Of late, he was considering giving up the fight to save Nohartinit, surrendering to the hopelessness of his mission.

There were times he gave serious thought to moving out by the lake and leaving the dismal city twenty long miles behind him. He did not envy Grampy, an old friend, but at times he acknowledged the wisdom of his decision to move away.

True, Nohartinit had not had a major crime in many years, not since a Madam had been murdered in her place of business on Third Street in by-gone days. But this was about to change.

For the Politnitroff men, things were about to change, too. Their quiet and peaceful lives were about to flip-flop, and they were on the brink of being roped into an unprecedented manhunt, spearheaded by, of all people, Grampy's long time friend and colleague, Professor Alexsandr Simon, Ph.D., retired.

The Politnitroff men dressed alike in gray trousers with cotton shirts. They wore khaki fishing hats, stuck through with fishing flies. In many ways, from a distance, one might think the one was a clone of the other. Up close, the blood relationship was unmistakable, but there the physical resemblances ended. The grandson had, however, inherited the grandfather's probing curiosity. And from time to time they loved to spar with one another on many sophisticated issues. This day, however, the grandson was searching not for banter but for truth.

They were tossing around ideas. It was a fine spring day, a good day for relaxing the body, warming the soul, and chewing the fat. Not a single fish had been taken, and they had been out for several hours. But they were like friends, and the fishing, in fact, was incidental to having time to spend together.

Richard Politnitroff, the grandson, was a graduate student taking a few days off from classes to work on his thesis. He was twenty-four years old. He was single, and seeing no one. He had shiny blue eyes, penetrating eyes, which sparkled in ways there was no way to mistake the lively mind inside the skull. Richard had smooth skin, high cheekbones, thin brownish hair, which shown as if strung with strands of gold under the high noon sun. He had a stubborn chin and jaw, thin lips, which were accented by perfect white teeth. He had inherited Grampy's propensity toward thinness.

The lake, this day, was calm underneath a quieting blue and clear sky. An occasional puff of wind rocked the branches of surrounding pines and broke the silence of an otherwise placid picture-like outing. An occasional bird fluttered now and then. Water gently lapped against the bow of the skiff. The only sounds otherwise, were the voices of the two men and the occasional splash of their fishing lines when they reset them. The skiff was old but well tended over the years. It was freshly painted, so it would be ready for yet another summer's use. For many years now the two men had been fishing buddies.

"What is good?" the old man said, repeating verbatim his grandson's question. "In my prime, I might have had an answer, Richard. But with each passing year, I seem to lose track of things. I've seen too many changes over the years. Standards for right conduct seem to change over time any more. That confuses me these days. What is good? Does anybody know and does anybody care?"

Richard looked upon the leathery face of his grandfather; this day his mind was hard at work, trying to make sense of the world he had inherited, and he was prepared to ask a lot of questions.

"I hope you don't mind the question, Grampy. You're one of the few people I know I feel like I can trust these days. You're an insightful and trustworthy man who would tell me things as they are. I have many more when we get through this one."

Grampy chuckled, for he was delighted with Richard's comments. "I warned you, didn't I, Richard? Those warmed-over Hippy hotshot quasi-professorials don't shoot straight, do they? You have to remember the people teaching now were the same people who burned down buildings, bombed police cars, murdered judges, and kissed the asses of every left wing radical in the world. I'll warn you again something like 'good' is much too traditional a subject for your thesis. You have to justify ignorance, violence, and moral corruption to reach those people."

"You are right about them, of course. If you remember, Grampy, I never disagreed with you, did I? It is frustrating...I'm searching for truth and all I get are stale and trite little summaries of human miseries and Liberal/Socialist dogma."

"Sounds a lot like elementary schooling these days. What did you say this was for, anyway?"

"I'm working on my Master's Degree, Grampy. My thesis. You know that."

"What for?"

"For my thesis, Grampy."

The old man chuckled again. "I heard that part, Richard. I'm old but not deaf. My question is: What for? What is another diploma going to do for you? And you expect to deal with a subject like 'good' and get any kind of decent grade? They're more likely to blacklist you for life, even if you can pin it down."

"I want to teach, Grampy. I want to be a teacher...at a college somewhere. Call me a dreamer, but I believe in right and wrong, good and bad, good and evil. I believe in truth, and reason."

The old man reeled in to check his bait. "In real world academic politics, Richard, you're like this worm here. They've got you dangling on a hook...right through your gut. They own the politics of the academy, and you're the pawn in their elaborate scheme of radical deconstruction." That said and the worm re-hooked, he cast out again.

"Well put, Grampy."

"Well, Richard, I can understand your dream...wanting to teach and all. In my day, teaching was an honorable profession. But back then we could search for truth. We didn't split hairs over what's right and what's wrong. We talked freely and openly about God. In those days, people understood God. They understood truth. They're not interested in truth any more. Just politics...left-leaning politics or anything so long as it is absent the all-powerful presence of God or negates the possibility of moral absolutes."

"I know things have changed, Grampy. Maybe I won't be able to teach anywhere because I won't fit in. But I can search for meaning on my own. And, to tell you the truth, Grampy, that's what I'm doing now. I'm trying to make some sense out of the world. You're a wise and learned man, Grampy. We both know this. That's why I'm asking you."

"It is a gift from God."

"What?" Richard queried.

"Good is a gift from God. Somewhere in the extra-dimensional scheme of things, good exists. It is an elusive quality, inside of and yet out beyond the normal sensorial range of human beings. Read Genesis. Good has been around since day one."

"A definition, Grampy?"

"No. Maybe...in more traditional times it might have served as a definition of sorts. An explanation, Richard. Listen carefully, if you really want to know. A person can experience good without fully understanding it. A person can also experience good and discern it, from among various experiences. It is a cross-over phenomenon, which bridges the gap between the sensorial world and the world beyond the sensorial range." The old man raised a bony finger and pointed skyward. "Out there...where God is." Then the bony finger tapped Richard's chest. "And in here." He smiled. "Listen to your inner voice, Richard. Explain that voice, and you will understand."

"Then why does good not prevail, Grampy? How do you explain a city like Nohartinit? You are saying it is ubiquitous, right?"

"No, not exactly. The ability to discern good is an innate human capability fair enough, and it can be developed in the individual inside the single most important human social unit people have – the traditional family. No other social structure can function as well for a child in this developmental process. Nohartinit has an extraordinarily high illegitimacy rate. The process is turning in upon itself."

"Now, I'm lost, Grampy. What's the connection? I see this much clearly, Grampy: The ability to discern good opens many doors for human beings. It enlightens the searching soul, guides the wanderer through the darkest of nights. It shapes lives, defines excellence. But what is it? And why do many people shy away from it, even try to deny it in the face of reality?"

"Look at it this way, Richard. The existence (presence) of good in the world is the liberal's worst nightmare. The presence of good in the world tears down liberal philodoxy, defines the parameters of acceptable human behavior, and contributes, in many positive ways, to the elevation and improvement of the human condition.

And look at it this way, Richard: Liberal philodoxy cannot stand in the face of good. The existence of good negates the plausibility of relativistic moral authority. Once parameters are in place, setting standards of any kind, liberal philodoxy weakens and begins to collapse. Sustainable only in fantasy, liberal philodoxy then shows its true colors.

And consider this, Richard: The presence of good in the world builds a powerful, indisputable case for God, the Creator. Nothing so complex, as good, could have possibly happened by accident, nor served the world's people as it has, without a Creator of intelligence far beyond even the highest possibilities of human understanding."

"What you're getting at is this: The presence of good in the world plasters the evolutionists and atheists with insufferable questions concerning God, chance, and Big Bang ideas. Moreover, the presence of good in the world forces to the forefront the possibilities of moral absolutes, an affront to liberalism answerable only by stale platitudes or their fantastic voyages into liberal never land, of toxic value at best."

Richard waited for a response, hoping he was on the right track.

Grampy tightened his line. He smiled, a weak acknowledgement to Richard that he was on the right track.

"But the existence of good does not mean people will discern good," Grampy explained. "Many liberals, for example, cannot understand good even in conceptual terms much less discern good in actuality."

"You're saying good is a stumbling block to relativistic mental meanderers, and good is a thorn in the side of the morally ill among us?"

"Precisely. But don't leave out the ungodly. Even though the ability to discern good is an innate human capability, it is also a fragile developmental process that can be thwarted, stunted, or even snuffed out during the formative first few years of a child's life. When it gets snuffed out, then the child is left undefended against the forces of evil; the child can be lost to evil, handed over, if you will, to satanic forces, even demonic possession. It is very important, then, that care be taken to allow children to develop this ability to its highest possible degree. We have several generations in Nohartinit where there has been no development of this kind."

"Are you saying there are common sense reasons many people in the last fifty years or so have lost touch with their ability to discern good?"

"Common sense reasons for you and me perhaps. One of these reasons is the disintegration of many families, Richard. And if you think you can sell that idea to your leftist instructors, more power to you."

Richard mumbled, knowing only too well, true or not, few academics would open their ears to such a proposition.

"You and I both know how things are these days, Richard. One of the great human tragedies of the Twentieth Century in America is the disintegration of the family. Broken homes are commonplace. In that school of yours I'm sure you heard it all: unwed birthing, high divorce rates, and other blame-the-system evidences are often credited for the unusually large numbers of broken homes. These are simply excuses, Richard, not primary causes. Root causes go much deeper. They are seldom addressed directly because, for many people, they are offensive."

"I can see where you're headed, Grampy. Offensive or not, nothing much can be done to improve conditions inside a broken home until root problems are addressed, without regard to hurt feelings. To discern good means, in fact, one must also define those things that are not good. But, Grampy, I still don't see the connections? It seems like your thoughts are sound, but disjointed in a larger sense...when families break up in sufficient numbers, the spillover has horrendous implications?"

"Ask yourself a question, Richard. With a sixty-eight percent illegitimacy rate in Nohartinit, where do you think the future lies for the people? Is such a high rate reversible? How far can one stretch ideas of victimism before reality slams home? Consider this: Children from broken homes are not victims. They are not doomed to secondary citizenship. Children from broken homes are not victims of social pressures, of economic pressures, or any of the many other lame excuses offered up to circumvent or explain away their disproportionately high incidences of inadequate meshing into mainstream life.

Children from broken homes have their lives messed up only when they are not nurtured to discern good, encouraged to develop their innate capacity to discern good. You get enough kids like this and you've got big trouble on your hands. A child from a broken home cannot learn to discern good unless a male heads that home. That's statistical truth, that's moral truth, and that's a humanitarian truth. That's God's truth."

"You're saying the ability to discern good is everything?"

"You're close, Richard: If one removes all the hype and the psycho-babble, one thing stands out among all others when dealing with children from broken homes. At the core is the simple fact many grown people have lost touch with their innate ability to discern good and are impotent when it comes to raising stable children, regardless of secondary circumstances."

"I see where this is going, Grampy, but I'm not sure what it means. Am I on the right track: Not all children from broken homes, for example, end up as thugs and socio-pathetic malcontents, although huge numbers do, especially when the numbers are weighed against child statistics from intact family units. Are you saying because adults do not discern good, their children will not discern good?"

Grampy hinted at a satisfied grin.

"You please me, Richard. Consider this: Challenging to all of us is defining the extra-dimensional ramifications of good within the human being's limited understanding of his own range of perception. How does one explain good to a child who has never been taught to recognize it when he sees it? How much good can one realistically discern in the everyday life of Nohartinit? How does one explain what races through one's total-package experience when he sides one encounter up to the next and concludes one, as opposed to the other, is good? One must take into account not everyone can discern good. Not everyone can distinguish between good and bad, good and evil, or even right and wrong."

"Are you implying that without some understanding of such conceptual gradations, the human being is little more important, sophisticated, or significant than a rat or a mouse."

"I don't think I'd take it quite that far, Richard. Consider this, however: People who cannot discern good view themselves and others in precisely that way. The implications should be self-evident, especially in a place like Nohartinit."

"Grampy, I love you dearly. But where's the connection? What's the link?"

"We're getting to that part, Richard. Here's the connecting link: What separates one person from the next, which enables one to discern good and one to float in a wasteland of relativistic thinking is a simple formula for human stability, explainable in extra-dimensional terms. Human stability has three elements: 1) Order; 2) Life-affirming values; and 3) Sex identity with affiliation to one's sex as male or female.

Broken homes break down the continuity of all three elements, and, if reparative intervention does not occur, the children involved in the breakdown will be cast adrift to float aimlessly in a world that will increasingly overwhelm them by its apparent complexities. The younger the child when the breakdown occurs, the more devastating will be the consequences in the long run.

Children between birth and eight are especially vulnerable when the continuity of the elements is broken. It should be easy to see and appreciate the implications of the disruption of developmental years as extremely important for the child as well as the adult."

Richard reeled in a little. He pondered the old man's words.

"Grampy? Are you saying the traditional family...mom and pop and Junior and Jane is central to understanding good?"

"Not exactly, Richard. The traditional family helps children stabilize, to move toward enjoying fully their humanity."

"But, Grampy, you know you can't just say the traditional family is, therefore it is best. People don't buy that any more."

"Yeah, I know. In my day many people didn't need research to tell them what they know by instinct. Here's how it falls together, Richard: If one fails to identify and affiliate with his sex as male or female he will never be grounded in a real world, for he will have no frame of reference by which to discriminate between not just the sexes but between one person and the next.

Children learn to discriminate this way by having a father, and a mother, who relate to their own sex and affiliate with that sex, as male or female. Without this discrimination, the child will never be able to understand or comprehend life-affirming values much less bring order into his life.

The failures in grounding in the formative years are later manifested in anti-social behavior, because, simply put, the person has to live in a relative world devoid of absolutes to affirm his own identity. Thus the ability to discern good is snuffed, and, in some cases, extinguished."

"The child, you say, who isn't grounded and affiliated to his or her sex will be lost to liberalism or worse?"

"Trapped by relativistic nonsense, to affirm his own existence."

"Whew! You're saying, then, liberal thinking and other anti-social proclivities are a direct result of broken homes?"

"In a way, yes. But liberal thinking is just the proverbial tip of the iceberg, Richard. All the so-called intellectual stuff, the radical psychologies, environmental nut cases, the gangs, the yakked-yak rights stuff...it all evolves when people never ground themselves in their natural sex and affiliate with that sex."

"You're saying it is an evolutionary process? That liberalism and worse is a natural consequence of broken homes? I understand the grounding implications...we've worked that before. But a natural evolutionary thing?"

"That's what I'm saying, Richard. When men no longer know what it means to be a man, when women no longer know what it means to be a woman, relativistic thinking – which is no thinking at all – is a natural process. Let me ask you this: If people are lost this way, how else, but in relative terms, can they affirm their own existence?"

"I get it. To affirm their own existence, they have to float away from absolutes. Which means, in turn, they have to deny or suppress their innate ability to discern good. To discern good would imply absolutes, therefore to affirm their own existence, they have to deny good to validate the world they live in and their own lives?"

"Very good, Richard. Now let me pose a question: Does this insight help you understand the reasons behind what might be called moral bankruptcy like that which prevails in Nohartinit?"

"It would seem to be self-evident concerning homosexuals," he mused. "But others as well? You're telling me millions of us – Americans – are morally bankrupt because of confused sex identities?"

"Check out the numbers, Richard. Then you tell me."

"And...I'll find what, Grampy?"

"Nohartinit is just a model of the nation at large, Richard. We've become a nation of morally, emotionally, and psychologically ill people."

Richard laughed. He tugged on his line, then began to reel in to recast.

"There's a loony around every corner, Grampy?" Richard said, sarcastically.

The old man frowned. His bright eyes took on a faraway look to them. He began to reel in. His whole demeanor changed. His lightheartedness faded.

"The numbers are in the tens of millions, Richard. Liberalism is a moral psychological illness. It is going to take a lot more than a thesis here and there to save this great nation. We're standing on the brink of internal dissolution." Grampy looked sternly at Richard. "Look at the stuff going on in town. Just like the adults, the kids are hostile, intolerant, and violent. They're wild, unschooled, unskilled, mean-spirited. They don't care about anyone or anything. There's your story and your thesis, Richard. The future is unfolding right before our eyes, in our own time, right in the middle of Nohartinit. And it does not look good."

"Let's head in, Grampy. I don't think we're going to catch anything. Besides, I want you to come with me into town. I'll buy you lunch and a cold one. Later, I want to go over more of this and share some thoughts with your old friend, Alexsandr. Now that he's retired, he has been working on a book, doing some research about broken homes and stuff. I'm working along the same lines. Maybe, between the three of us, the world's problems might be solved."

"You're referring to Alexsandr Simon of course," answered Grampy as he reeled in. "He and I are old friends, although I have not seen him in a long time. You were a little kid the first time you met him. I wasn't aware you knew him that well."

"I didn't actually. I knew his granddaughter, Ladonna. We spent a million hours playing together as kids. We were best friends for years. I never could get her interested past friendship. Then she got busy, I got busy. I have not seen her in a long time now. Maybe I'll get a chance to sit down with her again one of these days."

"So how was it you and Alexsandr became friends?"

"He was a guest speaker in one of my classes at school. Boy, did he get a cold shoulder! Liberals are a cold blooded and intolerant bunch, Grampy. I admired the way he handled himself. He stood up to them like he was made out of concrete. After his talk, I introduced myself. We talked about you. We talked about Ladonna. He said he met me a long time ago, when the two of you were at some kind of conference or something. Actually, Alexsandr and I have seen quite a lot of each other recently. He's agreed to help me out with my thesis."

"They didn't want to hear a word he had to say, did they? Probably tried to talk over him, drown him out, and smother him with their absurdities...right?"

"I think he lost them when he told the female students to throw their books in the trash and go get married, stay home, and have babies."

The old man laughed. "Alexsandr never was one to hem and haw. How's he doing, anyway?" The old man put his gear in the bottom of the skiff and started rowing toward shore. "Last time I saw him he was complaining about arthritis or some such."

"Seemed basically fine to me," answered Richard. "Said his joints hurt."

"Hmm. Last time I saw Alexsandr he was grumbling about morality and politics," Grampy said. "We were sitting in his den. Old Alexsandr threw a book at the television set."

"Are you free this afternoon, Grampy? Alexsandr set aside two hours to go over some notes with me."

"To visit Alexsandr? You bet. He livens up my days from time to time. Did he ever tell you about the time he got shot at when he was speaking at Cal State in the sixties? Some stinky Hippy tried to pop him. Alexsandr has dodged a lot of bottles, books, barbs, and an occasional bullet in his time. Never was too popular, as far back as I can remember."

"I've read some of his recent work, Grampy. He's a smart son-of-a-gun, isn't he?"

"He's more than smart, Richard. He's worldly and wise. I've never known Alexsandr to jump to conclusions. When Alexsandr speaks, he speaks with authority. He's always prepared to hold his own."

They headed for shore. Grampy pulled off the gauze patch. "If it isn't aches and pain, it's itch, itch, itch. I hate getting old," he mumbled, as he tossed the patch to the wind.

BOOK ONE

Chapter One

Professor Alexsandr Simon was puttering in his rose garden when the men drove up. He looked up briefly, taking mental notes of his company over the rim of his dark glasses. He was a chubby, jovial-looking fellow, sort of a Santa Claus character with black hair. He stood, dusted his trousers, and walked slowly, apparently painfully, to greet his guests. His greetings were authentic, and his handshakes were firm and manly.

"Richard," he said. "What a pleasant surprise to see you've managed to pull Grampy from his skiff long enough to visit an old friend. You'd think a twenty mile drive would not be that hard to manage from time to time."

"It is a multi-directional highway, Alexsandr," said the old man. "The pleasure is mine. Richard tells me you've been helping him with his thesis. I appreciate that. Thank you. I have high hopes for my grandson here. Between the two of us maybe we can do something for him."

"Enough said, Grampy. Let's go in. Have you eaten? I'll have Rachael prepare something if you wish."

"No, we're fine," Grampy said. "We just finished lunch downtown. How is Rachael? I have not seen her since what, the late eighties? Back in her save-the-children, feed-the-children days."

"She's fine. Still the chatterbox once you get her going. She'll be pleased to see you again. She gets a little grumpy now and then...my retirement is a hard adjustment for her. But, otherwise, she has not changed much. She's still very active in children's crusades...new stuff for the hospital's pediatric unit...Toys for Tots...volunteer time at the local Day Care...helps out with tutoring at the Elementary school. She and Father Wyman have some scheme in the works as we speak."

Inside the modest house, Alexsandr led them into his study. It was a well-lit room, with a huge oak desk occupying a lot of floor space. Two walls were lined with bookshelves. Open books, stacks of notes seemed to be strewn everywhere.

"Pardon the mess," he said. "I'm working on a book. I've got notes spread everywhere, as you can see."

He pulled up two chairs in front of his desk, and then planted himself behind it. He scratched his unshaven chin. He took off his glasses and put them aside.

"Richard, what are you working on now? Your notes on the statistical relationships between father absent homes and criminal

3

proclivities are affirmed. By the way, I found an interesting piece of information for you, although I have not confirmed the correlation." He picked through a pile of notes. "Here it is." He handed the paper to Richard.

Richard studied the graph that Alexsandr had clipped from a newsletter.

"What's it mean?" he quizzed. He handed it to Grampy.

The graph showed an amazingly parallel relationship between rising crime rates and welfare spending.

"Looks to me like it affirms the obvious," said Grampy. "No correlation exists to link crime to poverty."

"If I get some time, Richard, I'll see if I can confirm the figures from other sources." Alexsandr picked up another stack of notes. "I've been going over your notes, Richard. I think you're on to something. Where are you headed? The pathway does not exactly jump out at me? Am I missing something?"

"Grampy and I were discussing good this morning. I'm heading toward discerning good as an essential tool in social development. Violence among the kids in town has my attention. Trends seem to be setting a pattern among the young. I know of your intense interest in moral education, and I was wondering if you might share your ideas along these lines?"

"Alexsandr," Grampy said. "We've been toying with our ideas...remember them...about broken homes, the health of society, and the impact of broken homes on the future of America as a viable nation."

"Your Grandfather and I used to discuss such things for hours at a time. I always expected a book out of him, but he never got past his thesis." Alexsandr grinned. "We agreed about half the time on key issues. I always wanted him to write that book so I could answer with one of my own and prove him wrong. I looked at things in terms of Moral Education, and he saw things as a Psychologist. The two views often collide." Alexsandr thumbed through the notes. "I've been reading your material, Richard." He picked one out one of Richard's ideas and read it.

"I like this, but you're going to have a hard time selling your conclusion on this one, Richard. The politics of the academy just won't let it fly" He looked at Grampy. "The boy is smart. Back him, Grampy. Listen to this: The relationship between broken homes and the discernment of good can be seen by the inability of the developing child in a female headed household to ground himself as an affiliated male or female. This is not always the case, however, depending on the age of the child at the time the family is dissolved. A child firmly rooted in his sex identity and affiliated to his sex (after the age of six or thereabouts) will be grounded to what must be considered a cautious degree, although reaffirmation through male presence is workable through surrogacy. Without this grounding, the child will have no frame of reference by which to judge moral or immoral, good or bad behaviors, because he simply will not have the basics in line in his own life to judge any personal or interpersonal actions with any degree of certainty."

Alexsandr looked to Grampy for a nod of approval, which he got. Then he read on: "For younger children (if one is to accept the statistics) it should be absolutely illegal for a female to take sole custody of children under the age of twelve, regardless of circumstances, if the best interests of the child or children or society as a whole are deciding factors."

Grampy hummed his approval, but agreed with Alexsandr the conclusion, although valid, would not fly in the academy.

"Richard," said Grampy. "The academics these days are not interested in truth. They are not interested in evidence or supporting data. They'll chop your head off."

Richard protested. "Statistical evidence affirms overwhelmingly that single parent homes headed by females are disasters in human terms, as far as children are concerned," he said.

"You're missing the point," Alexsandr said.

"Not so with male headed single parent homes," he continued.

"Richard," Grampy said, as he put a sympathetic arthritic hand to his grandson's arm. "We know and agree statistical figures are no measure of the real damage done to children by broken homes. Statistics measure such things as income, propensities toward crime, illegitimate birthing, and the like. Statistics affirm the lack of developmental skills in broken home children, but they do not (and cannot) explain why such children develop as they do."

"So?"

"The academics these days do not care what the evidence or data mean," Alexsandr said. "They have an agenda, Richard. A social/political agenda. Truth is not in the equation any more." He looked deep into Richard's eyes with his own, penetrating Richard's eyes, as if his own could somehow imprint on Richard's brain.

"Statistics do not explain, for example, the unsettlingly disproportionate rates of various crimes by people from broken homes when they are matched to their counterparts from traditional family settings," he continued. "They do, however, set up legitimate cause/effect relationships worthy of deep examination. These cause/effect relationships are what you must work with. If you don't push the cause/effect aspect, they'll cook you over an open fire. Liberals are an intolerant bunch, Richard, merciless, and mean spirited."

Grampy joined in. "Listen, Richard. I dropped out of psychology partly because it fell apart in my mind as a legitimate science, a fact that took me years to accept. It turned into a political circus. Of course, psychosocial engineers cite poverty as a major cause of crime. Poverty can be linked to single parent homes headed by women. But the leap from poverty to crime is unacceptable, as a cause/effect relationship. It is nonsense, of course, because there is no correlation between poverty and crime. However, there are links between broken homes (especially father-absent homes) and anti-social proclivities such as rape, long term incarceration, teen homicides, unwed birthing, teen suicides, liberal political inclinations, and homosexuality, among other things. These are the facts. They are irrelevant when you are playing hardball with academics. They're no different than Psychologists. They don't care what the facts are; they have an agenda, a stinking Hippy holdover agenda. Truth be damned."

Richard protested again. "It does no good to skirt real issues (which can be approached with real answers) by fabricating false causes for real problems. Many of the social theories surrounding social problems are pure conjecture based on pure conjecture, independent of common sense and hard facts."

"Now, you're getting somewhere, Richard," said Alexsandr.

"You know that," said Grampy. "Alexsandr knows that. I know that." Grampy folded his arms across his chest; a sure sign to Richard Grampy was getting riled.

"Richard, look," said Alexsandr. "Here's the real problem: Problems associated with broken homes are not social problems, and there are no social answers. Dumping money and perks into broken homes is not the answer to anything. There is no way to legislate morality, and there is no way to legislate away personal deficiencies that contribute directly to broken homes. Only in America do people try to hold the government responsible for their personal mistakes...and get away with it."

"So we bury truth to accommodate political goals? I can't do that!"

"You don't bury truth, Richard," Alexsandr explained. "You use it as a secondary support agent to refute their political objectives."

"Truth plays second fiddle to the politics of the academy?" Richard protested again.

"Yeah...now you're catching on," said Grampy. "You play to the house, as the entertainers say."

"I'm not an entertainer, Grampy."

Rachael entered the room. She looked like the perfect mate for Alexsandr by the way she carried herself. Brisk. Lively. But not the pick...pick...pick fastidious woman who might trail him around and move his stuff. She was slightly smaller than him, but not less jovial.

"I heard the talking," she said. "Grampy? I thought that was you! How are you? I have not seen you in years."

Grampy had risen to greet her. She looked him over.

"You look well and fit," she said. "What brings you here? It is so good to see you again!"

Richard had risen also, and he greeted her politely.

"Rachael," Richard said. "Its good to see you again. I'm here close to getting broiled, and it's a good thing you came in. I feel like I'm being led to the slaughterhouse without benefit of a trial."

She laughed.

"Alexsandr, you go easy now...especially in front of Grampy. I don't need you two getting into anything. Not after all these years of peace." She approached Alexsandr's desk. "Can I get you anything, Alexsandr?"

"No. Leave us, woman," he joked.

She looked back toward Richard and Grampy.

"How about it, you two? Soda? Coffee? Tea?"

They declined.

"Well, then. I'm going out. I'll leave you brainies to your work. Grampy? Will you be here for a while? I'd love to just sit and chat...for old time's sake. When you're finished grilling Richard, maybe we could spend a few minutes filling in some gaps. I've got a great project in the works for the Elementary school...I'd love to tell you about it."

"Certainly, Rachael," Grampy agreed. "How long has it been?"

"Late eighties, right after that bonehead tried to kill Reagan."

"So it was."

Rachael left the room. The men returned to the business at hand.

"Where were we?" said Alexsandr, returning directly to the thesis notes. "Oh, yes. Richard, as I was saying, even though your conclusions may be valid and justifiable and backed by reams of data and supporting evidence you cannot assume your liberals in the academy are open-minded, fair, or even interested in legitimate research. These are the people who draw their conclusions first then hunt for supporting data. If they can't find it, they invent it. You are not addressing intellectually pure scientists or searchers. You are trying to convince a bunch of mental and moral midgets there is a better way."

"Is it as difficult as you seem to imply...getting through to them?" Richard asked.

Alexsandr laughed. "I have the scars to prove it. You won't get through to them, not ever if you insist on taking a rational or common sense approach."

Grampy cleared his throat. "Richard, we're not questioning the validity of your research. You just have to reinvent the way you present your conclusions. Let's look at the example Alexsandr pulled out. What are the numbers of custody cases in which men get custody? Do you have them, Richard?"

"Roughly ten percent of all custody cases are decided in favor of men."

"Here's what you have to do. You conclude by questioning. Rather than by making statements or suggesting reforms, you present your case, summarize your case, and then pose your question. Something like this: With the evidence being overwhelmingly one-sided, in that single parent homes headed by women are disasters in human terms, for many legitimate and important reasons, one has to wonder why only ten percent of custody cases resolve in favor of men. One might conclude the criteria used to resolve custody issues are neither scientifically justifiable nor socially prudent..."

"Therefore," Richard interrupted. "One can be safely led to conclude such arrangements, while not serving science, society, or prudence must have other reasons for being. And one may safely ask: What are they?"

"Now you're getting there, Richard," Alexsandr said. "You don't conclude that female custody of minor children is an idiotic idea, you merely present the facts, ask the pertinent questions, then move on to other things."

"Then you find the reasons behind the stupidity, examine them, and question them. Then move on again."

"And I must save my suggestions for reforms for a separate section of the thesis text."

"Precisely," said Alexsandr and Grampy, almost in unison.

"You see, Richard," explained Alexsandr. "By doing it that way, you allow the reforms to stand alone, so those grading your thesis can separate them out, tear them apart, and yet let you slip by. That way they won't have to accept the facts, the evidence, and the data. They can pretend these things don't exist and satisfy themselves that your suggestions, however meritorious, are intellectually inferior to their own. They'll be able to tell you they don't agree with a thing you had to say, but that you have every right to say it. End of case."

"If they don't see it that way?" quizzed Richard. "What then?"

"You won't be the first grad student thrown out of school for what you have to say," answered Grampy, with a frown of sorts creasing his jowls.

"Anyway, Richard," said Alexsandr. "Proceed along these lines. Then, here's what I want you to do. Write a full draft version, not more than two hundred pages or so. They'll want you to chop it down to no more than one hundred and sixty pages. In the meanwhile, we'll do as we do now. Drop by from time to time, and we can go over some stuff. My door is always open."

"Alexsandr and I used to collaborate on a lot of things," said Grampy. "We have a pretty good idea how to help you. I'll open my archives, if it is okay with you, Alexsandr. Between us, you'll have a very good thesis. No guarantees after that."

"Fine by me, Grampy," answered Alexsandr. He opened a desk drawer. He removed a stack of pages from it, about an inch thick. "In return, Richard...and you, too, Grampy...if you can tear away from your skiff now and then...I want you to look over my latest manuscript. I've been thinking about this. We're barking up the same tree, Richard. Different sides of it, mind you, but the same tree nonetheless. Perhaps we can come up with something. Feel free to cite the studies if you wish. And, of course, feel free to make suggestions."

"I'm honored," said Richard. "I'd be happy to."

"Just like old times, Alexsandr?" said Grampy. "Leave it to you to drag me out of the water." Then Grampy stood to excuse himself. "I'm going to look up Rachael, and catch up on some empty spaces. Richard, we'll probably be sitting outside somewhere when you are ready to leave. Alexsandr. I'll see you later." He left the room.

Alexsandr returned to Richard's notes.

"Now, Richard," he said. "Let's see where we can take the rest of this material. I'll read your own words and you listen. This is a very good way to go over such things. I have Rachael read my own stuff to me time after time. Here we are...not to say the children from female headed broken homes cannot be taught simple life lessons like the difference between good and bad, good and evil, right and wrong. However, before any such teaching can benefit any child from a broken home, there are higher priorities: Order, life-affirming values, and sex identity with affiliation to one's sex as male or female.

Just because a family's integrity is shattered there is no logical reason children should suffer long-term consequences. For any child to be given a fair chance at success as a human being capable of enjoying his full humanity, with all the hopes and possibilities it offers, it is

9

necessary to aid, if and when necessary, appropriate developmental growth, to compensate for the elementary losses inherent in the violated integrity of the basics of human stability.

Certain minor adjustments inside the structure of a single parent household can make a lot of difference in the developmental possibilities of a child. Before any approach can or will work, however, a reality assessment of the needs and possibilities of the children involved must be given every due consideration, free of prejudice, free of conjecture and not based on purely rhetorical social/psychological theory. The structure must be conducive to stability and reality."

Richard waited for comment.

"I will suggest another line, Richard. I'll pen it in for you, if you do not object: The ultimate goal is for the child to learn to discern good."

"Is it, Alexsandr? Is it the ultimate goal? I can understand clearly you and Grampy think a lot alike along those lines."

"That we do...we spent many months trying to figure out good, Richard. We agreed a long time ago that good is one of those extra-dimensional things that is very complex, a phenomenon made up of component parts which combine into a whole experience, which defies the human being's capacity for complete understanding.

We agreed a long time ago that human beings experience good in sensorial and extra-sensorial ways, concurrently.

We also agreed even in the most basic form, when human beings experience good, it is an involved process that combines sensory perceptions (the five senses) and evokes responses on deeper levels as well, in mental, moral, psychological, emotional, and spiritual ways.

Where we have always disagreed was how people access good. I always felt to access good the basic elements of human stability must be in place, and the observer must be grounded in a real world populated by real people. We debated for years whether a liberal could experience genuine or authentic good. Perhaps you can enlighten us one of these days."

"You've got very little tolerance for liberals, right, Alexsandr?"

"That's another bone of contention between myself and Grampy. He thinks they're mentally ill. I used to think they're just plain stupid. The more I know about them, however, the stronger is his argument. In any case, we agree on the fact they're an insufferable bunch."

"That they are," agreed Richard. "I'm undecided, personally, just which assessment is correct. But I'm sure of one thing, Alexsandr...I strongly suspect Grampy is correct, but you are, too, except the explanation is rational, not just something they can, individually, overcome. Hear me out. The failure to identify and affiliate with one's sex as male or female reduces the individual to the pitiful level of relativistic thinking...liberal...and, if you take it a step farther, see this: There has to be a reality cap, a limited capacity for discerning things because at some point the frame of reference is exhausted. Liberal thinking is finite...it can only go so far then it exhausts its own future possibilities until it ventures into pure fantasy. Once based in fantasy, then it can take on a life if its own, never having to touch base with reality."

"Keep going...please keep going."

"The search for meaning capability, Alexsandr...understanding. Consider that it is not innate, but learned."

"And...extinguishable?"

"Not only that, Alexsandr...unattainable to start with without training and exposure."

"Anybody can think, Richard."

"Of course they can, Alexsandr. It is the shift to the high level...understanding...that is most formidable as a reparative barrier. Liberal thinking notwithstanding, teaching people to understand stuff is a difficult process, especially when the person or persons involved are not grounded in their most basic human identities as affiliated males or females."

"You're saying they've got nothing to understand because their frames of reference are too limited to move into the deeper areas of comprehension?"

"Think about this, Alexsandr: Homosexuals, for example, are seemingly improbable candidates for treatment or cures because they are phenomenally deficient in mental, moral, psychological, emotional, and spiritual ways. Yet treatments and cures are a matter of historical fact. Like homosexuals, liberals and other mentally, morally, psychologically, emotionally, and spiritually deficient people can also be treated and cured simply by widening their frames of reference."

"I see where you're going, Richard. In many ways, you're aligning with Grampy in his mental illness theory."

"Like the liberal's jump...poverty causes crime. Even though there is no connection, the understanding deficient makes the leap because it sounds good. So they jump from point a to point d and rest their case, regardless of the fact the conclusion has no basis in reality."

"You're saying they are not just plain old fashioned stupid?"

"No, Alexsandr. No exactly. I can't disagree with that. I'm saying their mental abilities are retarded, not fully developed. I'm saying they have no ability to connect points in a sequence and see the larger picture. They have no ability to enter into the larger picture. Picture it this way. People with no affiliation to their sex live in an air bubble in water. The skin of the bubble is so thick there is no way to see outside of it. No matter how many times they look around, it won't take long before their entire universe, so to speak, has been examined and re-examined. Not until the air bubble is popped by outside intervention will any kind of new environment open to them. They cannot connect the dots, Alexsandr. That's all there is to it."

"So, Richard, you're telling me when the liberals say guns kill people they are literally seeing an inanimate object (the gun) kill someone without making the literal connection of someone pulling the trigger?"

"Yes, Alexsandr. I am. They see an event, and then they see a solution. Rational evaluation of the circumstances is not only unnecessary but also impossible. The mental faculties are not there. I'd call that mental illness, wouldn't you?"

"That, Richard, is a leap toward the improbable."

"Does this ring a bell, Alexsandr: There's too much violence in the world so we need to get rid of guns."

"The leap from point a to point d without regard to the larger picture?"

"Precisely. The jump from a to d. And making cherry pies from apples and cranberries. These are the same people who will abort a baby without blinking an eye yet squander millions of dollars, ruin lives, and destroy entire communities to save a couple of trees...or flies...or bugs."

"So what do you propose, Richard? Mew up tens of millions of people?"

"That, Alexsandr, is the leap toward the improbable. The secret, Alexsandr, is to somehow teach them to, ah,...reawaken...their innate ability to discern good by widening their frames of reference."

"Move toward prevention rather than treatment or cure?"

"It could work, Alexsandr. Can you help me with that?"

"I can try, Richard."

Grampy and Rachael entered the room, chatting. Rachael was telling him about her latest efforts to raise funds to combat juvenile diabetes and some work she was doing with Father Wyman. They had obviously enjoyed the few minutes together. Alexsandr looked up from his desk and addressed Rachael straightforwardly.

"Richard is to have unlimited access to this room and my computer from now on, Rachael. Anything here is to be put at his disposal. Anything." He then looked at Richard. "Anything I can do, Richard, I will. You tell me what you need, and I will see to it you get it. Rachael, I mean it sincerely when I say this. You need to back Richard in every way you can." He scribbled something on a slip of paper and handed it to Richard. "Here's the password for my computer. The file name, also. Rachael will show you where it is. Rachael, Richard if you will excuse us, I need to speak to Grampy alone for a few minutes."

Richard stood and thanked Alexsandr for his offer. Rachael had a questioning look on her face.

"What is it, Rachael?" Alexsandr asked. "Is there a problem?"

"What about The Red Flag, Alexsandr?"

"What about it? I said anything, Rachael. That means anything."

"But Richard, be warned," Alexsandr said. "Do not breathe a word about The Red Flag...not to a living soul. I'll fill you in on the details later."

Rachael led Richard to the computer room that was tucked away and isolated in the basement, and she showed him around. The electronic whirring of sleeping machines filled the room.

"Wow! State of the art," Richard commented. "Impressive."

"He likes you, Richard. If you only knew."

"Are you sure I won't be imposing, Rachael? I mean, this is a gold mine, but I don't want to be in your way or anything."

"When Alexsandr opened up The Red Flag to you, Richard, he told me all I need to know. He's not let anyone see that file...not the best minds he's come to know over all these years. No one. Not even Grampy, and they've been the best of friends...and occasional collaborators...for decades. It was a commissioned secret study, privately funded."

"Have you seen it, Rachael? Have you seen The Red Flag? What is it?"

"As far as anyone is concerned," she whispered, "the answer is an emphatic: No! Absolutely not! Not at all. But between you and me, yes, I have seen some of it, and...as God is my witness...it scares the hell out of me!"

"Do you know what it is, Rachael?"

"Sort of."

"Sort of? That's not an answer, Rachael."

"It opens the door into another world, Richard. Alexsandr has moved inside a legitimate reality option. You better think long and hard before you go there."

Meanwhile, in the study, Grampy and Alexsandr discussed The Red Flag.

"You sly son-of-a-bitch!" said Grampy, somewhat amused. "I thought you washed your hands with that project a long time ago. How long have you been working on it, Alexsandr?"

"Off and on? Maybe a couple of years, Grampy."

Grampy sat down and looked Alexsandr squarely in the eyes.

"What's the deal, Alexsandr? General Perkins has been dead for quite a while now. Nobody wants the stuff, and he's certainly not one to have left any mention of it in his papers. What gives?"

"A year before he got killed, Grampy, he and I sat down and reached a gentleman's agreement. This was after you backed out. He came back to me, after he heard I was going to retire from teaching altogether. This time, he brought a few scribbled lines, a model, Grampy. It wasn't perfected, but it certainly was inspiring. It was far superior to his original work. I grasped the implications right away.

He fronted me the same twenty-five thousand to get started. Then he passed along another twenty-five thousand. All in cash. He died not long after. I had the money and I had a start on it. I had no way to return the money without tarnishing his reputation. So I kept it. And kept working on The Red Flag."

Alexsandr sighed to show he was somewhat relieved he could finally tell his friend about the project.

"Perkins was a good man, Grampy. His intentions were the best. He knew he had a hard sell even if we came up with The Red Flag. He was the only person who could have convinced anyone, anyway. We've got nothing to win and nothing to lose by completing the project. It'll never see daylight, and we both know it. At least Richard might gain something by the experience."

"Why involve Richard?"

"He's on the right track, Grampy. Besides, nobody is going to find out about the project. Certainly not from you, or me, or Rachael. I don't think Richard will tell anyone. What's the harm? He might even fill in the gaps."

"Are you not through with it?"

"No."

"I want in, then. Let's finish the damn thing…the three of us."

"Fine with me. Will you take Richard aside and fill him in? He may not want to participate, you know. Times are different now. People are different now. If word gets out, it could ruin his career before he ever gets off to a good start."

Grampy leaned imposingly across the desk, to look Alexsandr hard in the eyes, stopping but inches from his face.

"Did you break through, Alexsandr? Did you?"

"I turned the key, Grampy...but I just couldn't muster the courage to open the door."

"Anything testable?"

Alexsandr gloated, grumbling a thick throaty defiant, almost evil-sounding few grunts.

"Grampy, I can predict the outcome of decisions before they are ever put into motion with a hundred percent accuracy in a matter of mere seconds, with a margin for error...of zero...and an applicability factor that is...universal."

Grampy backed off and sat down, flabbergasted. He stared in amazement and disbelief. He gathered his thoughts and quickly regained his composure. His old hands quivered more than usual.

"If I didn't know you so well, I'd call the guys in the white suits. Are you sure of your results?"

"Absolutely. Relax, Grampy. Isn't that what we always assumed to be possible? Isn't that where we were most critical of the social sciences?"

"I presume you have a testable model as well?"

"Margin for error of zero and universal applicability...you bet! The General was very close, Grampy. A remarkable man!"

"You've tested and retested?"

"Of course."

"But no outside testing from independent, disinterested third parties, right?"

"Right. Not needed. The model and the tests hold, Grampy. I've cross-examined from widely diverse population samples, Grampy. It holds."

"How much does Richard know about this?"

"Nothing usable, depending on what Rachael has said about it. She knows enough to be afraid of the implications."

"Afraid? An understatement, isn't it, Alexsandr?"

"Perhaps."

"Alexsandr...a margin for error of zero and universal applicability? You're playing God, Alexsandr. No wonder you were afraid to open the door! It will rewrite or invalidate just about everything done in the social sciences over the last two centuries."

"You realize, of course, when The Red Flag reaches fruition, we might have to destroy every shred of evidence it ever existed. The standard established is a formula for chaos...or worse. We're on the brink of what General Perkins foresaw."

"The General must be smiling in his grave right now."

"Oh, don't get me wrong, Grampy. There is a long row to hoe still. But, the results so far are quite amazing."

Chapter Two

Alexsandr looked through the papers that General Perkins had prepared for him, years ago. The pages were yellowish and dog-eared. He wondered what it was that had stirred him then. Looking through the General's work, the preliminary stuff seemed almost trivial. But Alexsandr realized he had the benefit of hindsight now. In the time and place, the General's work had possibilities. His last written communication with the General, a few scribbled notes, had unlocked elusive secrets, although the General himself had never known exactly what he had stumbled onto.

He remembered their first meeting. Alexsandr had given his views to an assembled group of people from various backgrounds. He had been invited to sit in and participate in a round table type discussion group. A series of child and teen violence episodes had rocked a South Side neighborhood, and a few concerned citizens of Nohartinit were looking for answers.

The meeting had been called in the Baptist Church. As churches went, in Alexsandr's opinion, it was plain and unexciting as a building. It had a few stained glass windows, a few highly polished railings and picture frames here and there, encasing poorly balanced pictures of Jesus. In Alexsandr's opinion, the acoustics were lousy. Every one who spoke seemed to have their words bounced back at them.

Alexsandr was invited because he was well known as a moral education researcher. With him on the panel were various educators and professionals of the usual selection…psychologists, teachers, public officials, and such. Alexsandr participated, shared his views, but captivated few. His usual bland, matter-of-fact delivery was not what his audience wanted to hear. They were, in his opinion, wanting to hear a load of psychobabble or political doubletalk, and that he could not deliver.

General Perkins did not participate, but sat calmly, stiffly, in the audience throughout the whole discussion. Alexsandr had noticed him, but did not know who he was. He stood out in his tailored dark blue suit, very expensive shirt and tie. Before meeting him, Alexsandr figured him for a very rich and influential Real Estate Developer or businessman. After the discussion closed, General Perkins approached Alexsandr, introduced himself, and then he asked him for some time in which they could speak privately. Alexsandr got the immediate impression this was a man with lots of money, a blueblood education, and he was one who was used to getting things done.

17

"I have an interesting proposition for you, Professor," the General said. His voice was harsh and heavy handed, as if he would not even consider the possibility of a refusal. "It seems to me you're the only person in the whole batch who has any connection with what's real. Most of those folks sounded like blubbering idiots. I loved your line about the new-breed barbarians. Give me a few minutes of your time, and I might be able to help you build something of lasting value."

Alexsandr arranged to meet General Perkins in a coffee shop. They ordered coffee, chatted informally for a few minutes, against the noise of chattering people and the rattling of dishes, and they got to know each other. They seemed to mesh fairly well. After a few minutes, Alexsandr asked directly, what he wanted.

General Perkins was a fit man, battle hardened and battle scarred. He seemed firm as a rock, hard as nails. He had piercing dark eyes, as if they could somehow slice someone in half with a simple hostile glance. But Alexsandr sensed he was a man with an intensely involved and concerned inner core. A man with a mission. His assessment was confirmed when the General told him what he wanted.

"The kids, Professor. They're going nuts...running wild...mean as snakes. I spent my whole life defending this great nation, Professor. I don't want to spend my later years watching these punks tear it apart from the inside out. I want you to do something about it."

Alexsandr grunted. "What makes you think I can do anything about it, General Perkins? You saw the reception I got at that meeting. I'm just an aging professor nobody listens to any more. I'm as concerned as you are, but I'm a nobody...I can't even get people to listen to me to say nothing of trying to find ways to make things happen."

"You figure out what's going on, and I'll make things happen."

"You can do that?"

"I can do that. You figure out what's going on, I'll take it from there."

Alexsandr had his reservations. "General Perkins, I don't really have the time to take on such a project. To be more specific, quite frankly, I don't have the resources."

"I'll fully fund your research, Professor."

"You're talking a lot of money, General Perkins."

"I'll fully fund your research, Professor. I am a rich man, Professor, and I did some background checking before approaching you. You come highly recommended. A trusted friend of mine in the Police Department gave me your name. You're the right man for the job."

"Can I bring in a colleague, if he's willing?"

"Grampy Politnitroff? Will you need him?"

"Most likely. His character is beyond reproach, General Perkins."

"I know of him. I know his credentials. Between you and me, Professor, he was my second choice, if you turned me down. Done. By all means bring him in, if he will join you."

They arranged another meeting, a few days later at Alexsandr's house. Rachael was gone for the afternoon. Alexsandr invited Grampy along, to meet the General and consider the proposal. General Perkins had a briefcase with him this time. After a brief introduction, they got down to business. They entered Alexsandr's study, closed the door. General Perkins was straightforward.

He laid twenty-five thousand dollars in cash on Alexsandr's desk.

"Seed money," he said. "The only thing I ask is complete secrecy. There are some people who'd give anything to remove me, so nothing must leak out about the project. Let's just say there are people in high and powerful places who do not share my enthusiasm for preserving this great nation of ours. They feed off the amorality and seemingly endless stupidity of the young."

He took some papers out of his briefcase, and he handed them to Alexsandr.

"I'm on to something, but I'm not sure what it is. Read this. Get back to me. Maybe you can find what is evading me."

He handed Alexsandr a business card with a number scribbled on the back.

"Use my private number. It is secure. I will gladly tell you what I'm thinking and where my own research has taken me. Burn the card after our initial contacts are finished. Quite frankly, gentlemen, I'm in over my head. Give me bullets, tanks, bombs, and missiles...I can kick anybody's ass, but words and books and papers, I'm in over my head with this research stuff."

Alexsandr tried to hand back the money. General Perkins refused to take it.

"No. Sit on it for a few days. Talk it over. It is clean money, gentlemen. I'll match it within days of your acceptance. That ought to get you started. I'll always work with cash. I want you to do the same. No paper trails. And my intentions are honorable, I assure you. There's only one other thing. If you decide to take on the project, I do not want to hear from you again until the project is completed. You'll know how to find me."

"Why all the secrecy, General Perkins?" Grampy asked. "Are you so sure we'll find what we're looking for that it can, in fact, put you at risk?"

"Oh, no, Professor. It isn't me I'm worried about. If you find what I think you will, there will be hundreds of millions of dollars at stake, thousands of jobs put at risk, and some very impressive reputations...political, educational, professional, and otherwise, put asunder. If you find what I hope you will, the implications will become self-evident and horrific for a lot of people."

"Why me? Us?" asked Grampy. "I have a feeling your selection was not by chance...our reputation as colleagues...some people call us co-conspirators...is common knowledge."

"No. Not by chance, Professor Politnitroff. As I told Professor Simon before, I know enough about you both to have confidence in my choice. Why not you...you are learned and honorable men with impeccable reputations and very impressive credentials aren't you?" With those final words, General Perkins shook hands, thanked them for their time, and he said he would call to set up a meeting to finalize the agreement. "I'll be hard to catch in a few days, so it will work best if I make the final arrangement. For the next couple of days, I'll be reachable at the number on the card."

"Give us a couple of days, General," said Grampy. "We'll have an answer we can all live with, I hope."

"Professors...don't be shy about the funding. If this won't work, tell me what will. I'll see to it you get what you need."

"General Perkins? One last question or two?" asked Grampy.

"Certainly."

"You are acting alone for your own private and personal reasons?"

"Do you mean is the military involved? Oh, yes, gentlemen, I am very much alone. Very much alone." He intoned his words so Grampy would make no mistake about it all.

"Why, sir, from personal funds would you put out this kind of money for a project which may or may not pan out?"

He smiled, for the first time since they met.

"I've been in all kinds of battles and skirmishes, all around the world. It has been my life to fight for the dignity of man. It dawned on me, not too long ago, while I've been out parading all over the world, I somehow did my part to let my own country slip away, to fall into the hands of barbarians. I realized I just might be able to win a very important war...the war for the hearts and the minds of our children...to bring them to the good...without firing a shot. The pen, they say, is mightier than the sword. Gentlemen, I want you to prove them right."

Alexsandr put aside the recollection, read a few entries from the original material:

20

THE RED FLAG:

This report concerns itself with prevention. In many ways, it is an attempt to classify problems, make recommendations for solving the problems, suggest workable reforms, and, in summary, espouse expectable results. It is hoped the report will shed more light on the unthinkable proposition that children from broken homes, more than any other segment of the population, are at risk to become morally (psychologically) ill, with the illnesses manifested in moral turpitude, mental illness, and perpetual childhood – the trademarks of the modern liberal.

This report concerns children from father absent and other broken homes. (The reparative techniques espoused herein, however, are usable under other applications for a wide variety of maladjusted individuals.) The ultimate reparative goal is to reach the children before permanent damage is done.

The purpose of my proposed extra-dimensional education approach is to prepare the children to move into adulthood armed with reality perspectives within the stabilizing parameters of order, life-affirming values, and sex identity with affiliation to one's sex as male or female. Once the elements of stability are in place, the rest (mental, moral, psychological, emotional, and spiritual preparedness) will fall into place.

The reparative process, however, does not begin with the children, but with the adults in the children's lives. Broken homes leave gaps in all the lives affected. When a marriage collapses, or a spouse dies, the three elements of stability break apart. Continuity is disrupted. Sometimes restoring some sense of stability in affected lives takes weeks, months, or even years. It is unquestionably the responsibility of the parents to re-stabilize the home environment, as quickly as possible, for the sake of the children.

Many males from father absent homes themselves do not take on the responsibilities of raising children. This is not an unusual response given the background of the individual from such a beginning. It has little or nothing to do, in fact, with rejecting one's personal responsibility, but is tied to one's affiliation to one's sex as male or female.

An unaffiliated male see his sex identity through the genitals, if he has them, the reasoning goes, then he is male...a man. The idea manhood may be more involved than rutting never enters the scenario.

21

Because the male is unaffiliated, he does not recognize the female as anything important other than just another toy, and the unseen child he recognizes not at all. Such a person will not attach any kind of "value" to the impregnated female or the child she carries because he cannot.

He does not have the ability to understand or even comprehend the implications of the pregnancy.

Many such fellows are great at copulating but fall short of anything else resembling fatherhood. Women who use themselves or allow themselves to be used in such ways are usually unaffiliated as well. These are the same women who can, without blinking an eye, abort their baby.

This lack of affiliation brings up the truly dark side of human nature. In many cases, people do not just fall shy of affiliation with their sex; they do not come close to affiliating with fellow human beings. This is not as far-fetched as one might think. The newborn babe, for example, enters the world with a sex identity (presence of genitals) but no awareness of sex, has no values to speak of, and is indifferent to order or disorder. A person who never graduated from this state of being, in any direction, could be capable of anything, from cold-blooded murder to intercourse with animals. A person who never learns how to discern good could easily fall into this category. The truly amoral sociopath is most likely to show up through illegitimate birthing or inside the framework of a father absent home.

Illegitimate birthing, rather than imposing a disruption upon the child begins, develops, and ends in instability.

In a society that really cares about its children, illegitimate birthing should carry the stigma of a crime against a child.

Parental abandonment is not a one-sided proposition, for it does irreparable damage to the developing child.

Alexsandr put the pages aside. He remembered now how Grampy backed off the project after going through the General's original stack of notes.

"They drag on and on," Grampy commented. "It is like he's punching away at something, some illusion, and doesn't have a clue what he's fighting with. There's nothing to build on. There's a missing key ingredient, no starting point. Sorry, Alexsandr. Count me out."

Alexsandr remembered clearly picking through the notes, line by line. He remembered that certain something that kept pecking away at him. He remembered thinking to himself: It is here...somewhere inside these lines...it is in here! He remembered Grampy calling the project aimless, and choosing to go on toward other things. He remembered meeting the General and declining the offer. He remembered the day General Perkins came back to his house, to try to sell him the idea one last time. He was, once again, dressed flawlessly. Alexsandr guessed his shoes alone cost close to a thousand dollars for the pair.

He remembered the scribbled model, in all the grand simplicity. He remembered General Perkins handing him the handwritten notes, insisting: "The key is in here somewhere. I know it! I'm just too damn close to it all to see what I'm looking at! I'm a soldier, not a researcher."

Alexsandr remembered going over the notes time after time, in the privacy of his study. He remembered picking his brain to isolate the key. It came to him quite by accident, a few days later.

He and Rachael sat on the porch, at sunset, to relax and idle some time away with senseless chatter surrounded by the co-mingled odors of blooming flowers. It was a colorful sunset, with all the right hues bouncing just right off some stringy, scattered clouds. Off in the distance somewhere a bird sang. There was no traffic to disrupt the peace.

"What's got you so preoccupied these days, Alexsandr?" Rachael asked. "Ever since that gentleman visited, you've been preoccupied. Can you talk about it?"

"In all confidence, Rachael, yes I can. Not a word to anyone, okay?"

Rachael knew, once upon a time, that meant, literally, not a word to a living soul. Years back, one of Alexsandr's papers had been compromised by idle chatter, and another man built a career on the basis of Alexsandr's research. These days, it meant no one outside Alexsandr's most trusted circle of friends. Alexsandr was simply too far up in years to worry too much about someone stealing his work.

"The gentleman is a General, Rachael. He's spent years fighting wars, all around the globe. He wants to commission a study to find the root cause of the incredible decline in young people's increasingly deficient social awareness and their amorality. He's sincere. He's agreed to fully fund the research if I will take it on."

"Are you going to do it, Alexsandr?"

"I can't get Grampy interested, and I'm not sure I can do it...if I want to do it...alone. I have a feeling it is a very complicated undertaking."

"What's the hold up, Alexsandr? You've studied this kind of stuff all your life."

"I know. There's something challenging about the possibilities," he answered. "I've spent decades pouring over excuses for such stuff, but never, anywhere, have I found a legitimate non-speculative root cause or causes for amoral and anti-social behaviors."

"Alexsandr, might I make a suggestion?"

"Of course," he answered. "I value your input, you know that."

"On something like this, Alexsandr, walk away from the books and documents for a while…tap into your plain old-fashioned common sense. Then proceed from there."

Alexsandr smiled. He remembered the quiet evening, and the words that kept ringing in his head for day's thereafter…common sense. Common sense! Common sense!

In time, he recalled, these two simple words sealed his fate and brought the dreams of General Perkins a scant few steps from fruition. He looked up from his desk, put his glasses aside, rubbed his eyes. With the most simple of nods, he mumbled to himself, "Common sense. Such simple words…what an evasive and irritating rascal you are!"

Chapter Three

Alexsandr sat behind his desk, going over some notes. He was expecting visitors shortly. He gathered his notes, leaned back. He closed his eyes, and recalled, with a hint of a smile on his face, how The Red Flag project initially took off:

He had explored endless possibilities after that fateful day when common sense entered the picture. He spent hours on end in his study, taking no calls, no visitors. At one point he banned Rachael from entering or bothering him, explaining a fire or an earthquake might justify an interruption...nothing less."

Human behavioral phenomena occupied his mind, and he tumbled possibilities to and fro, juggling ideas and more ideas searching for, of all things, logic behind illogical behavior. Through stacks and stacks of papers and paper, he scribbled, tested, re-tested one idea after another, until his trash cans overflowed with wadded up balls of paper, accumulated discarded ideas, by the hundreds.

In an exhausted rage one evening, very late, he wadded up what seemed to be his thousandth idea for the session and threw the wad angrily across the room. If one had laid eyes upon him at that moment, they would have seen a red-faced, blurry-eyed man in a wrinkled suit, his tie pulled open and dangling around his neck. His hair would have been a stringy mess from running his hands through it time and time again. They would certainly have seen a side of Alexsandr Simon few people knew existed.

"Good God Almighty! Where's the key! It has to be here!"

He called it a night, got up from his desk, walked toward the closed door of the study. Feeling something akin to rage tempered by exhaustion, he paused in front of the door to regain his composure. He took a deep breath. He scratched his chin. He closed his eyes briefly. He bowed his head, and his brow furrowed. He opened his eyes again.

He was about to open the door when he changed his mind. He returned to his desk, scribbled one last idea, and placed it in full view on his desk.

"I'll be back, you little pickle! Tomorrow...you and I are going to war!! I gotcha! Praise God...I gotcha!"

On the paper he wrote, in heavy digits: $1 + 1 = 1$.

He felt a certain shivery tinge of joy mixed with satisfaction as he left the room. Though very tired, he took the time to sip a glass of wine before turning in. That night, he curled up beside Rachael in bed, put his arm around her. He slept harder than he had in weeks.

The next morning, Alexsandr woke refreshed. He showered and shaved. He scrubbed his teeth. He ate a hearty breakfast, of pancakes and eggs. Then he and Rachael went for a walk. It was a beautiful wind-free morning. It smelled fresh. The sky was clear and pale blue and cloudless. Birds chirped. When they got back home, Alexsandr removed himself to his study. Rachael went shopping. She was going to pick up her granddaughter, Ladonna, and take her along. She was going to pick up a few toys to distribute at the hospital. She could not wait to mention the fact Richard and Alexsandr were going to work together. Although she liked Ladonna's boyfriend, David, she had it in her mind Richard was better suited to her.

Alexsandr began writing in earnest. He let the thoughts flow as they might, to return to them later to thin them out, tighten them up if necessary. He let his years of research dictate the route of the entries. He grouped his entries as the ideas flowed.

Alexsandr's recollections were interrupted by a knock on the door. He looked up from his desk, as Rachael stepped in, escorting Richard.

"I hope I'm not disturbing you, Professor," Richard said. "Grampy filled me in on some details, and I'd like to pursue a few things pertaining to your research."

"Come in! By all means, come in, Richard. I've been expecting you." Alexsandr rose from his desk, and greeted him with a hearty handshake.

"I was just remembering a few things. You woke me from my trance." He walked Richard to a chair in front of his desk. "Be seated. Where's Grampy?"

"He'll be here, shortly. He said something about bringing your research to a satisfactory conclusion?"

"We'll see what develops, Richard. I'm going to introduce you both to The Red Flag project. I think you'll find it very interesting…challenging, at the least. It might give your thesis a well-defined direction to take." He asked Rachael to take a few refreshments into the computer room. "We'll be down there for quite a while, I think."

Before she left the room, she nodded a warning finger toward Richard. Her eyes relayed her sincerity.

"You be careful, Richard. Don't let Alexsandr draw you into something you have no business tampering with."

Alexsandr chuckled. "Give Ladonna a big hug for me, Rachael," said Alexsandr.

Rachael left.

"How is Ladonna these days, Alexsandr?" asked Richard. "What's she up to? It has been quite a while since I've seen her."

"She got herself a good job in Nohartinit, got herself a nice apartment, got herself a boyfriend – a really good and decent fellow named David Wilson – a law student. I like him, but I always thought someone like you would be better suited to her. I don't like lawyers. She makes enough money to have some extras, saving some to buy a better car. She's turned into quite a beautiful young women; maybe you two ought to get reacquainted."

"The next time she comes over, would you give me a call, Alexsandr? I'd sure like to see her again. We had some great times while we were growing up. I never could get her to like me in any way but as a friend. I doubt she would have changed her mind." Richard looked at Alexsandr. He could see from the beam in his eyes he was very proud of Ladonna. Richard then changed the subject. "What's got Rachael so dead set against this project, Alexsandr?"

"She knows just enough about The Red Flag project to be afraid of it," he said to Richard. "It is about knowledge, Richard. We're not going to be doing anything but trying to bring order to chaos."

"Why did you call it The Red Flag, Alexsandr? Seems like an unusual name? What is it about, Alexsandr...some kind of left wing commie plot, maybe?"

Alexsandr smiled. "General Perkins considered the facts he had gathered, brought enough order to them to postulate a conspiracy of some sort...subversion. I just kept the title he used. He was, however, way off the mark with his conspiracy ideas, but not the possibility of conspiracy altogether. He made good sense, for the most part, but, in that, he missed his mark. I have to admit, his ideas made sense; until I rerouted his ideas, I did not, as he did not, understand the relationships existing in various ways. I have since discovered a lot of reasons to endorse a conspiracy theory...of a strange kind, anyway It is an evolutionary conspiracy, a turn of potentially unstoppable events."

"I get the eerie feeling there is some kind of organized plot behind events as they turn, Alexsandr. You know, like when bad social policy keeps getting worse, as if by design and deliberate manipulation of systems."

There was a knock on the door, and the door was pushed open. "Am I interrupting?" asked Grampy.

They both turned toward the door as Grampy entered. He smiled, and approached them. He had dressed casually in jeans and a blue cotton shirt, rolled up at the sleeves. He wore sandals, with no socks.

"I see you started without me," he joked.

"Grampy, Richard...let's go to the computer room. I'll bring up The Red Flag, and we can discuss the ideas as they have evolved. This way." He led them to the basement. In the basement, he grouped three chairs near the computer. He then pulled up the file. It was formatted in paragraphs labeled, simply, IDEA 1,2, and etc.

IDEA 1 came on the screen:

IDEA1: There are extra-dimensional elements involved in all human lives. They are. They exist. They are present. They are beyond the human being's sensorial grasp. The ability to think, for example, is one such entity. The ability to discern good is another. Order is another. There must be dozens, at least, if not hundreds. These entities are found in five realms of human experience...mental, moral, psychological, emotional, and spiritual.

Thus, it is easy to see why people's lives sometimes evolve around patterns of perceptions, without regard to sensorial interpretation, in which that which is perceived equates to what is. In this reality optional sphere, standard rules do not always apply. One's covenant with God, for example, cannot be literally measured in intensity as it affects one's life any more than a schizophrenic's radio-in-the-basement can be literally measured in intensity as it affects his life. However, in the sensorial reality world, the results of these perceptions can be seen to manifest through behavior, legislation, law and other ways as well.

When extra-dimensional perceptions take on the characteristics of fact even though they are pure fantasy, for example, they are sometimes quite potent as moving forces in the sensorial sphere. In America fantasy is big business. For example, the most obvious shortcoming of American social legislation and law in the last few decades is the accommodation of, catering to, and financial support of deviant behavior.

We live with social policy in which fantasy serves to legitimize that which is illegitimate, homosexuality, for example. With the switch from moral absolutes to oppressive and damaging relativistic moral assumptions behind the legislation and law, the social values which bind people, encourage prosperity, and define the individual as worthy and important have been pushed aside for political expediency with no view of (or consideration given to) the defining down of deviancy and the impact, in larger social terms beyond the individual, this redefining can have.

If there is, in fact, a logical explanation for deviant behavior, then a grievous and potentially dangerous situation has been aggravated by social engineering.

Common sense allows that rational or irrational behavior in mental, moral, psychological, emotional, or spiritual ways has a logical basis, in the extra-dimensional sphere, otherwise changes in social thinking would not affect the outcome of such changes. Outcomes are certainly measurable over the last forty years or so. Order, on the human plane, rests in the extra-dimensional sphere, and there is no reason that order of some kind does not govern that sphere. Einstein, for example, projected that a straight line, if it goes on long enough, will return to the point of origin. Is such a presumption: Fact or Fantasy or both?

In this optional reality, for example, things can make perfect sense but outside that sphere...in the sensorial reality world...they may appear to be lucid and sensible or utter nonsense. The desire to encourage deviancy on the personal level, for example, is understandable among the morally ill, but the desire to legislate immorality as a basis for social policy is not easy to understand. A look inside extra-dimensional realms may hold the key.

For example, the mathematicians swear that one plus one equals two (1+1=2). And there is no disagreement among us in the sensorial reality world. Simple math does not work if operated from a relativistic base. However, when one enters into an extra-dimensional sphere (the reality option) one plus one can and does equal one (1+1=1). Although it is necessary to move into the extra-dimensional sphere to accept and validate this equation, we can verify it in our sensorial real world. In simple math, we do not tolerate deviancy. But in matters of the extra-dimensional reality world, we allow that anything goes. All this accomplishes is disorder and confusion. Yet one can allow that disorder begets disorder.

There is no reason to believe the extra-dimensional reality world is not also ordered and orderly, even though things taking place in this optional reality may seem erratic and even chaotic.

A male and a female coupling can produce a child, 1+1=1. Thus we have a circumstance in which the mathematicians are right and those who disagree with them (on a different plane) are also right. But we also have a dimension (verifiable) in which 1+1 might also equal 2,3, or 4 etc. In the spiritual realm inside the extra-dimensional sphere, this same equation is again validated through the Father, Son, and Holy Spirit, three yet one. In the first example, each successive child is a separate individual, with the same 1+1 point of origin. In the second example, 1+1=1, with no extenuating attachments.

"Alexsandr?" asked Grampy, hesitantly. "You're saying, if I understand you right, there is a logical or rational foundation to even the most bizarre of thoughts or behaviors?"

"Yes."

"1+1=1." Richard thought about it for a few long moments, and he quizzed, "Are you implying that is the logic you're looking for?"

"That's why I've asked you here. Is it? Is this the key?"

"Verifiable in one plane, although originated in another?" hummed Grampy. "I can live with that; the creative process. But…right in one plane, wrong in another…yet both equally credible? A very interesting concept."

"An extra-dimensional sphere…and a sensorial sphere…both equally credible, yet one sometimes directly in opposition to the other…yet, maybe, right in both planes or wrong in both planes?"

"Yes! Isn't it beautiful!"

"But Alexsandr," cautioned Grampy. "Can you take it anywhere?"

"Think about it?" explained Alexsandr. "Suppose one a) knows how to bond both spheres, and; b) one does not know how to bond the spheres…what kind of individuals have you? Here's my hypothesis:" He pulled up IDEA 2.

IDEA 2: The breakdown in this extra-dimensional sphere comes when there is no extra-dimensional bonding. If one does not, in fact, join these elements as a legitimate reality-based bonded entity, the equation falls apart. In other words, if order does not prevail in the extra-dimensional optional reality, it, like the sensorial reality world, for the individual, will also break down. In effect, the individual will follows path of disunity and disorder.

For example, if there are no mental, moral, psychological, emotional, or spiritually based ties between a male and a female, then the equation for reproduction changes accordingly. The complete package child (1+1=1) cannot exist but is displaced by (1) + (1) + (1) and there is no answer in any dimension. One cannot, for example, deny a part the Trinity and still find God, any more than two people with no extra-dimensional connections or commonalities can extend extra-dimensional qualities to their offspring.

In theory, perfection can be achieved only when all the elements of both spheres are conjoined and pushed, each and every one, to absolute fulfillment, which is, of course, impossible for any human being. Stability, however, is possible, and is manifest in both reality worlds as a matter of routine human business. Not all children enter the world untouched by extra-dimensional qualities bestowed by mentally, morally, psychologically, emotionally, and spiritually healthy parents.

The child born to parents who are married and bonded in both worlds, will have offspring equipped to lead a fully human life. The child, an individual person from conception onward, will find his or her full completion only if nurtured by his or her biological parents. Being part father, part mother, yet totally separate as a human being (1+1=1) or (+1), the child, to fulfill his biological destiny, needs the extra-dimensional and sensorial influences of both parents to reach a state of complete bonded harmony in both worlds.

This is not to say the child will or will not thrive. The deck will be stacked him, however. In a broken home, a very real part of the child will always be missing.

Richard rubbed his chin, moving toward a high state of mental activity. "You're saying that unless one ties extra-dimensional thoughts to sensorial realities, he falls flat?"

"No. I'm saying the extra-dimensional elements must bond in the extra-dimensional plane first, and then...and only then...will they reconcile with the sensorial reality world. Then thoughts, as you put it, will mesh with the sensorial reality world. Liberals, for example, take the thoughts – no matter how irrational – then try to bend the sensorial reality world to meet the criteria of the thoughts, which is, of course, impossible."

"The 1+1+1 as opposed to the 1+1=1?" said Grampy. "A liberal, for example, will equate the =1 and +1 when, in fact, there are light years separating them. They connect the dots in fantasy alone and proceed from there."

"Precisely," Alexsandr answered. "You see where it is going, don't you, Grampy? The +1 scenario, I think, is the key to maladjustment and anti-social proclivities. If the extra-dimensional elements don't mesh, then they cannot contribute to the discovery of truth in the sensorial reality world."

"You're saying, then, that God is?" Grampy queried.

"Of course." Alexsandr said. "Otherwise religion would not shape and form the twists and turns of humanity. Saints are real, Grampy. And, once again, we're back to 1+1=1. At the other extreme, you take the +1 extreme and you have satanic influence."

"I see," said Grampy. "And the closer one tunes in toward the perfection of the 1+1=1 scenario, the closer he gets to God? The more distant one goes, the closer he moves toward satanic possession?"

"Faith is a power beyond the grasp of human understanding. Where else than through the 1+1=1 scenario (The Father, Son, and Holy Spirit) do miraculous conversions take place. All the psychiatrists in the world, combined, cannot touch the power of an authentic

31

conversion or transformation of even the most gruesomely troubled character in the land. Through Jesus Christ comes peace and hope and forgiveness when nothing else in the world can. And where does this conversion take place?"

"In the extra-dimensional sphere, manifested through behavioral changes in the sensorial reality sphere," Grampy said. "Just as demonic possessions take place in the same extra-dimensional sphere."

"Absolutely," said Alexsandr. "The +1 becomes an =1, a legitimate part of a larger something. And, if you read between the lines, you will see as well moral absolutes are...they exist. They're real. Moral rejection is equally real."

He looked at Richard. Richard seemed totally bewildered at this point. "Saints and sinners...where's all this going, anyway?"

"Read on, Richard. Perhaps this will help," Alexsandr said, sympathetically.

He keyed in the next page.

IDEA 3 came onscreen.

IDEA 3: In many ways, bonding is like gravity and other existences in the extra-dimensional sphere. You can't see such existences but you know they are there. The person must bond with extra-dimensional elements in mental, moral, psychological, emotional, and spiritual ways for the extra-dimensional element to reach fruition and manifest itself in the sensorial real world. The bonding or lack of bonding can be verified in either direction in the sensorial sphere. Nobody, for example, can miss the aura surrounding two people bonded by love, but no one can measure it, either. It is. It exists. It is present. And that is all. The intensity of love depends on how tightly bonded the two people are (as individuals) in mental, moral, psychological, emotional, and spiritual ways.

"In other words," Richard probed. "If the extra-dimensional elements conjoin a certain way, the individual will behave in a certain way. If the elements do not join, or fail to join completely, then the individual will behave in an entirely different way? If one loves intensely in all five ways and one loves less intensely in but two of the five ways, there is an imbalance in the total package. With this imbalance, you get the +1, or the powerful =1, depending."

"You're getting there, Richard, but that's not the case," replied Alexsandr. "The elements do not bond to one another, as in atomic theory. The individual creates the bonds...he takes the bond from part to part...by his learned ability to search for meaning, to discern the difference between the +1 scenario and the =1 scenario, to discern good. To recognize a moral absolute when he experiences it."

"But, Alexsandr? Where does it all begin? Wouldn't there be some kind of automatic connection made once the process begins?"

"If one has a sex identity and affiliation to his sex as male or female, it starts there. The rest is evolutionary, but not automatic. And the individual will live happily ever after," said Alexsandr, playfully, "if he can search for meaning and he continues to search for meaning."

"You mean if someone develops normally with his natural sex, he will begin the bonding process?"

"Precisely. That's why we are not yet swamped to overflow with mentally ill people. Not yet."

"So you're saying anti-social behaviors are rooted in sex identity?" asked Grampy.

"Not in identity but in the inability to affiliate with one's natural sex, as male or female. It goes way beyond the possession of genitals. Affiliation rests in the extra-dimensional sphere, Richard."

"Hmm," mumbled Richard. "Without affiliation we're looking once again at the +1 scenario. Existence with no frames of reference."

"Read on, Richard," said Alexsandr. "It may lead to clarification." He pulled up IDEA 4.

IDEA 4: One might suggest the bonding element in the extra-dimensional sphere determines which direction people will take in the sensorial reality world. Behavior, in this world, would be determined early on, depending on the circumstances surrounding the child in his or her earliest years (from birth to three), the time span in which the experts tell us gender recognition begins to take hold. The simple boy/girl distinction is a simple beginning. But this beginning is not enough. Other simple answers must be found: What is a boy? What is a girl? What is a man? What is a woman? Without moving toward understanding the real differences between the sexes, the individual cannot rise above the +1 scenario. In this scenario, for example, there would be no distinction between the sexes. The +1 scenario would apply. With this distinction rooted, no matter how elementary this rooting may be, the scenario changes to the =1 scenario, the individual being elevated into a larger and relatively stable scheme of existence.

Those who do little or no bonding whatsoever would be expected to mesh with little or no manifestations compatible with the sensorial reality world. Such people, like the homosexual or other amoral socio-paths, would manifest nearly complete aversion to the sensorial reality world's minimum levels of expected behavior. This could also explain the characteristic lack of social affiliation through unwed birthing demonstrated by children from broken homes, where the extra-dimensional bonding does not take place; the child of such a union is brought into the world as a solitary being (+1) not an integral part of something larger and more stable than mere existence (=1). Although they may be totally out of line or incompatible with the sensorial reality world, such individuals would be totally compatible with their own thoughts and behaviors in the extra-dimensional sphere.

Such a child, denied this extra-dimensional bonding, fends for himself, if intervention does not enter the scenario. The child would never experience the total package, the full human experience. They would be living in half-life and never know it. They would experience the sensorial reality world but never the extra-dimensional sphere, which rounds out the human experience.

The half-life scenario fits, for example, the homosexual quite literally. Thus we can search for the genesis of the homosexual condition, manifested in an almost total absence of mental, moral, psychological, emotional, and spiritual development, possibly the loneliest, most incomplete, and most empty of human existences one can imagine. One cannot, for example, make water (H_2O) from oxygen atoms alone. Without hydrogen atoms, there is no water, as simple as that. Without bonding with the sensorial reality world in extra-dimensional ways, there can be no completion as a human being.

"What we have here, Alexsandr, is the beginning of the search for meaning...somewhere in the first three years of life?" asked Grampy.

"Suppose, Grampy, a child never affiliated with his or her sex. They are, and that is all. How would they validate their existence?"

"Richard? Do you see where this is going?"

"They would validate their existence through fantasy, Alexsandr. Otherwise, they would negate their own existence by acknowledging there is more to existence than genitals, and, having no frames of reference, they would, by doing so, invalidate themselves. So they live out the +1 scenario, because they have no other choice."

"Now, Richard...do you see where the evolutionary possibility of inevitable detachment takes root?"

"The conspiracy, then, is nothing more than an evolving reaction to ungrounded children?"

"Precisely."

"And as the real numbers of ungrounded children grows exponentially, the chances of social recovery correspondingly decrease."

"The conspiracy, then, is in the confused meaning of compassion espoused then manifested in social, legal, and other ways. The more our people and our government subsidize broken homes and personal irresponsibility and stuff like unwed birthing and other personal mistakes the closer we move ourselves to social collapse and chaos."

"People are trying to fix personal problems at the expense of society as a whole," added Richard. "My research seems to indicate social pressure is by far the better medicine than all the money in the world. Does this fit the scenario, Alexsandr?"

"Of course it does. All the money in the world cannot repair anyone's lack of perception or inability to discern good or encourage one to search for meaning. Money can't buy back a ruined soul."

"What we are looking at, Richard," explained Grampy. "...Is the genesis of liberalism and other forms of mental illness. Irrational solutions to real problems." Grampy chuckled, and he looked at Alexsandr with a twinkle in his eyes. "Are you ready to concede my ideas of mental illness are stronger than your ideas about ordinary stupidity, Alexsandr?"

"I made that concession months ago, Grampy. I just didn't want to say anything to you." Alexsandr laughed heartily. "But now, Grampy, we can at least affirm your suspicions without much ado. Liberalism and other mental illness have a root cause, which means there has got to be a cure, at least a treatment somewhere. But stupidity is not out of the picture altogether. Not yet. Irrational thinking and stupidity often run hand in hand."

"Isn't it all tied to the ability to think, but not necessarily to think clearly or in some sensible way? It all moves on the ability or inability to decipher not just meaning but legitimate meaning from the thinking and experience processes? The ability to understand is not the same as the ability to think?" asked Richard.

"Precisely," answered Alexsandr. "Thinking, per se, is nothing. Any bonehead can think. Ah, but understanding! That's an art."

"Thinking is a very important part of the bonding process, then," Richard added. "Anybody can think, but understanding stuff...that's the part liberals and others don't quite latch on to."

"I get it. Thinking is the first step, but understanding is the bonding agent, so to speak," Grampy said. "One can think until he turns blue but never make the connections necessary for legitimate understanding" Grampy hesitated to ruminate. He appeared penetratingly thoughtful. Then he looked at Richard, then Alexsandr. "Thinking is a universal quality."

"But how can we validate this proposition?" asked Richard. "It will, if we can affirm it, validate the mental illness hypothesis. We all know liberals do nothing but think, think, think...then think some more. Never met one yet that understood the first blessed thing about anything. Do we separate out thinking as a process in and of itself, totally unrelated to anything else? A pure process, so to speak, independent of all others?"

"That would certainly help explain liberalism and street crimes and social crimes and moral crimes, wouldn't it?" added Grampy.

"We're getting there," said Alexsandr. "In the next few sections, Grampy, you will find some of our old work. I was struck by something, which the General also came up with...our formula for human stability...slightly modified. He took it a little beyond what we had done. Using his model, I extended it again. I figured, between the three of us, we had to be on to something. It just about drove me nuts getting past our original formula."

"What was the key, Alexsandr?"

"Something Rachael said one evening, Grampy. It goes back to what Richard just said about thinking. The key was plain old fashion common sense. And then something else, something I said, as I was about to break my desk into splinters after a long and fruitless day."

"Let me guess," said Grampy, his eyes shimmering playfully, recalling many such times in the past. "You probably threw something across the room and yelled: Good God Almighty! What's the key!...Hence the 1+1=1 scenario."

"Precisely."

"I see it now...we've had our heads buried in books for so long we forgot about the world going on outside the pages. You simply started looking at what is, and then you took it from there?" Grampy commented.

"I had to rethink how I looked at things, Grampy. It was, actually, as simple as that. I began to see what was...and is."

Richard smiled, slightly, and said, "Just because you see an occasional three-legged dog does not mean you have to cancel out the proposition that dogs have four legs."

"Precisely." Alexsandr moved them next into IDEA 5. "In this section, you will notice a logical case can begin to form. You will find the model beginning to solidify, common sense reasoning shaping and forming the development of a workable and testable hypothesis. Read it, and then we'll see where it goes. I'll walk you through it."

Richard leaned forward to get a better look at the screen. Grampy sat a little closer. Alexsandr began to read:

IDEA 5: "It seems not just possible but totally logical human behaviors can be measured against extra-dimensional bonding (or lack thereof) and manifested sensorial reality world behaviors and activities explained in logical terms. To find these logical terms, one must look at the extra-dimensional sphere as a thinking sphere.

To do this, one must start at the foundations of human stability, order, life affirming values, and sex identification with affiliation to one's sex as male or female. All three of these foundations begin and end in the extra-dimensional plane and are manifested in the sensorial reality sphere. To move from one element to the next (and there is a logical progression) one must not only think but one must also understand."

"Alexsandr?" said Grampy, as he scratched his chin. "You're separating thinking and understanding into two separate functions altogether?"

"Remember, Grampy, we're working with common sense here. Look at it this way, Grampy. When we were trying to develop our model, remember how we went over the possibilities time after time, revising time and time again? What was it that we were doing?"

"Thinking, Alexsandr."

"And why was our thinking unsuccessful for the most part? Why did we trash so many ideas, Grampy?"

"They didn't add up, Alexsandr. They just didn't add up right."

"In other words," offered Richard. "They did not add up because they did not lead to understanding?"

"Think of it this way, Grampy. We can gather stacks of data, papers, and the like. We can ruminate over the information, and we can try to discover what the information yields. Until it adds up, you have nothing testable, no workable hypothesis."

"The thinking part means absolutely nothing without the understanding, right?" added Richard.

"Now, listen to this: The extra-dimensional sphere is a thinking sphere, in that it is reachable by mental processes commonly called thinking. Anybody can think. Not everyone can make sense of the sensorial reality world, however. Many such people live out their lives barely even touching base with that world. Many touch base with it but never understand it. Many stay put in the purely mental (thought-originated) fantasy world of their own creation and never venture into living to their fullest potential as a human being. They think, therefore they assume they have reached the peak of human existence, when, in fact, they have barely touched the surface."

"Correct me if I am wrong, Alexsandr," said Richard. "You're implying that some people confuse thinking with understanding and never move that extra step toward productive thinking? They never add two and two?"

"Let me continue," said Alexsandr. "The ability to think is not so important as one might think. What is important is what one does with his thoughts. It comes to mind right off hand the child who can recite and rattle off the ABC song flawlessly, but cannot tell anyone what letter follows S without going back through the whole song. They have the letters, they have the song, and they have everything but they do not grasp the reason behind it all.

Many people live out their lives that way. Many people sing the songs, or repeat the phrases, but do not have a clue why they are singing or spouting the phrases. Many people simply cannot move their ability to think that necessary little step toward a search for meaning, much less accomplish some form of understanding. Such people define and live out their lives (and behaviors) one word or one thought at a time."

"You can justify that, Alexsandr?" quizzed Grampy. "How are you going to build a case for such disjointed thinking...one word or one thought at a time?"

"Remember we're dealing in common sense here."

Richard read the paragraphs carefully. He had another question. "Alexsandr, you're breaking the process into three distinct movements rather than two?"

"Right, Richard. It seems obvious to look at it. First: Thinking. Second: Searching for meaning. Third: Understanding. Not too far removed from the so-called scientific method."

"Hmm?" grumbled Grampy. "I'm not sold yet, Alexsandr."

"Back to common sense, Grampy. Consider this: Some people, for example, can abort a baby and never connect the taking of a human life to the process. Such people would confiscate guns and blame the inanimate object for violence. Nothing rational needs to enter the scenario because, for such people, the continuum can not and never will exist because their thought processes leap from word to word, resting where ever it might be convenient to stop, usually at the point it sounds good. Such people, for example, will speak of a woman's right to choose. But they would never phrase it a woman's right to kill her unborn baby. Or, better yet, guns kill people."

"Are you proposing they cannot make the connections rather than they refuse to make the connections?"

"I am proposing a legitimate form of mental illness, Alexsandr. Consider this: These are the same people who will take an isolated incident involving a few people out of the total population of the whole country and push for laws to guard against a repeat of the incident, even if it means shackles for millions of innocent people. These are the same people who favor throwing God out of public life to pacify a bunch of atheistic social ingrates, for example.

The lie is these people are so compassionate, so in tune with their fellow human beings, they must, at any cost, protect minorities (human or animal or insect, no matter how insignificant are their real numbers) from the evil hordes.

In truth, however, these are the same people who will sit passively by while millions of unborn babies are slaughtered each year, who will destroy lives and livelihoods to protect a bug. These are the people who will commit murder and mayhem to protect a tree, or a rodent, or a whale, or a gnat.

These people are, in many ways, very sick. There is a logical reason behind this sickness. They are sick because they cannot push their ability to think to any useful level of understanding. They cannot discern good, or truth, or anything else of a civil or civilized nature. Many have nothing but utter contempt for their fellow human beings, but will lay down their lives to save trees, rocks, insects, or rattlesnakes.

These are the same people who will chance upon a freak of nature and never accept the notion...never ever again...there is order in the natural world. The problem is not such people are stupid. The problem is they cannot think past one word or image at a time, and they cannot connect events or experiences in a chain or conceive of things as integral parts of a larger entity. They can think, but they understand very little."

"Go on, Alexsandr," Grampy said. "I'm beginning to see what's up ahead of us. I think I do, anyway."

Alexsandr continued reading: "These are the same silly and disjointed people who would discriminate to end discrimination.

These are the same people who would destroy the life and livelihood of a human being to save a kangaroo rat, but who could not (or would not) shed a tear at the death of Mother Teresa. These are the same people who would donate more money to save a mountain lion than they would to help out the children of a woman ripped to pieces by the same mountain lion.

These are the same people who would never give up their rights to consent before their teenage daughter could get her ears pierced, but who will, nonetheless, allow her to have an abortion without that consent.

These are the same people who would blow up a multi-million dollar medical research center to save a few chimps but who would fight to the death to keep the door of an abortion mill wide open.

These are the same people who hate and despise big business but couldn't give a reason behind the hatred if they had to.

What is it about? It is about some inability to think? Or is it about stupidity? Is it about mental illness? Is there any logic behind the chaos? Is there any kind of order behind the apparent lack of order?"

"Where's it going, Alexsandr?" quizzed Grampy.

"Are you saying they can think, Alexsandr, but cannot separate themselves from thinking long enough to see the absurdity of their thinking?" asked Richard.

"They sort of run around in a thinking trance-like state...pure thinking, without meaning, without closure, without substance, or any kind of development beyond mere thinking," answered Alexsandr. "But...it has order. There is order and logic and common sense behind this tragic mental illness."

"I can see the logic," agreed Grampy. "Thinking, if taken alone, standing alone, can mean nothing, lead to nothing, amount to nothing. But I find it very hard to believe people can exist in such a state and never tune in to planet Earth."

"Look at it like this, Grampy," explained Alexsandr. "Suppose Richard here has his thoughts fixed on an absurd notion...hmm, let's see...rocks can communicate with one another through telepathic means. That's a good one. Now, here we have a thought process that has awakened the possibility of an absurdity. But to Richard, it is not absurd. It is real...as real as anything...in his mind and his mind alone.

Thinking is beautiful...it can conjure absurdities, harmlessly. We can mentally picture the destruction of the world, for example. Now, as long as Richard thinks this absurdity, he feels secure in the idea rocks can communicate through telepathic means. Under normal conditions, Richard would process the idea and take it to the next level, the search for meaning. He would, being a reasonable man, dismiss the idea forthrightly. The thinking has come and gone, and everybody lives happily ever after.

But suppose Richard cannot move the thinking to the next level. He simply cannot do it. His brain won't allow him to do it...or whatever. Now we have a man saddled with an absurdity he can't dismiss...it lingers and he can't do anything with it. Can't throw it away. Can't backtrack and pretend the idea never entered his world. Now what? Suppose this is the high point of Richard's intellectual life? He would, of course, treasure his grand discovery, which, of course, is nothing, but to him it is everything. It is what sets him apart in the world. He knows what he knows!

Still, there's nothing. Not until Richard convinces others his rocks can, indeed, communicate with telepathy will his thought take on what he will perceive as truth. Ten people believe him, and they convince ten others. Soon Richard is surrounded by believers; in this group, the absurdity becomes truth, when it fact it has never left the point of origin...absolute nonsense. And then what happens?"

"And then he gets a government grant to further his research?" joked Grampy.

Richard and Alexsandr laughed heartily.

"And then DOD pays him handsomely to train rocks for use as spies and forward observers?" added Richard.

"And he begins to teach telepathy in rocks at Berkeley," added Alexsandr, playing along.

After they had a good laugh, they took a short break, had some coffee, and they got back to business.

Alexsandr explained where it was going: "We can agree the telepathic rocks example is absurd. Now, look at substituting telepathic rocks with something that sounds better, is more widely appealing, but still has no basis outside of pure thinking and fantasy."

"Confiscating guns will end violence," Richard offered.

Grampy nodded his agreement.

"A good example," Alexsandr agreed. "Now where are we?"

"Back to the government grant and tenure at Berkeley?" Grampy offered.

They laughed again.

"Precisely," said Alexsandr. "But this time, we have added something to the equation. What we have developed is a very appealing absurdity, pure thinking from start to finish, never moved to the search for meaning stage. But we have opened a door leading toward power and control. The appeal will be not just widespread but it will reach epidemic-level attractiveness and gather in followers by the thousands upon thousands. And, in time, it may be moved into the realm of legislated social policy."

"The genesis of liberalism," hummed Grampy, frowning.

"I'll be damned," mumbled Richard. "Nothing but pure thinking, absurd in and of itself, taken to the stature of law."

"Here's the beautiful part," added Alexsandr. "It fits a pattern of logical progression, predictable, but not necessarily containable. Read on." He brought up the next page:

The politics of this apparent mental mush is, in fact, by design. There are two things, of all else, these people do not have and will go to any lengths to get – even murder and mayhem – and these are power and control.

Their thinking ability yields no power because it is next to worthless in a real world. The +1 scenario must be terrifying for the individual.

Not only is he alone, un-bonded, he is alone in the world and has not a clue who he is (no affiliation to his sex as male or female), what he is (no life-affirming values), or where he is going (no order). He cannot even think clearly.

They have no control of anything because they cannot connect the dots in a real world...not even in their own thinking. They cannot validate their own existence except through fantasy, and this, too, must be terrifying.

So, inevitably, they will turn political, in a very broad sense. They will exert themselves any way they can which will satisfy their need for self-identity through power and control. These are the people who will shape their lives on the shaky proposition that a consensus can somehow validate their inept thinking and their empty lives.

Thus they clump, generating one crisis after another, to empower themselves, to validate their existence. The cause for which they fight does not have to be sensible, as long as it gives them a feeling (as illusionary as it is in a real world) of power and control. By clumping in whatever numbers they can muster, they generate their own reality through a consensus of their kind. That is to say they seek safety in numbers.

They validate themselves through the only mechanism they have...thinking. If enough people agree on the same songs and phrases, they find safety and security in a scary world. It does not matter that their songs and phrases make no sense at all. What matters is how many people join the chorus.

This thinking mechanism allows the most fear-filled of the bunch to fight the fight from his armchair, thinking in unison with the mob while not moving one inch in any direction. He can join the chorus without having to be involved at all! It is the perfect thinker's scenario to satisfy, in absolute safety in a scary world, the need for power and control.

There is a logical way to look at this. It makes perfect sense to see the +1 scenario played out through a consensus process. As it runs, it approximates the 1+1=1 scenario, except the closure never happens because the closure mechanism is missing. A cheap imitation (consensus validates) falls short of the authentic process. The thinking is that when enough people agree on something, they have rooted themselves in the sensorial reality world, which is not possible under the 1+1+1+1 etc. scenario.

The consensus validates scenario is very useful to those who need it because it allows them to participate in living out the fantasy (achieve the illusion of power and control) while not putting forth any effort to get there. An imitation, at best, with the consensus validates approach the individual does not have to think too long, too hard, or too far, or think at all. He is free to skip and skim in his fantasy world and find acceptance, regardless of the absurdity of his personal visions through thinking. Understanding is not in the picture at all.

The most frightening and damaging part of the picture is with the need for power and control in these otherwise empty lives, violence will inevitably follow. These people will eventually strike out (or strike back) at the world they cannot find a place in, in a world that will not validate their absurdities. It will, in time, become essential they force their thinking on others, if for no other reason forcing it will validate their existence, even if it is in pure fantasy.

"I see the progression, Alexsandr," said Richard, when he finished reading the page. "Are you sure about the inevitability of violence, Alexsandr?"

"Common sense, Richard. When these people fight for power and control, by definition and human nature, they will meet with resistance. In our example, do you think people are willingly going to give up their guns just because some lonely bonehead...or ten thousand lonely boneheads...want it in the name of right social policy?"

"I would think forces beyond the human being would also move them toward violence," offered Grampy. "You cannot begin with nothing, proliferate nothing, force nothing onto a reality, however it may be defined, without some kind of collision, most likely violent and formidable. It would be like trying to force the mating of a bear to a wild horse. Violence would be inevitable. You just cannot do it, not when dealing with people...and not when you're dealing with truth and forces above and beyond the human experience. I think there are truths in the human and the natural world that will inevitably prevail, in spite of what may be thrown against them. No matter what, you cannot make an untruth into a truth. You cannot begin with nothing and make it something, no matter how you package the illusion. Creation, from nothingness, is reserved to God alone. It cannot be done by mere humans."

"But, Grampy, liberals do create huge barriers to human progress and potential. These barriers exist," Richard queried. "Wouldn't that negate your proposition?" He looked to Alexsandr, for an opinion. "What do you think, Alexsandr?"

"They're all on paper," said Grampy. "Words, words, and more words. They are artificial barriers. Inventions of sick minds."

"Nothing translated into words is still nothing," said Alexsandr. "These barriers you speak of, Richard, are based in nothingness and doomed to failure, even if they go through the motions of putting up the appearance of working, of being real."

"But abortion, Alexsandr? That is very real...and very permanent."

"If you happen to be the baby, yes. But how long can a society slaughter the replacement generations and still stand? There is nothing that says the confrontation between truth and nothingness will not take time to develop."

"It is inevitable," Grampy added.

"Look at our own society, Richard," said Alexsandr, as he moved the page.

Richard read the page:

In our own society, we see this violence manifested in abortion, in school shootings, church bombings, murder and mayhem to save animals or trees, drive-by shootings, homicides, and various other manifestations of this obsessive need for power and control.

The manifestations of social tolerance for violence are strange, and it should surprise no one that the +1 scenario plays out. Outrage is not tied to any particular kind of violence, but to the political muscle the various incidences can be milked for. As a liberal-leaning nation (+1), for example, it is not unusual that abortion is not just legal but socially sanctioned, even though abortions claim more than a million lives a year. Blowing up a church is deemed wrong if the congregation has political use, but numbers of casualties are insignificant in real terms compared against the population as a whole; still, to bomb a synagogue or a Baptist church, for example, is considered by many to be wrong (more wrong if the congregation is predominantly black, or perhaps Jewish or some other politically correct select group), but for the government to burn men, women, and children to death (as happened in the Waco, Texas, Massacre) is tolerated.

What seems apparent in how +1 people see acts of violence has little or nothing to do with casualties or body counts; sentiments seem tied to +1 political leanings, the exercise of power and control.

Liberal politics and the +1 scenario run hand in hand. It should surprise no one, in liberal politics, that killing millions of unborn babies is okay, but to put a mass murderer to death is wrong. In liberal politics it is wrong to bomb one church, but not wrong to massacre the people of another.

+1 thinking permeates American social policy and has subverted the social and moral conscience of the nation. Where violence is concerned, the leapfrog thinking of the +1 personality prevails. Outrage against violence is a process of selectivity, not something drawn from a base in any kind of moral absolute. The cries of indignation against the rape of women, for example, are politically correct and thus very popular. That more males are raped each year than are females carries no political weight, thus no outrage.

Because violence and the +1 scenario are inseparable, it should surprise no one that the more people who are born and bred into the +1 scenario, the more likely are we, as a society, going to move toward a violent society which answers not to principled behavior or moral discipline but to violence that will be addressed by more violence.

This is the tragedy of multicultural thinking, for example. As internal groups lose their identity as Americans, the +1+1+1 scenario kicks in. People begin to cower into ethnic, religious, sexual, racial or other pockets to hide from living. It is the consensus validates scenario manifested in a ghetto mentality. Instead of a common identity (=1) they opt for the +1, a position in which they become accountable only to their peers. Thus we see blacks clumping with blacks, homosexuals with homosexuals, and liberals with liberals.

The same things reappear...no recognition of a larger perspective, safety inside the consensus validates shield, it is easy and requires no effort to gain acceptance in the herd. Inside these pockets, there is safety, security, and rational thinking, the search for meaning, or understanding of the larger perspectives plays no role whatsoever.

Thus, for example, homosexuals can hide from their moral illnesses rather than face them, blacks can yell racism to explain away problems everyone confronts as a matter of the daily business of living, liberals can live in their fantasy worlds unmolested and unchallenged by reality.

These pockets play out the 1+1+1+1 scenario, and, in a social sense, divide people into factions, which will inevitably fight for power and control, and move, in time, toward violence as the ultimate solution to the most minor of problems.

"You're saying, Alexsandr, the consensus validates ingredient does not call for a large following, but merely a sufficient number of people to satisfy the needs of the individual?"

"How many people does it take? Who knows? What we do know is it takes a considerable number to grab the political processes. On the individual level, probably a single person can validate, to some degree, the lost and the aimless. The +1 individual who cannot find this consensus however is a different type of character." Alexsandr scrolled the page, and he read the next few paragraphs:

45

"There are signs this (violence as the first answer) is happening now.

It should surprise no one, for example, that young black males have an astoundingly high homicide rate, given the +1 scenario and the sixty-eight percent unwed birthing rate among blacks. Nor should it surprise anyone if this homicide rate skyrockets in coming decades.

Nor should it surprise anyone that crimes committed by children between ten and seventeen are among the highest among all the population groupings in per capita crimes, with boys heading girls in real numbers of crimes, but with girls closing in fast to cut the margin of separation by sexes.

And it should surprise no one if violence becomes the rule rather than the exception among all factions of the population as a whole.

The farther into pockets +1 people go, the more behaviors can be expected to gravitate toward the amoral or the bizarre. If a +1 person moves into the loneliest pocket of all (himself with no one else to validate his existence), there are logical reactions one can expect from that person. They will find a way to validate their existence.

Interesting and tragic is the violence associated with the +1 individual who never finds his or her consensus validation mob. When they are alone, they become deadly, walking time bombs, or they will try to lose themselves through drugs or alcohol. These +1 individuals, stripped of everything human (not excluding companionship), cannot find their validation except through some exceptional presentation of themselves to the masses. They will take validation any way they can get it.

When these individuals strike out (as they inevitably will!) it is by way of angry, mean-spirited crimes. By the time they have let their unsatisfied needs fester enough to strike back, they will strike, through crimes motivated by the need for validation through the only means at their disposal: power and control; by the time they are ready to pop, they will have been stripped of everything except power and control...and physical sensations.

They will be able to commit just about any crime without burdening themselves with moral, ethical, or other implications or associations. They have only one goal: Validation, confirmation that they exist. They will be able to murder for money. They will be able to murder for the sheer excitement of the act. They will be able to do just about anything. They will go after any target that will fulfill their needs...babies, young children, boys and girls, men or women of any age. They will go after their false gods...money, television sets, and cars. They will do what they must to experience a physical presence, even if it is momentary.

Many power and control +1 crimes are manifested through carnal dominance. This is logical and understandable. The physical sensations of sexual acts, regardless of what they are, attach the empty +1 individual to existence. It requires no thinking to speak of, requires no exterior validation. The +1 can at least feel his existence, if only for a little while. These hapless souls have no other way left to validate their existence. They have no consensus validation mob, they have no identity, they have no friends, no enemies, and no place in the world they can call their own.

Rape, for example, according to the experts, is not about sex...it is about power and control. Arousal during rape, although temporary, validates existence, but power and control moves the act.

Child molestation, spousal abuse, and such crimes are about power and control. Homosexuals, for example, need youngsters to proliferate their lifestyle, to supply replacement generations, to validate homosexuality as a lifestyle; this is attainable only by power and control over the youngsters. The youngsters are needed to validate the homosexual's existence, to legitimize the same sex preference as acceptable. Pedophiles take it a step farther and use children to satisfy their needs and then discard them. Pedophiles, at least, don't go through the motions of a mock legitimacy. Anal rape in male prisons is commonplace, another example of carnal manifestation of the need for power and control.

Bondage, torture, sometimes mutilation, and murder are a fairly common set of conjoined occurrences among homicide cases, especially where young females and other women are involved. Analyzed, this represents manifestations of power and control, taken to absurd dimensions, and a complete absence of human connections to the situation. Arousal can be conjured, in behalf of the perpetrator, although the better interpretation may be the transference of pain and suffering, of helplessness, of unanswered cries for rescue or salvation. It may be some imagined transference of agony, of transferred isolation from love, from identity, from meaning, from existence.

Why else would one bind then torture a fellow human, degrade this fellow human, render this fellow human powerless and defenseless, then extinguish the light of life if not to act out, through this fellow human, one's own life experience?

Is it possible: Through such brutality, the ultimately pitiable +1 person acts out his resentment for his own life, devoid of form, substance, meaning, and identity, and, possibly, all things considered, transfers his unhappiness to another, to find and enjoy, however temporarily it may last, sensual existence while accommodating his only

47

connection possible with the demands of his station in life – power and control?

One thing is for sure. No matter how far into the =1 scenario his victim is, the +1 lunatic, in this scenario, can – and does – reduce the whole of the circumstance and situation to his level, to act out the play as he sees it in his own life…1+1 is the sum total of human existence…the level playing field.

Such behaviors mirror the +1 individual in another way. They degrade the victim, to compensate for (or transfer) their own degradation as a human being. On other levels, the +1 individual will often run down another individual to elevate his own imagined stature. This works (in some imagined way) to make one look better by tearing someone else down. This allows the +1 a sense of superiority simply by making someone else look really lousy when compared to himself; in point of fact, the tearing down does nothing but move the standard of superiority downward, and it elevates no one. Degrading someone does not elevate the one doing the degrading. Making someone else look bad does nothing to erase the +1 stigma…nothing is still nothing, no matter how it comes packaged. Thinking one is superior to another does not make it so."

"Alexsandr, you're getting pretty cold-blooded here," said Richard. His concern was genuine. "Although it seems to make sense, I'm inclined to believe something is missing…or not quite right. It has the odor of speculation, not science."

"I'm searching in this section, Richard. I asked the question: Is it possible?"

"Sounds feasible, Alexsandr," said Grampy. "I think we need to flag this section for future study."

"Duly noted," said Alexsandr. He scribbled a note on a piece of scrap paper, and put it aside. "I want to add a side line here, if I may," said Alexsandr. "Concerning the step from thinking to searching for meaning and then the step from searching for meaning to understanding is not automatic once that first step is taken. I'll give you an example.

Ladonna was sick when she was but four, maybe five. She felt really bad. Rachael put a thermometer under her arm to take her temperature. She fell asleep before the thermometer was removed. The child woke the following morning feeling much better. The child explained it this way: If you go to sleep with a thermometer under your arm, it will make you well! She was pleased with her conclusion. What she had done is take the thinking to the search for meaning, and then blew it on the understanding part. We see this a lot in liberal thinking…they stop short of authentic understanding, even though they may have right data or whatever to work with."

"This would seem to back up the contention that thinking, the search for meaning, and understanding are separate functions altogether, not automatically connected," said Richard.

"You ought to insert that anecdote, Alexsandr," said Grampy. "It illustrates the contention quite well." Grampy smiled.

"Duly noted. Now, put this idea into the context of the next part," said Alexsandr. "I'll read it:

This need to reduce circumstances to the lowest level is a common trait among the +1 individuals, whether they act independently or in the herd. It can be seen not just in the actions of the super-empty but also in the social goals of the slightly less unbalanced.

Liberal social policy, for example, gravitates to the lowest common denominator, the so-called level playing field. Liberal social policy is a manifestation of the false closure scenario. This false closure stems from taking thinking to the next level, the search for meaning, but stopping there, instead of pushing ahead to understanding. Thus we see many examples where the facts are there, but the conclusions just don't add up. Many liberals and other +1 people are locked into a perpetual childhood because they cannot pass by the search for meaning step toward closure. It takes time and exposure and practice to develop the faculties sufficient to arrive at some authentic understanding of anything.

Liberal social policy, instead of encouraging order, life-affirming values, and sex identity with affiliation to one's sex as male or female, pushes – always relentlessly – toward the chaotic +1 scenario, manifestations of childhood. The ultimate goal, of course, is power and control, achieved by affirmation of one's existence through the consensus validates approach (defining down deviancy). The level playing field has but one primary objective and that is to destroy anything and everything that promotes or encourages stability, self-development, separateness, competition, the search for meaning, or understanding. The level playing field is a fantasy, the +1 playground. There is method to their apparent madness. They jump to conclusions before they understand what they are talking about.

The level playing field is an excellent example of taking thinking to the next level, the search for meaning, but moving no further, toward closure. It is a way (and this is the most damaging flaw in all liberal policy thinking) to make people equal whether they are or not, a way to ignore human nature and reshape the human being to an engineered hypothetical social robot, a real world impossibility. Yet circumstances seem to make it plausible…just spread the wealth, punish achievers, and bingo! Everybody's equal. Thinking is thus moved to the next level, the search for meaning. There, the process breaks down. Where the understanding never shows is people cannot be manipulated that way. Nor can they be redesigned to fit some wild-eyed social assumption based on nonsense. It is not the nature of the beast, so to speak. There is no way to force the mating of a gorilla and a kitty cat."

Alexsandr waited for a reaction.

"This, then, fills out what was said earlier about stopping queries when something sounds good," mumbled Grampy. "This would be consistent with the second level and nothing more. The search for meaning can sound good, but conclusions drawn at that basic level are not necessarily correct conclusions."

"Like Ladonna's conclusion about the thermometer. She took it to the search for meaning and quit when the answer sounded good. A child's perception of real events."

"Suppose she never rose above that child's perception…because she could not, her brain would not allow it?" Alexsandr asked.

"She would live out her life convinced, in her own mind, that sleeping with a thermometer under one's arm would cure illness," offered Grampy.

"Of course, as she grew older, the perception changed as she developed her ability to push her thinking from stage one, to two, to three," explained Alexsandr.

"But, Alexsandr, why would she develop the ability and others would not?" quizzed Grampy. "What is the decisive determinate?"

"The determinator, Grampy, is that her parents won't let her sit on nonsense. Nor will I. Rachael won't put up with it either. We make her think about what she says, we make her push her thinking to higher levels."

"Without that involved interest, then, she would be left without a developed capacity to move from thinking, to searching for meaning, to understanding?"

"She would probably never know the capacity exists, much less use it."

"There's still something missing, Alexsandr," said Grampy. He was obviously not sold on the idea. Not yet. He got up and refilled his coffee cup. He stood, stretched. "Let's go outside a few minutes. I want to think about this stuff. I see where you are going, Alexsandr. I like it. But there's still something missing. On the one hand you imply some people's brains just can't go there, yet, on the other hand, you say people can be taught to go there? It has to be one or the other, doesn't it, Alexsandr?"

Richard stood, in agreement with Grampy; it was time to get some fresh air. Alexsandr joined them, and they went upstairs, down the hallway, outside to sit for a while on the front porch.

Richard sat on the step. Grampy and Alexsandr sat in chairs. Richard looked back over his shoulder. Grampy was rubbing his eyes.

"Grampy?" said Richard, as he settled his back against a post. "What's your take on the maybe yes, maybe no with the understanding step?"

"I'm kind of stuck on the total lockout thing. Would your granddaughter, for example, still make the breakthrough if no one set her straight?"

"How could she?" quizzed Richard. "If she is never introduced to the heightened possibilities of a new frame of reference, she would be mentally immobile."

"Do you remember, Grampy, how we once used a river to illustrate a point similar to this one?" asked Alexsandr.

"Oh, yes. You know, Alexsandr that might have some bearing here. Here's how it goes, Richard. See what you can make of it: Person A looks down upon a river from a high vantage point. He has never seen a river before. What he sees is a ribbon-like, mirrored body of water. What he sees is purely a surface impression on a sunny day. If he does not get a closer look, by actually diving into the water, his understanding of it and his perception of it will be essentially the same. But when he dives into the water, he discovers it is murky, thick with debris, cold; once this new discovery is made, he can never see the river – or any river – the same way again. He has touched base with the reality of the river, and it will never let him go back to the pure joy of looking upon the shimmering ribbon-like spectacle in the basic undefined terms."

"So, if a new frame of reference is introduced – no matter how it is done – the process will kick in?"

"It would seem, then, my granddaughter would have made the discovery herself if she chanced upon the right circumstances?"

"Not exactly," insisted Grampy. "Let's go back to Richard's air bubble in water. As long as she was content with her discovery – no matter that it was wrong – she would have no reason to re-examine her discovery. On something like connecting a thermometer to curing illness, the disclosure of the real use of a thermometer would come in time anyway, providing someone broke her air bubble. What we are dealing with in the +1 scenario, however, is ideas without substance –

pure fantasy from start to finish – that cannot and will never have a foothold in the real world. To say, for example, we can have world peace if everybody just quits fighting makes perfect sense. Indisputable sense. Nobody can say it is wrong, but nobody with any sense at all will see it as possible…people are not going to quit fighting. So we have now an example of the two-step conclusion in the fantasy world. There is no connection with reality, even though it seems possible. It breaks down, of course, when the third step kicks in…human nature will not allow world peace."

"The thermometer example, then, has the element of reality in the physical presence of the thermometer," Richard said. "The function, in your granddaughter's mind, was not taken to the step of understanding because she did not have the exposure in the world to make the connection. Because it is real, it is inevitable she will make contact with the reality sooner or later, and, like diving in the river, the thermometer will never, in her mind, be the same again, assuming she accepts the new explanation."

"She will, in time, understand the thermometer and separate the error from the facts and reach a legitimate stage of understanding, unless the new discovery posed a real threat to her," explained Alexsandr. "If the new discovery threatened her existence, she would, of course, have to deny the possibility that the new discovery is genuine. If she was locked into the +1 scenario, to preserve her own existence, she could never accept the 1+1=1 scenario. But dealing with something concrete, she would find it very hard to reject the presence of the thermometer and get away with it. She could, however, reject the new discovery, not from lack of information but because she has no interest in changing her perceptions; in all probability, if she did not change this perspective at an early age, the change would be less likely to take place as the years rolled on. Look how long, for example, it took people to change their minds about the world being round instead of flat. She would have to conjoin the mental perceptions with what is real to arrive at a sustainable reality…understanding. Now, look at it in terms of the +1 individual. Richard, using your air bubble: where are we now?"

Richard took on the challenge. "Inside the +1 scenario, no one deals with the concrete; these people deal in fantasy and fabrication, bits and pieces put together into a sound-good package with no basis in reality whatsoever. This sound-good package is derived in one of two ways, pure thinking with no advancement toward a search for meaning or through thinking through to a search for meaning but no farther than that. The +1+1+1 scenario always prevails; otherwise they cancel out their own existence, which they cannot accept. They opt for the political...ideas, power, and control.

There would be no power or control element in dealing with a thermometer. It does what it does, and it will not go away, and no one can stop it from doing what it does. It is real. The example of the thermometer is good for illustrating how the search for meaning does not automatically lead to understanding, but it has no validity in dealing with the +1 scenario otherwise, because it is, in fact, a real object that must be confronted. The +1 individual cannot simply think it away.

The world peace gambit, however, sits in the air bubble. Although it holds up to the two-step examination, when the bubble is pierced by the reality of human nature, the whole proposition is invalidated, cancelled out by the presence of what is, in fact, real. The world peace gambit is safe and secure, a win-win situation.

I think the underlying factor we have overlooked is this: The two-step examination is safe. Understanding is not. Fear, another extra-dimensional element, inhibits the passage from the search for meaning to understanding. It is a conjoined element with fantasy in the blocking of passage or transition from the search for meaning to authentic understanding. +1 people will sell their souls for safety and security. The thermometer is not a threat thus even the most dedicated +1 individual can live with the thermometer and accept it for what it is. It would be the same with a brick, a flowerpot, or a refrigerator. The air bubble is safe and secure. An air bubble with a punctured shell is not. Ideas and ideas alone pose the unapproachable threat."

"The element of safety and security plays an important role?" quizzed Grampy. "This would explain a lot...the mothering government fanaticism, for example, the herding proclivities. As you said before, it would also explain the consensus validates idea."

"My granddaughter would be unthreatened by the thermometer and what it does. She would have no problem accepting the real story behind it," said Alexsandr. "She could go about her business, no matter the depth of her insecurities, and live...co-exist...with it. It is mentally safe, also. It exists, undeniably, and it does what it does without challenging her right to exist."

"The behavioral implications begin to solidify only when ideas threaten the +1 scenario. And then the +1 individual becomes agitated, fearful, even violent," offered Richard.

"Thus we find our +1 individuals accepting machines which they see as safe co-inhabitants of the Earth, sometimes to the extent they measure the quality of their lives by the numbers of machines they surround themselves with," said Grampy. "This could explain the blind battles the +1 individuals engage in to upstage the Jones family next door. It is not a measure of success, but a fanatic need for the safety and security of material possession of a non-threatening kind."

"Somewhat off the track," interjected Alexsandr, "...but let's look back at the thermometer. We have a material object, a defined use, and it is worthless if not used for what it is made to do. We have the object...1. We have the defined use...1. We have the reason it is...1+1=1. The =1 cannot be until the thermometer is used. Now, look at it this way: We form a mental picture of it (useless in and of itself)...1. We add the next step. We know what it is called, how it is made, why it does what it does; we combine these things as we view it and search for meaning behind the combination of glass, mercury, whatever and define it in the real terms of what we have...1. We use it as it is intended to be used and get results from the use...=1. We have the 1+1=1 scenario. If we simply look at it, handle it, name it, but never go beyond that, we have the +1 scenario; no matter how long we study it, photograph it, pass it around, if we don't use it for measuring temperature, we end up with the +1 scenario...it is a worthless contraption sitting quietly on the desk."

"The 1+1=1 scenario in this context takes on the appearance of a constant or law," said Grampy, as he sipped his remaining coffee. "Alexsandr, I may not show it, but the prospects are exciting, to say the least."

"If the thermometer is never used, we get the +1 scenario," said Richard, repeating the observation. He read through the lines. "Alexsandr, you're on to something. The idea of a constant, even in the physical world, is challenging, to say the least. Does it hold in the metaphysical world, the extra-dimensional world as well?"

"I think maybe it does, Richard," said Alexsandr. "Actually the two are probably conjoined, bonded, as we said before."

"The heart of man's creative powers can be found in the 1+1=1 scenario," Grampy added. "Think about it: Those things which elevate the possibilities of mankind have their beginnings in the thinking, the search for meaning, the understanding scenario. Why would they not be interpreted in such terms?"

"Two extra-dimensional elements combine to create a single sensorial reality element?" quizzed Richard. "If they fail to combine, as when you and Alexsandr discarded idea after idea because they never came together, the +1 scenario returns. The worthless ideas float on their own, having no redeeming qualities?"

"The difficulty is we're dealing in things which exist and that is all...they are present," explained Grampy. "We're in territory human beings do not usually try to visualize. The thermometer, for example, came into being when someone put the thinking and the search for meaning in proper order, but only when they understood the elements surrounding the development of it. It did not have to be physically present to have been created, but it could not be made physically attainable without presence in the sensorial reality sphere."

"You have a blueprint drawn up before a building appears on the horizon," said Richard. "Everything exists except the finished structure."

"Your car existed a long time before it rolled off an assembly line," said Grampy. "Translated into ideas, if they are not two parts in the extra-dimensional sphere and one part in the sensorial reality sphere, the 1+1=1 scenario cannot be. They cannot be made attainable without presence in the sensorial reality sphere."

"It is quite possible, then, the 1+1=1 scenario is, in fact, a constant?"

"Quite possible, Richard," answered Grampy.

"Hold those thoughts, gentlemen," Alexsandr said. "Let's go back to the computer room. We're about to get into the testable hypothesis, and I think you'll find it intellectually exciting. There is a practical way to use the +1 scenario to accomplish some remarkable things. Think of the 1+1=1 scenario, like this: It is two parts mental, in the extra-dimensional sphere, one part, the sum total, in the sensorial reality world. In other words, if thinking and the search for meaning don't add up to what's real, the 1+1=1 scenario cannot be. Just like plans tucked away right now will be the automobile of the future, I'll show you how to predict behaviors in human beings long before the behaviors are ever manifested in actuality. Certain predictors outline, just like a blueprint, how certain people are going to end up as a direct consequence of decisions they have not even made at the time the prediction is made."

Alexsandr had whetted their appetites, and they wasted no time following him into the computer room. He anxiously pulled up the next page for them to read, as they refilled their coffee cups, and then resettled in their chairs:

To achieve success for their two-step nonsense, liberals have to attack certain social institutions and destroy them. The +1 scenario cannot come to fruition without destroying the barriers. Wounding the opposition is not enough, because as long as institutions stand for something grounded, in one way or another, in both the sensorial reality world and the extra-dimensional world, they pose a threat.

Among these targeted institutions are the family, legitimate organized religions (Christians, in particular), the educational system; they must break down the extra-dimensional ties which hold a nation together...a national identity, a common language, a social conscience based on moral absolutes, a legal system which is built on establishing minimum levels of acceptable human behavior and standards for right conduct.

The war, of course, is waged on the political level, because the goals of liberal social policy have no authentic intellectual or other realism to offer anyone. The ultimate goal is the complete destruction of the 1+1=1 scenario, and the dominance, through power and control, of the +1 scenario.

It should surprise no one that over the last forty years or so, liberals have attacked these institutions mercilessly, using every political tool at their disposal. It should surprise no one so long as +1 individuals are born and bred, in sufficient numbers, the trends will not change.

The only real questions left for Americans to decide are the basic questions all civilized nations must face from time to time: What do we do with liberals and Liberalism?

To find the answer, it behooves us to better understand what liberalism is all about, how it evolves, and by doing so try to discover what, if anything, can be done to treat this very peculiar form of mental illness.

"Now Grampy, Richard...pay close attention to this next section. I hope you see what I saw when it finally came together: Universal applicability and a margin for error of zero! I won't read it to you. Take your time. Study it. Start right here, at IDEA 6. You will begin to see how extra-dimensional existences bond and produce a sensorial reality, a total package human being or human life form...that is to say, an unborn child. You will also see the genesis of behavioral patterns. I hope you see what I do...the bonding mechanisms that connect extra-dimensional elements, such as thinking and the search for meaning."

Alexsandr paused. He smiled, somewhat smugly. Grampy recognized it as Alexsandr's I dare you to prove me wrong smile. "Pure existences, gentlemen, can be verified...soon, very soon, you're going to touch the face of God."

Richard shivered. Alexsandr's contention caught him off guard. Grampy nearly chocked on his coffee, and almost dropped his cup.

"Alexsandr?...Alexsandr?" stammered Grampy. "You're saying you can verify God in the sensorial realm? Whoa! You're losing it, Alexsandr."

Alexsandr chuckled. He got up out of his chair. He approached his old friend, put a sympathetic hand on his shoulder.

"Grampy...bear with me, okay?" Alexsandr said, patiently. He backed off a little. He extended his arms, holding his palms upwards in a pleading pleasant way. "You're going to see something so simple, so incredibly brilliant, it almost evades human comprehension. We will actually be able to enter into the extra-dimensional sphere, albeit in an unsophisticated and crude way. We will reach into pure existence, simple presence and presence alone...and validate existences and entities within the ken of plausible deniability."

"Don't do it!" cried a stern female voice from the doorway. Rachael stood akimbo in the doorway, obviously in a bad mood, upset about something.

The three men looked around, somewhat startled by her sudden appearance at the doorway.

"Stay away from that stuff!" she said. "If God wanted us peering into the un-seeable realms, He would have made them more visible."

Alexsandr approached her, inquiring as he walked, "Rachael, what's wrong? You look upset. You're back early? What's going on?"

"I need to talk to you, Alexsandr. There's been another incident. They want your help." Her words flowed uneasily, nervously. She was on the verge of tears. It was obvious to all three men something was terribly wrong.

Alexsandr slowly approached her, to comfort her, saying as he walked, "Let the police handle those damn kids...they don't listen to me, anyway. Call them and tell them no. I'm busy. Unavailable. Whatever works."

"Alexsandr," she sobbed. Rachael whispered something in his ear. Alexsandr whispered something back to her. He then turned to face Grampy and Richard. His face turned ashen. His eyes burned.

"Read on," he said. "I'll be back in a few minutes. I have some urgent business to take care of."

"Is there anything we can help with, Alexsandr?" asked Grampy.

"I think not. Not right now, anyway."

He and Rachael went upstairs, talking quietly as they went.

Grampy and Richard looked back to the computer screen.

"I hope they're okay," mumbled Grampy.

"If they need our help, Grampy, I'm sure they will ask for it."

"IDEA 6:" said Richard. "When one looks at extra-dimensional development in three possible ways, it comes clear how the human being gravitates in certain behavioral directions." He looked at Grampy. "That's it for IDEA 6?"

"Scroll it, maybe Alexsandr skipped some spaces and didn't know it."

Richard scrolled but nothing else showed up.

"Maybe he's just setting the stage for something else," said Grampy. "He does imply, however, with the right setup, a certain level of clarity develops which can, if I read this correctly, explain why certain people gravitate toward behavior in certain ways. Alexsandr never says something becomes clear unless he has seen the clarity for himself. That doesn't mean we will see it. I used to squabble with Alexsandr all the time about how he presented things. He tends to take for granted other people can perceive things as clearly as he does, which is not always the case."

"Well, let's move on, Grampy. Maybe things will clear up a little."

Richard scrolled until he found IDEA 7:

IDEA 7: All people come into the world having neither ordered nor disordered lives, they have no values, and they can be identified as male or female and carry traits peculiar to their sex, but they have no affiliation to their natural sex.

From this humble beginning, the child will develop along certain lines:

1st: He will never go beyond his initial state...1+1+1 scenario.
2nd: He will develop order, life-affirming values, and a sex identity with affiliation to his sex as male or female...and become an actively involved member of the human race...1+1=1 scenario.
3rd: He will thrive on disorder, life-negating values, and sexual confusion...1+1+1 scenario. (Eventually, without reparative intervention, he will evolve into the SE/Super Empty scenario, i.e. existing in a physical presence only.)

Into one of these three classes, any living human being (or human life form) can be categorized, making this a universally applicable model. The margin for error is zero. The same person will never fit two zones simultaneously.

"Now, we're getting somewhere," said Grampy.

"Are we looking at an extra-dimensional constant, Grampy?"

"Can it be that simple, Richard?"

"This, Grampy, is not simple. The implications are extraordinary and magnificently complicated."

"Hmm," mumbled Grampy. He leaned forward, to more closely examine the information before him.

"What is it, Grampy? What are you looking for?"

"The connecting link, Richard. If it is truly universal, there has to be a common thread applicable to every living human being...and, as Alexsandr put it, every human life form."

"Sex identity? Of course...of course," said Richard. "How much more universal can you get, Grampy?"

"Hmm," mumbled Grampy. "Two parts extra-dimensional and one part sensorial reality? Hmm?"

"It fits the 1+1=1 scenario, Grampy."

Grampy sat back and rubbed his eyes.

"Richard, it appears to hold...do you realize how revolutionary this is, if it is testable and can be affirmed, even proven? Do you understand the damage this can do? Do you appreciate the implications of a universal social science model with a margin for error of zero? This thing...if it holds...is a deadly weapon with incalculable constructive and/or destructive potential."

"Alexsandr was right then? We may have to destroy the whole project when we get done with it? Is there an up side, Grampy?"

"Hmm? I'm not sure at this point, Richard. Right now I'm thinking maybe Rachael's instincts are right. Maybe there is no reason we should head into the un-seeable realms."

"Grampy...we both know we can't back out now."

"I'm not so sure, Richard. What I'm looking at is very simple...something an old fellow like myself does not want to know. If this thing holds, Richard, it will negate just about everything I've dedicated my life to. I'm not sure I'm strong enough to take that."

"Let's look at the rest of it, Grampy," said Richard, as he scrolled a bit more into view:

Restructured, the model looks like this:

(B) THE POSITIVE ZONE: Order, Life-affirming values, sex identity with affiliation to the sex as male or female.

(A) THE NEUTRAL ZONE: Indifference, no values, sex identity without affiliation to the sex as male or female.

(C) THE NEGATIVE ZONE: Disorder, life-negating values, sexual identity disorientation.

They studied the model for a few moments.

"Let's see what Alexsandr has to say here," said Richard. He shifted the page.

One can look at the model, and then logical conclusions can be drawn. Logically, the child, if not taught the fitting developmental processes, will not graduate to the higher plane of human existence, (B – THE POSITIVE ZONE), from the point of origin (A – THE NEUTRAL ZONE). Because the child has to learn the things necessary to graduate, it is fair to say the child is inclined otherwise to an unfulfilled or otherwise corrupted life or lifestyle. Simply put, what the child does not learn, he will not understand. Without understanding, he will live life in the never-land of indifference, or in varied degrees of disorientation, devoid of order. There is no reason to believe the graduation, into the Positive Zone will be automatic. The movement into the Negative Zone by the untrained, undisciplined child is inevitable but not predestined.

Understanding, in many ways, affirms the extra-dimensional qualities that contribute to human stability. It does not take a lot of common sense, for example, to acknowledge the existence of order, although it has no qualities other existence. It is. It is present. But acknowledgement does not constitute affirmation. It takes something akin to evidentiary proof to affirm some simple existence-only entity. Can it be done?

The evidentiary proof can be found which, in many ways, taps into the extra-dimensional world. This proof can be found through an open examination of standards for right conduct. Before such an examination, however, it might be helpful to look at aspects of extra-dimensional development in more detail.

People do more than get born, live a while, and die. They are layered, in a sense. Full humanity has more to it than a simple presence in a physical world in a physical body. Human beings grow in many ways…mentally, morally, psychologically, emotionally, and spiritually.

Top experts in early childhood development offer a window of opportunity for this whole process of this layering development to take place within the first eight to thirteen years of a child's life, with all basic components in place between six and eight years into the child's life.

Also important during the layering developmental years is gender recognition leading to sex identity and affiliation to one's sex as male or female. This developmental process, of all the others, is the singular most important developmental any human being can go through. Without sex identity with affiliation to one's sex as male or female, there can be no full humanity development, and there can be no stability for the individual in mental, moral, emotional, psychological, or spiritual ways.

Some components, like sex identification with affiliation to the sex, have roots in the first three or four years of the child's life, and they are refined before the child reaches the age of nine. Other components of full humanity take years to refine, even though the basics are in place within the first six to eight years of life.

The consensus is what the child is (personality, etc.) between six and eight (in rudimentary terms of mental, moral, psychological, emotional, and spiritual development), he will still be at eighty-six, but more refined in the finer points of development. In other words, if the child is not prepared to enter into a mature adulthood (THE POSITIVE ZONE), in rudimentary ways, by the age of eight or so, he is not going to make it into a matured adulthood without reparative intervention somewhere along the line.

The reparative possibilities of intervention diminish as the subject (client, student, etc.) ages. If reparative work does not begin with the child, reparative possibilities fall sharply off as the child grow older. This is why there are very few rehabilitative programs for criminals that work. There comes a time when the bonding possibilities in the extra-dimensional sphere fade completely, and the extra-dimensional fantasies become real.

In time, fantasy fuses with itself to the degree the person has no other conceptual or perceptual resources left to draw upon (the sensorial reality world ceases to exist), and he cannot be reached with alternative possibilities. There's a lot of truth to the old adage once a crook, always a crook; in the absence of early reparative intervention, once the fusion process has run the course, there is little hope left for reconstructive intervention.

In this context, it should surprise no one there are many lifers in our prisons. It should surprise no one that older homosexuals spend their lives lost in moral (psychological) illness. It should surprise no one that young victims of abuse who let their wounds fester for years before seeking help do not repair well. It should surprise no one that liberals can live out their lives completely out of touch with the sensorial reality world.

"Grampy, where do you think Alexsandr is going with this standards of right conduct?"

"I don't have a clue, Richard."

"I'll gladly explain that later, gentlemen," said Alexsandr, as he reentered the room.

They turned to face him. He seemed agitated, angry. He struggled to maintain his composure.

"Is everything all right, Alexsandr?" asked Grampy. "You seemed somewhat disturbed when you left the room."

Alexsandr returned to his seat.

"Everything is not all right. If you will, gentlemen, move around so I can discuss something with you without having to twist my head from side to side. I'm kind of creaky these days."

"What's up, Alexsandr?" asked Richard.

"There's been another episode in Nohartinit. This time, it was more than vandalism and a few fights. This time, a man has been stabbed to death and another man beaten to a pulp with a pipe. I want your help. The battered man was Ladonna's boyfriend, David, and this time things have hit a little too close to home."

"Is Ladonna okay, Alexsandr?" asked Richard. His concern was genuine.

"Shaken. Scared. Damn near hysterical. She's staying with her parents right now, at the clinic. We're not sure yet what condition David is in. We're bringing her here for a while, where she will be safe."

"Surely they don't think that she'll be targeted, too?"

"They don't know what this psycho might do," said Alexsandr. "We're going to be cautious, that's all."

"What can we do, Alexsandr?" asked Grampy. "Name it – anything."

"The cops don't have much to go on. They think it was just some random act. The think it is a single individual gone off his nut. If we can't help them find this guy, soon, he may kill again. I know you have not had time to finish reading the project. I believe it holds the key to identifying this thug. I'll run hard copies for you both. Take them home, and read them. Then get back to me. I believe we can test this hypothesis and affirm the essential elements by profiling then tracking this slime ball."

"Do we know anything at all, Alexsandr? Anything to go on?"

"The cops said it has all the appearances of a random act, with the victims being targeted for no reason that was discernable. No robbery. Nothing to indicate he or they knew the victims. Nothing. Not even the weapons that were used. These were separate attacks, in different parts of town. The cops are playing a hunch...they think the same person or persons attacked both victims."

"Why would they assume that, Alexsandr?"

"Nohartinit is not big enough, they think, to be home to two psychos capable of such violence. They think he might have just been someone passing through, and he's gone by now. But if he does live here in town, we've got to nail him."

"They have nothing but a hunch to go on? So if we can't come through, it may never be solved?"

"That's about the size of it, gentlemen…unless they get a confession or catch the guy in the act. They're hoping to stop him before he takes another crack at somebody else."

"Do they think it was a kid, Alexsandr? Some kid gone nuts?"

"You know as much as they do right now," he said.

"Alexsandr," asked Grampy in all seriousness. "This is way outside our areas of expertise. Do you really think we can profile this guy using The Red Flag?"

"I know we can," he answered. "We have the skeleton, the +1. We just have to pack the meat on the bones, and we'll nail this son-of-bitch!"

Alexsandr clicked a few buttons of the keyboard.

"I'll print the whole document in two copies," he said. "I'll bring them to you later. Richard, will you be at Grampy's house in a couple of hours?"

"Yes, I'll be there."

"I have to go now," he explained. "We're going to pick up Ladonna and check on David. I'll see you in a couple of hours."

Chapter Four

A few hours passed, Richard and Grampy waited patiently for Alexsandr to arrive. A police officer arrived before Alexsandr did. He introduced himself as Bud Elbudro, an investigator on the case. He was a firm, ordinary-looking man, with dark eyes and short brown hair. He was wearing brown slacks, a white shirt, and black shoes. He had a scar above his left eye. Richard guessed his age at mid-forties somewhere. He brought with him the texts Alexsandr had copied for them. He met Richard and Grampy on the front porch of Grampy's house, where they were sitting and chatting.

He handed over the neatly prepared papers to Grampy, one stack laid across the other to keep them separated.

"Alexsandr wanted you to read Ideas eight through ten before he gets here," Officer Elbudro said.

Officer Elbudro seated himself.

"Alexsandr thinks you fellows can profile this guy. Can you? We've got squat to go on. When the coroner's report comes back, we might have something...right handed, left handed, strong or weak assailant, approximate height, stuff like that. I really don't think we will get much further than that. We're not set up for finding much trace evidence. I'm hoping we won't need it."

"Officer Elbudro, how well do you know Nohartinit...the people in it?" asked Richard. "If we do profile the guy, can you find him?"

"Call me Bud. Everybody else does. In answer to your question, I know the people who can find him if I can't. We'll get the guy if you can tell us what we're looking for. I know every shyster and sleazebag in Nohartinit. I've worked here for just shy of fifteen years now. You describe him, I'll find him. If we find this guy, there's an unsolved murder from years ago you might want to take a look at, too. A prostitute. I've been investigating this one on my own for quite a while."

"One case at a time," said Richard. "You realize we won't have a name...maybe not more than a general description of expectable behaviors, family background, stuff like that."

"I'll find him."

"One thing, Bud? Do you think it is a kid? One of these new-breed barbarians?" asked Grampy.

"My gut tells me no...it is not one of the kids. He's first or second generation grown-up version of the new-breed barbarian."

"What else does your gut tell you, Bud?"

"This guy lives in Nohartinit. This was not just some loon passing through."

"Why would he knife one, use a pipe on the other?'

"Who knows? He'll have to tell us that. I would guess he disposed of the knife, decided his urge wasn't satisfied, and so he used a pipe on his second victim, a spontaneous choice, probably. I would guess the pipe was handy, nothing more to it than that."

"Anything else?"

"Call me nuts, but I think he just got up, got dressed, did what he always does in the morning...and decided to go out at night and kill someone. He probably planned on killing someone for a long time, and, he just decided the time had come. Then he did it...or thought he did. The man he bludgeoned, David Wilson, is going to be okay...sore as hell for a long time, a broken bone or two, a lot of black and blue, and a head the size of a pumpkin, but he'll be okay."

"That's a relief," Grampy said. He sensed by the way Bud settled in he was not just on a delivery run. "Bud...you didn't just come out here to deliver the news about David and drop off these texts, did you?"

"No. I'm going to be working right along beside you guys. You see guys, General Perkins was a personal friend of mine. I was one of the very few people he confided in concerning Alexsandr's project. I know all about The Red Flag. I'm the guy who recommended Alexsandr for the research."

"Bud?" quizzed Richard. "Do you think there's some kind of predictability factor or constant which can explain what's going on with the kids? You're a cop. Can you tell me with certainty you have seen changes in the behavior of kids over the last fifteen years? The way I see it, if changes in behaviors are real and seem to follow certain demographics, then there must be something which can pinpoint the genesis of the behavior."

"I've watched this town grow, Richard. I've watched it change. I've seen the people change. The kids have changed. There are your decent hardworking kids, and there are your punks. That's nothing new. The punks, gentlemen, have changed from tough-talking, image conscious, and roguish rebels to cold-blooded barbarians. The decent hardworking kids are no different than they were fifteen years ago; they just have different names and different dreams and they're very few in numbers any more. If you can isolate the cause or causes behind the transition of the punks, you'll have what you are looking for. The punks of by-gone days had some values, even if they were not exactly right on. This new breed has nothing...some of them don't even seem to rest even a half-a-step toward being human."

65

"Did you buy into the General's conspiracy theory, Bud?"

"No, Not at all. What I see every day is not part of a conscious conspiracy. I can't isolate it, but there is an underlying shared sense of hopelessness or isolation or evil among these kids. It is like they share a common lost cause and purposely destroy their own possibilities and opportunities. I see kids with loads of potential stuffing themselves down the toilet...I run into it more and more every day."

"I hope you don't think I'm grilling you, Bud," apologized Richard. "I'm...we're...looking for answers. Do you, based on your experiences, see any connection between economic or social class and the tendencies of a kid to turn sour?"

"Class? No. Economic status? No. I was fascinated by the General's work. If I had the time, I would like to pursue it. There's no connection between crime and social status or poverty. The common thread I see...keep in mind I work the back streets and alleys...is drugs. But I am a firm believer drugs are a symptom not a cause of a kid's self-destructive tendency. As a parent, I hate and despise drugs. As a cop, I despise dealers."

"Drugs? In this town...surely there can't be much traffic in drugs in this town. We're not big enough."

"One addict is one too many," said Grampy. "I worked with druggies during my private practice days as a Psychologist. Believe me, one addict is one too many." Like something had really struck a nerve, he continued on, unlike Grampy in a usual discussion. "They screw up their own lives...they screw up the lives of everyone around them. Drugs...I hate drugs and druggies. I've been party to too much human damage. One addict is one too many!"

"Gentlemen, I pull twelve and thirteen year old kids out of the gutters a couple of times a week, and many have been selling themselves for quite a while before I get to them. I want to puke every time a little girl, hardly past puberty, bares her bottom and offers sex for a fix. I want to puke every time I pull some pre-pubescent boy out of the fag bar on the backside of Main. I want to puke every time I jail some guy for pounding on his wife, or molesting his kids. Don't let the size of Nohartinit fool you...we have an underbelly that is sick and evil to the core."

"What keeps you going, Bud?" asked Richard.

"In a lot of ways, I'm like General Perkins...I can change things, or at least do my best to make a difference...to bring some sense of balance or at least sanity back into the equation. You can't count the numbers of times I've felt like giving up. It might sound hokey...but I love kids...and I keep telling myself somebody has to care."

Grampy thought he detected tears beginning to form in Bud's eyes. He did not question his sincerity. He was in the presence of a man of high morals and convictions toward the good.

"Bud," asked Grampy. "Correct me if I'm wrong, but isn't the trend toward violence against unknown victims becoming more frequent? Aren't the kids, in particular, just striking back...at anyone who seems handy...for whatever reason they can find to justify the violence?"

"That I cannot say, Grampy. What does seem to fit is the lack of conscience as an evolving factor. More and more people seem able to commit crimes against people or property with no pangs of conscience whatsoever. Kids, in particular, seem to be gravitating toward bizarre behaviors...so-called adult crimes...to the extent many states are rewriting their statutes to try children as adults. Schools don't deal with foul language, talking in the halls, or chewing gum any more. They deal with drugs, teen pregnancies, abortions, assaults, mass murders, rapes, and suicides."

"Isn't it true, Bud?" asked Richard. "Kids are increasingly becoming victims as well as perpetrators in alarming numbers? Kids are killing kids for candy, jackets, tennis shoes...kids are being abused, molested, and exploited."

"I don't read statistics any more, gentlemen; if they are right, I'd have to accept the fact the good guys are losing. I can't live with that notion and still get up every day and do my part. In Nohartinit, I can safely say the good guys are losing. The General used to tell me he could understand the minds of men who fought for their convictions. But he also told me he was completely at a loss to understand people who fought for the sake of fighting...no reason, no convictions, and no purpose...violence for the sake of violence. They were, he said, his most formidable foe...and the most unreachable of all."

"Drugs, then, aren't behind the changes?" asked Richard. "You don't deal with fried brains...you deal with people totally lacking any kind of morals or values? They gravitate toward violence for the sake of violence? Is that the key, Bud?"

"I know it sounds trite, gentlemen, but I think there is no question these kids have no moral upbringing. Many of them couldn't tell you the difference between right and wrong if they had to," said Bud. "It is almost like they literally cannot see or appreciate the difference between a human being and a tree stump. But why resort to violence? I don't know."

"Any ideas where it all went wrong?" asked Grampy.

"Where? In the home, the churches? In the schools? TV? Movies? Gentlemen, my best guess is these people have turned their backs on God. In our own way, gentlemen, we're fighting a Holy War."

"Ephesians 6:12-13," said Grampy. "It isn't science, but it is true."

"Amen," said Richard. He then looked at Bud. "Do you see any kind of simple solution, Bud? Can it turn around one kid at a time...or is it, like General Perkins seemed to think, too big to handle without real clout?"

"If it is institutional corruption, the best we can ever hope for is one kid at a time. General Perkins was hoping Alexsandr could be convincing enough to sway some big guys. That's a tall order. The big guys are as corrupt as the kids...they just wear it better. I don't know if we've got a chance, in real terms, gentlemen. All we can do is take our best shot."

"The General was convinced the big guys, as you call them, were dead set on undermining this country," said Grampy. "Do you also think along those lines?"

"General Perkins had access to people and information none of us can ever get near. He was sincere. I, personally, do not think it is an active subversive effort. I think it is just happening...quite by accident or through the process of some natural – or unnatural – phenomenon."

"From what we have seen of Alexsandr's work, the natural phenomenon idea looks like a good possibility," offered Richard.

"Here's the deal, gentlemen," explained Bud. "If we can nail this killer, it will draw a lot of attention to an idea which may catch on." He sighed. He looked out toward the lake. Then he looked back at Grampy and Richard. "After we nail this guy, can I spend some time with you and see if we can't package something that'll work? I'm getting tired, gentlemen. Tired of peeling kids off the streets. Tired of beat up women and children. Tired of dopers and dealers. I worked with General Perkins from time to time, and I shared his sentiments. We can't let this nation slip away. I believe he was on to something. I can offer something useful, I think. I work with these punks day in and day out."

"Bud, do you know anything about the +1 scenario?" Grampy asked.

"Hmm?" Bud answered. He pondered momentarily; he said he never heard of it. "General Perkins never mentioned it; I've never come across it."

"I never did either until a short time ago, and I've been teaching philosophy for a long time now," Grampy said. "To tell you the truth, I think it belongs to Alexsandr...and I'm beginning to think it holds the key we're looking for. We'll find some time to go over it with you, Bud. You won't be disappointed."

"Tell me something, gentlemen...do you honestly think something will develop?"

Richard smiled, weakly. He nodded toward Grampy. "Bud, I think Alexsandr is heading in a right direction. If we can toss ideas around long enough, I think something quite surprising will come of it. This +1 scenario he has discovered is pretty amazing stuff."

"Here comes Alexsandr now," said Grampy. He stood, painfully, to walk down the steps to greet him; aching joints and various pains could not keep him seated. "Looks like Rachael and Ladonna are with him."

Alexsandr drove up. He parked the car. All three of them got out and started walking toward the porch.

Grampy, Richard, and Bud went down the steps, walked the short distance to the trio. Richard embraced Ladonna, and he asked her how she was holding up. She hugged him tightly, explaining to him she was tired, frightened, and edgy. It was a bad time for a reunion after all the years, so they agreed to spend some time together in a few days to get reacquainted.

They spoke for a few minutes, chattering among themselves. Then Bud asked Ladonna if she felt like talking. He wanted to know if she might have any information that might help him find David's assailant. She agreed to step aside with him for a few minutes to provide any information that might be helpful. She explained she probably did not have much to offer, and Bud said he understood the circumstances. He also told her as far as he knew David would be hurting and sore for a while, but he would be otherwise fine. He would be back on his feet and back to normal in a few weeks. She had already heard as much at the hospital, but she told him it made her feel better to hear it again.

Meanwhile, Alexsandr explained that Rachael and Ladonna were going to drive back to Nohartinit and come back for him in a few hours. Richard offered Alexsandr a ride so they would not have to make the trip back, and Alexsandr accepted the offer and explained it to Rachael. "Most likely very late," he said. "Don't wait up for me."

"I have to be back to school tomorrow for a few hours, anyway," Richard said. "I'm going to see if I can't extend my leave to get a little farther into this case. I'm sure my advisor will go for it."

After Bud questioned Ladonna, he rejoined them. She sat by Richard and exchanged pleasantries; he comforted her the best he could. Alexsandr asked Bud if he though there was anything to fear, whether the assailant might go after Ladonna for some perverse reason.

"I don't think you have anything to worry about, Alexsandr," Bud explained, loud enough for all to hear. "The attack on David Wilson has all the appearances of a random act...David was at the wrong place at the wrong time. Ladonna," he assured him, "...is in no danger. But she will probably feel safer away from her apartment for a while. With you she won't have to be alone. Her parents, as you know, both work. I see no danger, but we're dealing with a psycho, Alexsandr. You never know."

Then Bud drew Alexsandr aside out of earshot of the rest of them, under the pretext of discussing his research project. They walked around the corner of the house.

"Do you own a gun, Alexsandr?" he asked.

"I thought you said there was no danger?"

Bud slipped a small caliber pistol into Alexsandr's hands.

"It is fully loaded...if you have to, just aim and fire. Just make sure you kill the son-of-a-bitch using no more than two shots and make sure he drops dead inside your house."

Alexsandr casually slipped the weapon into his pocket. "You think he's coming after Ladonna?"

"All my instincts tell me no. But I couldn't live with myself if I am wrong, Alexsandr. Most homicide victims have some contact with their assailants, Alexsandr...close associations, relationships, or family members. Murderers usually know their victims. The ladies don't need to know, Alexsandr. They'll be better off if you don't tell them, okay?"

"There is a danger, then?"

"If David Wilson knew the guy, then there is a good chance Ladonna did, too. I think...my gut tells me...David was a spontaneous target; it could just as well have been an old lady, a young kid, you or me. He was in the wrong place at the wrong time."

"Should I go back with them?"

"No. If you can, just go through the motions of living as you usually do. Treat Ladonna as if she is just visiting for a couple of days.

If the creep is watching, you don't want to give him the impression he has any kind of power or control over your activities.

Alexsandr I've already set up a watch on your house, her parent's house, and her apartment. If you don't tell the ladies, they'll never know our guys are watching. If this creep has been following them, following her, he might just try something. If he does we'll be all over his butt.

These creeps, Alexsandr...you just never know. As they say, it is better to be safe than sorry."

"Bud?"

"What, Alexsandr?"

"Do you think you can catch this guy?"

"With your help, Alexsandr. We need to get that profile. Quite frankly without it, we don't have squat."

"Let's go back. I'll have Rachael take Ladonna home. Then we can get started. I hope you have some time and don't mind late hours."

"If it will snag this creep, Alexsandr, I'll stay as long as I have to," agreed Bud. "Chief Renwall is fit to be tied, as you can imagine. I hate to tell him...and I don't think he would listen anyway, but Nohartinit is not the quiet little town it used to be. Things are going to get worse and worse. These attacks are just a sampler...what's lies just around the corner will make these episodes seem like kid stuff."

Chapter Five

The four men gathered around the kitchen table. A fresh pot of coffee was brewing, and they had laid out bowls of various snack foods, cookies, crackers, chips. Alexsandr briefed Bud on the +1 scenario, and then he read IDEA 8 to them:

"IDEA 8: The bonding process, then, can be traced to early childhood development. It is a developmental process that can make or break the child, in terms of mental, moral, psychological, emotional, and spiritual fulfillment as a human being. It enables the individual to place himself inside the mass of humanity and recognize his separateness as a human being yet recognize his space inside the mass of humanity. It enables – and makes noble – the individual by separating the one from the rest while maintaining his elementary identity – as a human being, one among many. On the other hand, if the processes are not developed, the individual will not fit in, and he will not find a place in the mass of humanity to call his own. Such an individual will be headed, inevitably, toward instability as a human person. This instability will be manifested in behaviors linked to mental, moral, psychological, emotional, or spiritual incapacity.

This is not the same type of bonding one normally associates as taking place, for example, with mother and child. This is a bonding with extra-dimensional life qualities that make civil living and civilization possible. It, as much as anything, is a search for meaning capability taken to the logical conclusion, understanding.

For example, to bond (bring meaning) to order in a larger scheme (how it enables people to peacefully co-exist) one must first step outside the limiting confines of the self and see the larger picture...the millions upon millions of other human beings out and around.

I will continue, if there are no questions at this point," said Alexsandr. "This next few sections will be helpful I think." He read the next few sections:

"IDEA 9: One of the traits that runs in common among most (if not all) social deviates is the inability of the individual to see, understand, appreciate, or even recognize the existence of another human being as worthy, important, or special. In this, the liberal, the homosexual, the rapist, the common criminal and other social malcontents manifest their inability to separate themselves as human persons, independent, and special, and unique in all the world by treating other persons like inanimate trash, by treating others as they see themselves.

The social deviate spectrum excludes no income or social class, race, religion, or gender. In recent years, the young have emerged as the dominant group for statistical increases in criminal activity, with girls racing fast to catch up with the boys in real numbers of crimes committed by children between the ages of ten and seventeen.

Class, social status or income levels have no direct relation to the genesis of childhood propensities to crimes and anti-social behaviors; this is not to say, there are no ties to moral crimes and other crimes based on such.

Indeed race, for example, does seem to be a deciding factor in some moral and other crimes. The statistics on unwed birthing and abortion are quite clear, for example. Blacks, as a group of the population as a whole, for example, lead the pack in unwed birthing, and they lead the pack in abortions. This should surprise no one because of the huge numbers of unwed births inside the black community. A whopping sixty-eight percent (68%) of all live births among blacks are illegitimate.

One can discount factors such as income or social class in measuring social incompatibility, moral psychological illnesses, and various crimes (moral and otherwise). These are merely excuses, a smokescreen for convenience and political purposes. Liberal thinking, for example, is widely infectious not just among rich and poor alike, it is well represented among the various races, and among the sexes; it is, in many ways, a white middle class disease.

IDEA 10: But can one, really, tap into race or liberalism or homosexuality or whatever, as causative bases for social ills ranging from lousy manners to mass murders? No. These disorders are the end result of something more widespread. They are symptoms, not causes. No matter how one looks at it, the inability to search for meaning is a disorder of origin in early childhood, without cause in any other source, except parental failures, more often than not manifested in the breakdown of the family and closely associated with fearfulness.

When a family breaks down, the same results can be expected in terms of social malfunctions as far as the offspring go.

Because family breakdowns cross every demarcation line – economic, social, political, racial – these breakdowns and these alone are common factors in the failure of children to mesh with social expectations. This is affirmed by statistical evidence. This being the case, it is inside the broken family where not only causes can be found but reparative possibilities as well. The breakdown does not have to necessarily mean anything but two married adults, one male and one female, united under one roof, neither of whom are affiliated with their sex as male or female, and this would cause sufficient confusion to stunt developmental completion in the children.

IDEA 11: There can be no legitimacy of an unmarried couple, or same-sex couple calling togetherness a union or a family. This would be tantamount to uttering nonsense. Anything short of a marital relationship between a male and a female is a farce; it is an unnatural misadventure working toward a social impossibility.

A family exists when the extra-dimensional barrier is breached, when two people of the opposite sex become one (1+1=1). The unifying element is called commitment. Without commitment, the togetherness is simply that (1+1) and equals nothing.

A legitimate marriage has three elements, order, life-affirming values, and sex identity with affiliation to the sex as male or female. A live-in relationship without marriage lacks stability. It lacks a strong sex affiliation, and degrades the participants. It is disordered from the start, because it is subject to disposal at will from the beginning. One or both participants are free to pull out at any time." He paused.

"Now," said Alexsandr, continuing. "Let's take a look at what we have." He asked Bud to describe as much as he could about the two events, and he asked him to speculate, as best he could, based on his own experiences as a street cop and an investigator.

"The knifing and the pipe attack took place after dark, and they seemed hurried. The assailant took no time with them; he rushed his victims from behind. He appears to have run out of hiding in dark shadows, landed his first blow. Then he swung blindly, and as long as he stuck the victim, he didn't care where or how he got him. This indicates to me there was no planning, no intent to make the victim pay for anything; the assailant was not getting even with the victim. It appeared the assailant was in a hurry to get it done, and this would indicate to me the assailant was scared, this was probably the first time he had perpetrated an assault against anyone. The attacks were sloppy...very sloppy. He probably did not even stick around to look at his handiwork. This is basically what David Wilson described also."

"There would be no prior record of any kind then?" asked Richard.

"Probably not. Nothing to lead anyone to believe this guy was capable of murder. I think he just snapped, decided it was time to kill. So he did. Why he struck twice, with the incidents so close together, is a mystery. I assume the first time he wasn't satisfied, for some reason, so he tried again. Then he probably fell back into his regular routine, whatever that is."

"So after he attacked David, he was satisfied?" asked Grampy. He shifted in his chair to try to get comfortable. His lower back ached something terrible.

"For how long?" mumbled Alexsandr.

"There's no telling how long the guy will hold still. Here's what we do know so far. The entry wounds indicate the assailant was right handed. He would, at best guess, be about average height and weight, maybe five-eight, one hundred sixty pounds. Not exceptionally strong...just average. As a matter of fact David Wilson indicated he used both hands to club him."

"I thought you said the coroner's report would tell us that?" asked Richard.

"It will confirm what I've said. I was at the scene. I've seen a lot of stabbings."

"How do you establish the assailant's height and weight?"

"By the depth of the wounds, and the position of the wounds relative to the size of the victim's body. David said he caught a quick glimpse. He described him as shorter than himself. David is well over six feet. This guy came up to David's chin. David indicated the fellow did not have a powerful swing. I'm not sure if that means anything at this point."

"A nobody," grumbled Alexsandr. "Nothing to distinguish him from hundreds of other people out and around. We can probably rule out a manual laborer, construction type, athletic type."

"Not really. We can speculate at this point. He could be the proverbial man next door," Bud said. "That's why I enlisted you guys. We need a description."

"Does the fact both victims were male have any meaning to you, Bud?" asked Grampy. "Or the fact the attacks were after dark?"

"Like I said before, I think this creep would have attacked anyone if the time and place worked to his readiness. He might have stewed about it all day long. I don't think he would discriminate between male or female, old or young."

"He's not likely to go back and try to finish the job he did on David, is he?" asked Alexsandr. He crossed his arms defensively across his chest.

"No. I think he's done with David Wilson."

"Gang related, Bud? Some kind of initiation, maybe?"

"No. A gang member is not likely to be so sloppy with a knife. And a pipe does feel right in a gang setting. Besides that, we don't have much gang activity, and when we do they usually try to hurt each other. These guys around here are just a bunch of wannabes. They're too gutless to kill each other...or anyone else."

"The +1 super-empty scenario, Alexsandr?" quizzed Grampy.

"That, Grampy, would be a good place to start," replied Alexsandr. He directed his attention to Bud. "Is there any way to establish an approximate age? It would help in reconstructing his earlier years."

"I would say late twenties to mid-thirties. I think the guy had to spend many years festering before he reached the breaking point. Some series of events or a single traumatic event led him to the breaking point. I also guess he has been working, doing the everyday grind routine for a number of years. This would call for some level of maturity...a somewhat settled individual until his breaking point was reached. This would help him blend in, leave no paper trail. I'm convinced we have no priors...probably not even a parking ticket."

"Married? Single? Divorced?" queried Richard. "Any gut feeling about that?"

"No guess. Any of the above," answered Bud. "We probably won't know that until we get him. Both victims were single males, in their twenties, but I don't think that has anything to do with anything."

"Coincidence?"

"Yes. Pure and simple."

"If your instincts are right concerning his age, we might be in luck, Bud. We may have to tax your memory circuits a little," Alexsandr said. "I think we can accurately reconstruct his early years, family history, and the like. It will be up to you to put a name and a face to our description. We can reconstruct the kid, and, if you know the kid...you will have the adult...your killer."

"You guys can do that?"

"Bud, we're going to test something new. Alexsandr developed it...the +1 scenario," explained Richard. "Alexsandr, I'm sure, already has some idea who we are looking for, right, Alexsandr?"

Alexsandr smiled, slyly. "Of course I do. We're looking for nobody...the biggest nobody...and soon to be infamous nobody...to live in this town in the last twenty to thirty years."

"Please continue," said Bud.

"The man we're looking for is what I call +1 super-empty. Lonely...even totally friendless, probably not even in contact with members of his own family, who is lost in a world way beyond his understanding, overwhelming in fact. He probably has no hobbies, bare essentials to live by, probably a menial – even a demeaning – job, and he has probably been on it for years, with no advancement, no past and no future. He barely makes enough money to scrape by. He has probably lived in the same place all his adult life. Right off hand, I'd say he came from a broken home...father-absent. His mother was probably a drunk or a druggie, probably second generation. This guy all but raised himself.

He probably learned his work ethic from his mother...who made sure he got to work every day to bring in habit money. He probably started working as soon as he was old enough to get a job. But there was something about him – maybe his physical appearance or some such...that set him apart from everybody else. Maybe extreme poverty due to his mother's drinking or drug habit or some such. Until I look into it a little better, I'd say we're looking for the daughter of some warmed-over Hippy chick who got herself knocked up in the late sixties or early seventies and didn't have a clue what to do with the kid. She was probably a prostitute or gave it away for drugs. The time frame would fit. Then her kid was herself knocked up, and repeated the cycle. The guy we're looking for was born in the mid-seventies or thereabouts, most likely to an unwed teenaged girl, either a prostitute, a drunk, or a druggie...or some perverse mix of all three."

"All this from your +1 scenario, Alexsandr?" Bud said. "How in the hell do you expect me to find the kid of a transient kid of some transient Hippy broad?"

"Alexsandr," said Grampy. "Don't you remember how many of them had flooded into town during the sixties? What makes you think you can trace such a thing?"

"Our guy is definitely not a transient. I'll tell you now how to find him, Bud. How old are your kids, Bud? Early twenties, maybe?"

"Twenty-three and twenty-five."

"I'm willing to bet bucks Richard here, Ladonna, and your kids went to school with this guy. He's lived here all his life."

"I think...no offense Bud...you ought to talk to them and see if they can help you pick out the most untalented and not-very-bright, overtly bland, and essentially un-liked, undistinguished, unpopular, and ugly loner kid they knew in school who came from a broken home with a real loser for a mother. I'd bet you match the names they give you with the background I've given you, and you will have your man."

"I can see why you would call him super-empty," said Bud. "Grampy, Richard...do you gentlemen concur with Alexsandr's assessment?"

"Perhaps, if Alexsandr explained how he is building his description, you will see why we do," said Grampy.

Alexsandr thumbed through some papers, and he handed a copy of the model to Bud. "What we are looking at here is the Negative and the

Neutral Zones, Bud. The +1 scenario indicates an individual who has never become affiliated with his sex or who has never settled in his own mind what sex he is...he lacks sex identity altogether. Because he does, he cannot separate male from female, one human being from another...they are all the same."

"You're saying I'm looking for a fag or a switch-hitter?"

"No. You are looking for a man more empty than a homosexual...you're looking for someone ungrounded in even the most basic of all human identities. Without any recognition of his own sex, he is totally ungrounded in the human experience in what we call extra-dimensional ways...mental, moral, psychological, emotional, or spiritual experience. He is, inside, totally and completely empty. The homosexual, even though ungrounded, still tries to fit in somewhere and he finds acceptance among his own...your guy does not. He's dropped a peg below the homosexual. He's withdrawn from the human race and the human experience. The homosexual lives in the world by fantasizing his existence as legitimate. This guy does not even have a fantasy world to keep him company."

"Did he withdraw? Or was he driven out?" asked Bud. "If he is as lonely, alienated as you seem to think, isn't it reasonable to assume he may have started out normal and was driven backwards toward where he is now?"

"No. That's not a reasonable assumption," Alexsandr explained. "A person fully grounded in his sex identity would certainly move toward the positive life experience. Our guy did not. This leads us to the conclusion he had no way to establish certain critical developmental processes...gender identification and separateness. These qualities develop within the first few years of life. He was denied this. His mother probably hated him for being male and never let him forget it. He never had the chance to make contact with reality. He was raised, if you can call it that, by a female and had no male influences whatsoever. Hence the single mother scenario. I would suggest he never got past the Neutral Zone. He learned to function a little bit...get around, speak, and even hold down some menial job. But he lived in the worst possible world...one completely devoid of anything...no joy, no sadness, no values whatsoever and nothing of value...not even the ties to his mother. Hence the drug addicted, alcoholic, sluttish mother. He probably hated her for what she did and who she was, and severed any ties he could have had with the rest of human kind. He probably never knew his father...she probably didn't either."

"And all of this would have been festering since early childhood until it has, after all the years, driven him over the brink?"

"Not exactly. He roamed around completely cut off from the rest of humanity. The more alien he became the more distant he became. This is why I would suggest he is bland, uninteresting, a non-entity in his younger years, more so as he aged. I might venture to say, he just got so tired of trying to fit into the world he blew a cork, so to speak, and he decided to strike back. Violence, in some form, is an inevitable expectation inside the +1 scenario."

"But why would he strike back, Alexsandr...if he is a walking empty shell, why would he strike back? You are saying violence is inevitable is such an individual?"

"In this case, I think it is his very last connection with being alive, Bud. He probably had a love/hate thing going with his mother, which provided him a rush any time they fought. Some how that important connection was severed. He probably has never felt so much alive as at the moment he started stabbing that guy. It is sort of like the S & M manifestation, Bud. One person feels alive inflicting pain, and the other feels alive receiving it. If you don't find him soon, he'll either strike again...for that momentary feeling he gets from the rush...or he'll kill himself."

"Okay, gentlemen...I'm going to stick my neck out. You all seem like sincere and honest men. I admit I don't understand this stuff yet. But what I need is some kind of composite I can use to put a few men on the case. I want something fairly concrete to go on. Can you do this?"

"We can do it," Alexsandr said. "For right now, can you do some snooping...maybe birth certificates? We're looking for a male child born around the mid-seventies to a single mother, probably an addict, alcoholic, or prostitute. She was probably not much past fifteen or so at the time. If you think you have found her, check her birth certificate for a single parent birthing. If that checks out, then go back, get the name, do some snooping. By then Richard and the others could have some names for you."

"In the meanwhile," Richard offered. "I'll get with Ladonna and your kids, if we can arrange it, and try to come up with a name or two. We might be able to poll others our age as well. We could go through yearbooks at the library if we have to."

"Okay, gentlemen. I'll leave you to your work. When can you have something for me?"

"How about tomorrow morning, Bud?" said Grampy. "I'd like to see this creep taken out of circulation...fast."

"That soon?"

"I think so," agreed Alexsandr.

79

Bud wrote down some names and numbers on a piece of paper, and he handed them to Richard. "I'll tell my kids to expect your call. They'll cooperate."

Bud left. Alexsandr, Grampy, and Richard began their description. Richard recorded items as they came across them; they tossed each item back and forth, to match the criteria of the +1 scenario before they added it to the list. It took them several hours until their description was finished.

Description:

KNOWN: Male, of average height and weight, somewhere around 5'9" and 160 pounds. Not especially muscular.

DESCRIPTION MEETING THE CRITERIA OF THE +1 SCENARIO:

1) Born sometime in the early seventies to a teenaged unwed mother, who was probably a drug addict, an alcoholic, or a prostitute, or some twisted combination of all three.
2) Most notable characteristics are blandness of character, boring to talk to, a loner, with few contacts, few interests. Lackluster. May have some distinguishing physical feature or deformity.
3) Self-conscious, withdrawn. Possibly severely confused and volatile, may be suicidal. Should be considered dangerous to himself and others.
4) Probably exhibits some child-like mannerisms, in his manner of speaking and possibly in other behaviors as well. Probably essentially anti-social. Probably unresponsive, unemotional in most situations. Probably not inclined toward expressions of emotions in any direction.
5) Has probably held the same menial, low-paying job for ten or more years. It is probably in some position that draws no attention and requires minimal exertion or physical labor. Possibly works alone and remains unbothered as long as he does his work. Has probably lived in the same place for a long period of time, quite possibly a one or two room flat, tucked away somewhere out of sight, on a back street. Maybe a basement apartment or some such.
6) Probably a bachelor, not known to have female companions, or any kind of steady girlfriend. Is probably very shy around women or afraid of women. Treats and speaks to men and women, boys and

girls on a plain even level, making no distinctions as to age, sex, or other distinguishing characteristics.

7) Most likely has an excellent attendance record at work. Has never caused trouble for anybody. Most likely a creature of habit. Probably dresses casually, wearing indistinctive clothes and shoes, nothing that would draw attention to himself.

8) He probably buys the same meal from the same fast food joint, day after day, week in and week out. Probably as regular as clockworks when he does so. Probably buys the least expensive, most ordinary meal available.

After completing the initial description, Richard said he had a problem with it.

"This regularity, Alexsandr, doesn't it contradict the model...the patterns speak to order, a very high level of order."

"I was wondering about that also, Alexsandr," added Grampy. "Why would the super empty +1 lead such a structured life?"

"Extremes like these, taken to the point our guy has, speak to a high level of disorder. Such behavior is anything but ordered. I'd almost bet every item he owns has a set place in his room, and I'd almost bet they fall within the tiniest fraction of an inch to the same spot when he places them each time. He has let the routine define his life. Remember, he does not exist in the extra-dimensional sphere...essentially, he does not exist. But there is one inescapable thing he cannot fight. He has fallen into the natural order...he follows, in everything he does, the path of least resistance. It is there he defines his identity...he does not have to participate in life; he just goes through the motions of living, never having to face challenges posed by change."

"Alexsandr, another question," said Richard. "How did you conclude if he doesn't strike again, he might kill himself?"

"The newspapers will pick up the stories. So will the television. People will be talking. There is a chance this publicity...drawing attention to what he has done...will be the pin that pops his air bubble. Not likely, if he is as far gone into nothingness as I think he is, but if that bubble gets popped, his world will end. He will be in a position he can no longer roll with the flow, and he will have no choice left but to face reality as an ingredient in his life. The only thing that will be left for him to do is end it; literally in every other way, it will already be over. We need to get to this guy before he does something rash and preventable."

"Are we talking about depression, Alexsandr?" asked Grampy. "I see where all this comes from, but is the end product depression?"

"No. It is not. The end product is mental illness; you see, Grampy, you cannot move toward depression if you have never lived inside the 1+1=1 scenario," answered Alexsandr. "I won't go into detail, but I'm working on depression as a regression from the Positive Zone to the Neutral Zone. Some day, I'll sit down with you and discuss it. The match is, to put it mildly, surprisingly pleasant."

They went over the description a few more times, to make sure they were not omitting what might be an important identifier. When they were satisfied with it, Richard took charge of it. He placed it in an envelope, clearly marked it for Officer Elbudro, and he tucked it safely away in his pocket.

It was late. Richard and Alexsandr said their good-byes to Grampy. Then they left. After the twenty-mile drive, Richard dropped Alexsandr off at his house; he then dropped the envelope off with the Desk Sergeant at the precinct station. Then he went to his own apartment near the campus.

It was a small apartment, with a small bedroom, a kitchenette, a bathroom, and a closet. It was furnished with a wall clock, a coffee pot, a chair, a desk, a reading light, a large loaded bookcase, and a computer. He sat at the desk, pulled up a file on the computer. It was essentially a collected batch of notes for his thesis, dozens of pages in all.

He smiled weakly, a surrender-type smile; it was not an admission of defeat so much as a resigned acceptance of inevitability and truth. It was, instead, a pat on the back; an acknowledgement to himself there was light at the end of the tunnel.

He moved the cursor to Edit, clicked the mouse. Then he moved the cursor to the Select All line. He clicked again. The entire set of notes took on a backdrop of black, confirming the command. Then, with a wide grin...pure satisfaction...he moved his cursor to the Delete line.

With one final single click of the mouse, nine months of tedious research, one hundred and ninety four pages of notes plus a long bibliography, vanished from the screen.

He took a deep breath. Then he began again. He typed in the title of his thesis, centered it, and then saved the page. It was time for bed.

The new material would begin to take shape in the morning.

A REALITY OPTION:
Extra-Dimensional Education
and the Evolution of Values.

This done, he called it a day, undressed, took a shower, brushed his teeth, and crawled into bed. He dreamed of his younger days – and of Ladonna.

Chapter Six

The next morning, Richard woke up earlier than usual. He got dressed, fixed a pot of strong coffee. He sat in his chair, which he deliberately moved away from the computer, and he planned his day.

His first stop would be to make arrangements with his advisor for a few more days away from classes. He foresaw no problems.

His second stop would be at a phone to call Bud Elbudro's kids and have them meet him at the library to begin their search through old yearbooks.

His third stop would be at Alexsandr's to pick up Ladonna and take her to the library. He checked his wallet to make sure he had enough cash on hand to take her out somewhere when they finished at the library.

For his last stop, he would seek out several professors, the older ones, the ex-Hippy turned Social Scientist turned part-time instructor bunch; they might be helpful in locating the mother of the mother of the guy they were looking for; the university was overrun with them in his opinion, even though only five taught there intermittently; so he figured somewhere in their huddles he might find what he was looking for. It looked like a long day, so he took his time, drinking several cups of coffee before heading out.

In the meanwhile, Bud Elbudro was getting ready to start his day. He and his wife, Gynna, sat quietly at their table, drinking coffee. She had agreed to go with him to search birth certificates. It would, they agreed, speed the search process. They had to wait for the Court House to open.

Open, on the table, was the description Richard had dropped off at the station the night before. The Desk Sergeant had called and told him it was there; Bud had told him to let him know when it arrived, regardless of the time.

"Bud...this description...does it help any? I mean...you know...can you find this guy based on what they tell you here?" asked Gynna.

"I'll have to convince the Chief he has to give me some men to check out fast food restaurants, look for menial jobs and the like. I'll need guys to ask questions, poke around the schools, and interview people. If I can convince him Alexsandr knows what he's doing, he'll do it. It could be a hard sell. Assuming the description is accurate, there can't be too many people in Nohartinit who fit this description. I think he will go for it. This murder is damn near unprecedented in Nohartinit, and I don't think the Chief will let it go unsolved. Besides, we don't have squat to go on other than this description."

"Are you going to pass this description out to the street cops?"

"Why not? Maybe some of the older guys can come up with a lead. How about you, Gynna...do you know any old Hippy-types who might know something? I admit finding the son of the daughter of a Hippy slut is not going to be easy. We're looking at a trail that's damn near forty years cold."

"Why not pass it out to everybody you meet, advertise it?" suggested Gynna.

"I'll check with Alexsandr about that. This is his puppy. He may have reasons not to. This +1 scenario is experimental, Gynna, and it might not work. If it doesn't work, I don't want to publicly embarrass a man like Alexsandr. His reputation is impeccable." Bud checked his watch. "Let's go, Gynna. We should get there just about the time they open."

On the other side of Nohartinit, Ladonna, Alexsandr, and Rachael sat down to breakfast. Rachael and Ladonna had prepared eggs, toast, bacon, hot coffee, and they heated a few cinnamon rolls on the side.

"What time is Richard coming by?" asked Ladonna. She still had a faraway sleepy look in her big blue eyes. "It has been a long time. I hope we get some time together. He certainly filled out, didn't he?"

"He's more your type than David," said Alexsandr. "You really ought to think about that...think about your future, Ladonna."

"You like him, Grandpa, because he's an academic type – like you. I always liked Richard...as a friend. There never was any...you know...chemistry." She swept back her shoulder length auburn hair.

"Chemistry. Bah!" said Rachael. She took a healthy bite out of a cinnamon roll. "Kids don't know anything about chemistry. That was what...ten, fifteen years ago?"

"A long time ago, Grandma. A long time. We have not even seen each other in years. I don't love Richard...I love David. Doesn't anyone understand that?"

"But can David make you happy?" Alexsandr asked. "You don't want to be married to a lawyer, Ladonna. No. No lawyer."

"That's not fair, Grandpa."

"They think about their careers and politics, and they sooner or later sell their souls to the highest bidder. You don't want that. I don't want that for you, either."

"Richard has been in love with you as far back as I can remember," said Rachael, with a sly grin creasing her face. "You need a man who can love you like that. And give you beautiful children. Lots of children."

"Please...Grandpa, Grandma...I know you mean well. I appreciate that. I love David...aspiring lawyer that he is."

"Love? Bah!" hissed Rachael. "What do you kids know about love? Look at yourself, Ladonna. Young. Beautiful. Bright. Great personality...why do you want to waste your time with a law student?"

"I am not wasting my time, Grandma. I love the man, doesn't that mean anything?"

"Love? Bah!" hissed Rachael again. "You know nothing about love! You just think you do!"

The doorbell rang. Ladonna saw her out and took it. She went quickly to the door, opened it.

"Richard, good morning," she said. She stepped back for him to enter. "You are just in time to save me from two well-intentioned matchmakers. Please come in. I'll get you a cup of coffee. Everybody is in the kitchen."

She led the way as Richard followed. She was wearing a tight black dress, which fit her form exquisitely, he noticed. Form-fitting but not tacky, very professional looking, he decided. She looks good in black, he thought. Hell, she'd look good in anything!

As he entered the kitchen, Rachael hastily moved a chair to the table, to seat Richard beside Ladonna. She looked at him, smiling widely.

"My, don't you look handsome this morning," Rachael said. "Here...you sit here. Ladonna, get Richard some coffee. Don't you think Richard looks handsome this morning, Ladonna?"

Alexsandr pointed briefly at Ladonna as she set up a cup of coffee.

"She looks beautiful this morning, don't you think, Richard?" Richard had already made that assessment, but before he had a chance to speak, Alexsandr continued. "Too beautiful...look how she wears that outfit...too smart...got a great job, making a good living...too much potential to marry some lawyer, don't you think?"

Richard looked at Ladonna. He chuckled. She smiled, widely, as he remembered from their younger days. They both seemed playfully embarrassed. But Richard decided to play along.

"Alexsandr, your granddaughter has inspired my dreams for several decades now." Ladonna picked up on the cue. She placed the coffee in front of Richard, bent down, and kissed him on his cheek.

"And my dreams of you, Richard, have warmed my bed on many a lonely and cold winter's night." She sat beside him, leaned slightly toward him, to brush up against his shoulder. She placed a hand gently on his arm. She looked playfully toward him, winked, and then spoke softly, to catch both Alexsandr and Rachael off guard, hopefully to put an end to their badgering. "We were talking about love and chemistry," she said. "Talk about chemistry...maybe we should tell them about the time in old man's Richter's barn...wow! You want to talk about chemistry!"

Richard laughed heartily. Although nothing of the sort ever took place, he could see that it worked. He could see that Rachael was visibly shocked and embarrassed. Alexsandr almost dropped his cinnamon roll. One last jab at it, he thought, and the matchmaking might come to an end.

"And the time we almost got caught down at the Platt Street Bridge...yeah...Chemistry!"

"Enough already!" Alexsandr huffed. "That won't be necessary! We get the message."

But Rachael was not quite finished. "You do make a beautiful couple," she whispered.

"Enough already!" Alexsandr growled again. "We have a lot to do today. Let's get with it, okay?" Then he laid out the instructions. "If you find your people, list them. Be sure to keep quiet about what you are doing, what you are looking for and stuff like that. If, by chance, you know where they live, what they are doing these days, write it down. Bud will be here this evening around six or so. If you can, we need to stick around and see if we can help him get this guy." Alexsandr reached into his pants pocket, took out his wallet. He handed Ladonna a twenty. "Buy yourselves some lunch."

Ladonna knew better than to argue with Alexsandr about the money, so she handed it to Richard and asked him to hang onto it. He tucked the twenty in his shirt pocket.

"Everything is okay at school, Richard?"

"Yeah, fine. I've got all the time I need. I explained the situation without going into details. Alexsandr, what do you think of me probing amongst some of the professors...the old Hippy bunch? They might lead us to mother number one."

"If you have the time, why not? It may be helpful."

"Everything okay with your boss, Ladonna?"

"Fine, Grandpa."

"Bud has asked me to coordinate the various efforts, so keep in touch. He and his wife are searching birth records this morning. If we can get enough put together by evening, maybe we can get this guy soon."

"What kind of method are you looking at, Alexsandr?"

"Well, Bud is trying to get some guys on the street to check out fast food joints, ask questions, locate the menial jobs. It won't be fast and it won't be easy. We'll match what the street guys find with the rest. We'll match what Bud comes up with in the birth records with what you come up with through the yearbooks. We'll match this to our description. If the same name pops up in the coordinated efforts, we should have our guy."

"Sounds like it just might work, Alexsandr," said Richard. He looked at Ladonna. "Ready?" They started toward the door.

"One stop along the way? I want to check in on David at his apartment."

"Sure. No problem."

"How's he doing, anyway?" He opened the door for her.

"He'll be up and around soon. Banged up pretty good, but nothing permanent. He said the guy jumped out of the dark and started pounding. Strangest thing, don't you think?"

"I'm not sure, Ladonna. If Alexsandr is right, it isn't strange at all."

"How's that?"

"If Alexsandr is right, it all has a perfectly rational explanation. That, Ladonna, would be strange...and scary as hell."

It took them about twenty minutes to make their way through traffic, which was backed up because the railroad people were hitching tanker cars. It then took another ten minutes to find a parking spot near his apartment. David lived in an older, rundown complex. It was all he could afford. It was one of those places strewn with trash, frequented by dopers and dealers. Loud music blared almost 'round the clock.

They visited with David for a short while. He complained his new cast itched like crazy and he still had a lot of aches and pains. But he assured Ladonna he was going to live. He had no new information to offer.

"I just barely got a glimpse of him, and that was it." His speech was slurred from swelling.

"Is that all you remember?"

"Something else...it might mean something. He used both hands on the pipe." He could not demonstrate, for it was too painful to move his arms that freely.

"Why would that mean something?" Ladonna asked, curiously.

"Even with both hands, he didn't hit hard enough to crack my skull. He did some damage...as you can see. But he just didn't seem to have the power to do me in."

After a few minutes, they left his room, and then left the complex for the library.

One of the few well-maintained buildings in the city, the library was sometimes used for drug deals by preteens and teens, and, on cold days, it served as a refuge for homeless men and women, who used the pretext of reading to stay warm, and in hot weather, every few hours, local cops peeled winos off the front steps. Now and then a few other people used the library to hold meetings or just meet for the fun of it.

There they met up with James and Stephy Elbudro, Bud's son and daughter. There was only one other person besides the librarian in the library, a shaggy and dirty drunk precariously propped up in a back corner. After a brief introduction, they got down to business.

They recognized one another, but they had not hung out together. James and Stephy had already gone through a small stack of yearbooks, and James, playfully, slid them the stack.

"We started in eighty-six. Nothing yet. Most of the familiar faces...and some not-so-familiar faces...don't fit the description."

"Let's work back. James, you're twenty-five? You graduated in ninety-three? I'm twenty-four. I graduated in ninety-two. Ladonna...ninety-two. Stephy?"

"Ninety."

"Okay," said Richard. "Let's find those...I, for one, don't remember squat from earlier than that. Stands to reason if he was in school when we were, then he's got to be in one of those years."

"Unless he dropped out at sixteen," said Stephy. "In which case, the mid-to-late eighties would be right."

"That would fit the menial job," said James.

"Hmm?" said Ladonna. "Let's split them up. Two of us take ninety and later. Two of us take mid-eighties to ninety. Otherwise, we have hundreds of pictures to look through, and we still might come up with nothing."

"Which ones? Junior High or High?"

"Both, I guess. We don't really have a fix on this guy's age."

"Boy, I don't remember much about Junior High," mumbled James.

"Me either," said Stephy.

"I don't either. Let's look anyway...maybe something will ring a bell," said Ladonna. "Hand me a stack."

An hour passed. Then two. The stacks got smaller, but none of them came upon anything that caught their attention.

"I'm taking a break," said James at last. "We've seen every nerd, every jerk, every jock, and every nit for years and years. Still nothing."

"Good idea," agreed Stephy.

Ladonna and Richard concurred. They put the books aside, asked the librarian to leave them, explaining they would be back.

"I understand," the Librarian said. She had huge brown eyes, dark hair, and fair skin. She had beautiful white teeth behind large, firm lips. "I spoke to Bud last night. We're old friends. Can I help you, maybe?"

"What year did you graduate?" asked Richard.

"Eighty-seven."

"You know who and what we are looking for?"

"Yes. I do. The ultimate loser? I probably dated him at least once," she joked. "I've dated every loser in Nohartinit at least once." She smiled, playfully. "I've done a lot of research for Bud in the past. He trusts me implicitly. You guys take five. I'll see if I can find something. I'm not proud of it, but there was a time I smoked the dope and made a general ass of myself. I probably hung out with the creep at one time or another."

The four of them went outside for some fresh air. James lit up a cigarette, inhaled, and he hissed the smoke out between his teeth.

"Are we going about this the right way?" he asked. He looked at Richard as if he expected an answer.

"What do you mean?"

"We have all viewed dozens of pictures. Nothing. Not only did we not remember most of the kids, we couldn't place most of them as even being in the school. Nobody stands out. Those people Stephy and I knew were not the type we are looking for. The same for you two, right?"

"I see what you're getting at, James," said Ladonna. "We need to find someone who hung out with the losers, or who got to know them."

"Bingo!" said James playfully. "We need to be talking to the school psychologist, maybe social workers, people like that. I don't think this picture thing is going to work."

"How are we going to find out who was the school psychologist at the time?" asked Stephy. "I guess we could talk to the Principal...who is it now?"

"I don't know," said Richard. "I remember Cannonball Jackson...is he still alive?"

"Retired," said James. "He lives over off of Fifth. Maybe we should visit him. In his prime he knew just about every kid in school by his or her first name."

"I'll call Dad," said Stephy, "...and see what he thinks."

"Good," said Richard. "I'll speak to the librarian, and then we'll head over there. You guys go on ahead. I'll be close behind you. What's the address?"

"The four hundred block, about the middle of the block. Look for my car...a red Ford...a worn out piece of junk."

Richard went back into the library. He sat beside the librarian at the table.

"Anything?"

"Nope. Not yet," she said. She flashed her huge brown eyes. "Talk to me. Say anything. I love voices. It is sort of a hobby of mine. I can identify most of my customers by their voices. I put the voices to the face to the names. It relieves the boredom sometimes. Are you married?"

"No."

"Are you gay?"

"Nope."

"What are you doing Friday night?"

"Not a clue"

"Good. Call me." She wrote her phone number on a piece of notepaper. "I get home about six."

Richard borrowed her pencil and wrote his number for her. "If you think of anything, call me. What's your name, by the way?"

"My friends call me Lalinduh."

"Lalinduh...Richard. I'll be in touch. I think we're going to give up this search and try something different. Thanks for your help." He got up to leave. "You're on for Friday night."

Richard left the library, drove to the four hundred block of Fifth. He parked behind the old beat up red Ford. James, Stephy, and Ladonna were chatting at curbside.

"Let's go," said Richard. They walked up to the front door and rang the doorbell. Mister Jackson opened the door. He peered out suspiciously.

"Can I help you?" he said, hoarsely.

"Mister Jackson, can we ask you a few questions?" Ladonna asked.

"Who are you? What kind of questions?"

Richard explained what they needed to know and why they needed to know it. Mister Jackson stepped outside.

"I knew hundreds of kids. Some of them had some pretty sour home lives," Mister Jackson said. "The fellow you describe sounds to me like Jacob Lewski, a scrawny little kid who lived somewhere out on the South Side. I felt sorry for him. Not too bright. Fragile-looking. Never caused any trouble, but was always screwing up something. Seemed like everything he touched went sour. The kid had a terrible home life, I think. Seemed like he could never concentrate on anything for very long. Wore dirty clothes. I don't think he ate very well. If I remember right, he had some kind of problem with his hand. Deformed fingers or something. I did my best to keep him in school. The other kids...you know how mean kids can be...tormented him. They made his life a living hell. He dropped out to go to work as soon as he was old enough."

"When was that, Mister Jackson? Can you recall?"

"Oh, Lord...let me see? That would have been sometime in the late eighties, early nineties. Thereabouts, anyway."

"So he's probably in his early thirties now?"

"Thereabouts."

"Any idea where he went to work?"

"No."

"I know it is a long shot, Mister Jackson," said James. "Have you seen him since...anywhere in Nohartinit?"

"No. I don't get out any more. The old bones just aren't what they used to be."

Richard thanked him for his assistance. They returned to curbside.

"Well, we've got a name. Now what?"

"Back to Dad," said Stephy. "Maybe now they can flush him out. I'll catch up with Dad at the Court House. It ought to be somewhat easier to find the birth certificate now."

"I'll run you over there, Stephy," said James.

"Will you be at Alexsandr's tonight?" asked Richard.

"Dad asked us to come along...he said we might learn something. We'll be there. See you there."

"Okay," said Richard. He escorted Ladonna to his car, opened the door for her. "How about lunch?" he said. He got in, and he started the motor.

"Lunch sounds good. But, on one condition, Richard," she said, lightheartedly. Her eyes shimmered.

"Name it," he said, as he pulled away from the curb.

"You have to tell me, you ass," she said, breaking into a wide and playful grin. "How in hell did you come up with the Platt Street Bridge?"

"And you with old man Richter's barn?"

"I guess we could not have hit on two places with worse reputations if we had to, Richard. I can hear it now...Rachael will probably rake me over the coals this evening."

"I'm sure Alexsandr won't let me slide, either."

"Should we keep them guessing?"

"Why not?" answered Richard. He turned from Fifth into traffic. "Tell me, Ladonna. How long are you going to stay with Alexsandr?"

"Until Bud thinks it is safe to go back to my apartment. Until we catch this guy." She stared blankly out the window. "You don't think this guy is stalking me, do you?"

"No...no. That you don't have to worry about. But it won't hurt to play it safe for a day or two. We're not sure what he's going to do next, Ladonna. We're hoping to get to him before anything else happens. Just stay with Alexsandr and Rachael until this blows over, okay? No heroics."

Richard put on his turn signal and steered into the parking lot of a hamburger joint called Paddy's Place. He parked the car.

Paddy's, as it was known, was an old block structure, with two carry out windows that opened directly into the kitchen. One of the windows was blocked off with a plywood panel, and on the plywood was an arrow, painted in black, directing people to the other window. The building itself was in desperate need of a paint job. Years of use had taken its toll. At one time, the building had been very white and probably somewhat attractive. A young boy played with a yo-yo as he waited patiently outside the carry out window. Nearby, two teens, wearing denim outfits, sat idly on the curb, smoking and chatting about something.

"Do you still do the bacon cheeseburger, chocolate shake bit?" he asked. "Remember this place?"

"Sure do," she said. "It brings back a lot of memories, doesn't it?"

"Let's go then. I'm starving." They got out of the car and walked to the door. Richard opened the door for her, and then he followed her inside.

"This joint has been here forever it seems like," she said. "I wonder if they still make the best burgers in town. I have not been in here in a long time."

"Me neither. I guess we'll soon find out."

The place was noisy and crowded, with mostly young teens filling the booths.

"Great timing, huh?" grumbled Richard. "It must be lunch time at the Junior High."

The kid in front of him looked back. "We're in friggin' double sessions, man...we're friggin' done for the day. Friggin' cool, huh?"

"Yeah," replied Ladonna, as she did her best sloppy tough kid imitation. "I guess it is, like, friggin' cool."

Richard laughed, for she had caught him by surprise. "Somehow, you don't exactly fit the part."

"Oh, yeah?" she chomped. "Just place the friggin' order, man," she insisted as their turn came; they placed their order; the clean-cut kid behind the counter took their money, made change, and passed the order slip back for the grill man to prepare. Meanwhile, they looked for a booth where they could be seated to wait for their number to come up and be called.

"I didn't know you had it in you, Ladonna?" He was still totally enjoying himself.

She struggled to keep a straight face. "Ya gotta have some friggin' fun now and then man," she chuckled. Then she straightened up. " I can't keep it up," she said. "I just can't do it."

They sat down at a booth, to wait for their number to be called.

What they did not notice, as they settled in a corner booth, was the deformed hand that reached for the slip; like the rest of the customers, they paid little attention to the owner of the hand, an ordinary-looking man in a white paper hat wearing a bloody and greasy cloth apron; busy prying frozen patties apart with a large knife in the kitchen by the grill, the grill man paid them no mind either.

As he slapped some patties and a few strips of bacon on the grill, Jacob Lewski thought back over the years, of the thousands of burgers he had cooked; it occurred to him, in all those years, not a living soul had ever told him they liked his burgers. Hell, no one, as far back as he could recall, ever even bothered to tell him he did his job well...lousy...or otherwise. He had not had a raise in seven years.

As the patties and bacon strips sizzled, he mumbled his reply to his own thoughts: "Who gives a care...not you...not me...not a living, breathing soul."

He watched the patties carefully; he would wait to flip them until the blooded water bubbled to the surface. He liked the blooded water. It had a certain appealing something to it...the color...the way it hissed when he flipped the patties...the distinctive odor it emitted when it hit the hot grill? In just a few minutes, he would send up front two bacon cheeseburgers.

He dared not try to understand any of it. It was; beyond that, was nothing more, lest it would lose the magic. And that he could not abide.

Once their order was up and their number was called out over the incessant noise and chatter, Richard picked up the order. Richard and Ladonna ate their lunch, and then, when done, went on to other business.

Chapter Seven

By two-thirty, Jacob Lewski had his meal ready and bagged, and he was ready to go home. He restocked the patties. He had bricked his grill, wiped it off. He had put his utensils aside, to drop them off at the pot and pan sink on his way out the door. He untied his apron, balled it up. He clocked out, tossed the bloody and greasy apron in a dirty apron bag. He tossed the sweat-stained paper hat in a trashcan. On the way out the back door, he put the utensils into the pot and pan sink. His relief cook was on. Jacob was done for the day. He would be back at six in the morning to sweep and mop.

He carried with him a brown paper bag containing a plain hamburger, some French fries, and a small glass of water. The meal was free at the end of each shift, one of the benefits of working for Paddy's. He could have any soft drink he wanted, but Jacob always drank water, at room temperature.

By leaving through the back door, he could avoid contact with people, and it put him a few steps closer to home…a small rented room opening into an alley, two blocks from Paddy's. He would make the walk in less than ten minutes, stopping for nothing.

He had followed the same routine for years.

The last time he broke his routine it was to arrange for the burial of his mother. He had stepped forward to keep her from going to a pauper's grave.

He broke it for the second time to see her buried.

That had set him back financially, wiped out his savings, and left him in debt. Many years of scrimping and doing without – gone overnight. Even now, years later, he did not understand why he did it.

He hated her. He had always hated her. In his memory, she had never been anything but trouble and misery for him.

In a year or two, he would have the debt cleared, and he could wipe her from his memory forever. For now, however, she still had her claws in him, reaching out from the grave to draw his blood.

Jacob always ate his meal as he walked, so he would not have to handle the bag, the paper wrappings or the napkin in his room. He would simply toss them in a dumpster in the alley; this way, he did not have to complicate his life.

Jacob's room was a simple place, with a cot in one corner and a single chair, a brownish overstuffed thing he had picked up for five dollars at the used furniture store down the block, filled in the other corner.

95

A small bathroom was off to one side; in the bathroom, he kept a glass jar full of drinking water.

He had a single burner hot plate with a cheap aluminum pot on it sitting on a small table; he seldom used either of them.

Under the cot was a coffee can he collected his change in. He was, someday, going to reestablish a savings account. Someday, he knew, would come if he could ever get past the debt and remove her from his life forever.

A single window opened to the alley side.

The room was dust free, impeccably clean, and totally free of extras. Nothing in the room had been moved in months, except for cleaning.

Folded neatly in one corner was a change of clothes, identical to the clothes he had on...light gray slacks, a light blue shirt, black socks, a change of underwear. He had heard somewhere that people who wore such clothes attracted no attention. That was the way he had always wanted it to be, as far back as he could remember.

Jacob sat in his chair and stared blankly at the floor. He would rest for a few minutes then go out, walk down the alley, turn right and walk the two blocks to the park. There he would watch the birds, watch the children play, and watch an occasional squirrel scamper around. He would speak to no one. He would find his usual bench, tucked under a tree; from this vantage point, he could watch in peace. Undisturbed. Disconnected.

That done, he would walk back to his room, shower, shave, and go to bed.

Sometimes, late in the evening, if he had trouble sleeping, he would go out to buy a cup of coffee from a local convenience store, black, no sugar, no creamer. But lately, he had been saving the money rather than buy coffee.

As often as not the thirst would be satisfied with a drink of water from his water jar. Sometimes, but not often, he would save a paper cup for his water. He did not like to keep a cup around because it always seemed out of place; by presence alone, the cup messed up his room.

Jacob got up from his chair. He knew what he had to do; all that was left was to do it.

Uninspired, he walked toward the door.

Chapter Eight

Six o'clock rolled around, and the people gathered at Alexsandr's house. Bud had arrived early, to greet the rest of them; he looked a little frazzled. His suit was wrinkled and his tie was loose and hanging freely. He had a headache from too much chatter and not enough results: a long day at the office. His eyes burned. The description had been passed out to the street cops, but nothing had come of it.

Grampy was not there; he was busy researching something at home, and he would not attend the meeting.

They gathered in the living room, sat where they could, and each, in turn, presented their findings.

"We've got a name, Bud," said Richard. "Jacob Lewski."

"Where'd you get it?"

"Old Principal Jackson said this fellow fit the description. Right down to a deformed hand," Ladonna offered. "He knew just about every kid to pass through his school for several decades now. We gave up on the yearbook idea...it went nowhere."

"Hmm," mumbled Bud. He thumbed through a little brown notebook to check his own notes. "I've got him on the list of possibles from the birth certificates. Born in June of seventy-eight to an unwed girl, aged sixteen. Her name was Monica Lewski. Father unknown. I had a buddy run her, and she's got a sheet a foot long, everything from drunk and disorderly to prostitution. A few years back, she simply dropped off the record."

"Anything else, Ladonna?"

"He used to live on the South Side...as a kid. From there, we don't have anything. Isn't that where the stabbing took place? On the South Side?"

"Does the name Donald Bell mean anything to anyone?" asked Bud.

Nobody made any association.

"How about Jack Kim Grayborn?"

Nobody made any association.

"Gynna stayed on to search these three back to their grandmothers. She should be along soon," Bud explained. "They were the only three who came close to the description. None of them had a record. Donald Bell had a few traffic tickets recently, but, otherwise, they're clean."

"What do we do now, Dad?" asked James.

"We'll wait for your mother. Then we will figure out some way to find these guys. The rest, once we find them, should be fairly routine."

"Alexsandr...have you come up with anything else which might separate the three possibles...narrow down the list?" asked Richard.

Alexsandr got up, crossed the room, and picked up the local phone book. He tossed it to Richard.

"He will not be listed," he replied. "He does not even own a phone. And Donald Bell is most likely out of the running. Our guy does not own a car, either."

Richard found no listing for Jacob Lewski. He moved on.

"Grayborn. What's the spelling, Bud?" asked Richard.

Bud spelled it, and Richard searched the phone book. He found a listing.

"Here we are...Grayborn, J.K."

Stephy picked up the phone as Richard read her the number. She dialed, and someone on the other end answered.

"May I speak to Jack Grayborn please," she said.

He answered.

"Is this Jack Kim Grayborn?"

He answered.

"A friend told me you might be able to help me out finding a good affordable car?"

He told her he worked at a local supermarket.

"Sorry, I guess I have a bad source. They told me you sold cars. Sorry. Good-bye."

She looked upon expectant faces.

"No way," she said. "First his kid answered. I could hear a houseful of others in the background. I doubt this is our guy. He works at the supermarket on Grant Road. That is hardly the kind of job that would fit the description. Sounds to me like this guy got his life together."

"More power to him," said Alexsandr. "Bud, I suggest you find this other guy...Jacob whatever. He fits the description. But how are you going to find him? I can't help you with that. He's melted into the milling crowd. I don't have any idea how you might flush him out."

"Publicity, Alexsandr? Burst the bubble?" suggested Richard.

"No. Not yet," said Bud. "I'll put my guys out. Now that we have a name, it won't take long to round him up. What about the other two, Alexsandr? What are your feelings toward them?"

"Off hand, I'd say no. It might not hurt to question them. They're too open, too public. But, I never said the +1 scenario was flawless. They may still fit the description to some extent. We're dealing with interior stuff, primarily. A house full of kids does not mean the stability is there. All these guys had unbalanced mothers, no fathers around, and unstable home lives as kids themselves, don't forget."

"Is there anything else we can do, Dad?" asked Stephy.

"No. It is all a waiting game now," Bud explained. "We will pick these guys up, or just ask a few questions, and then we will take it from there. I thank you all for your help."

"We'll be going then," said James, speaking for them both. Stephy and James were on the way out the door when Gynna showed up.

She hugged them each in turn, and then handed her report to Bud. Richard and Alexsandr listened attentively.

"As you suspected Alexsandr," he said. "Their grandmothers were pretty messed up individuals. Each of the mothers of these guys was also born to unwed teenage mothers. One of them...hmm...Donald Bell...his mother was thirteen when she gave birth. No indication the baby was put up for adoption."

"Alexsandr," said Richard. "How can you explain the one fellow, Jack Kim Grayborn, who got his life together?"

"Assuming he has," cautioned Bud. "We don't know that yet."

"If he did...and I'd bet he did...he got religion. Probably converted to Christianity many years ago. I'd bet you'll find him and his family in church every Sunday without fail."

"Do we know anything about this Donald Bell fellow?"

"Nothing...except he apparently owns a car."

"Check your phone book, Richard" coaxed Ladonna. "There are probably lots of Bells in Nohartinit. It probably won't tell us much."

"Three listings under D. Bell, two at the same address...Junior and Senior. Our guy is the third one, if he is the one. East Second Street."

Bud had written down the phone numbers as Richard had called them out. He planned on making a couple of calls in the morning. If the listed men had alibis and witnesses, they were clear. He decided he would put the word out on the street to snitches and informants to locate Jacob Lewski; he wanted to talk to him in particular.

Alexsandr, Richard, Ladonna, and Gynna moved to the kitchen table. Rachael had prepared coffee and laid out some cookies. Bud followed close behind.

"Do you mind if I sit in, too?" Rachael asked as she entered the kitchen from the basement.

"Sure," said Bud. "We need ideas, Rachael. At this point, the more the better." He then filled her in on the list of possible suspects, and gave some of the background information.

"Alexsandr," asked Bud. "I don't want to put you on the hot seat or embarrass you, but is this +1 scenario reliable enough to use it to bring in this fellow, Jacob Lewski?"

"It would never stand up in court, Bud. You'll either have to get some hard evidence or a confession."

"Why not burst the bubble, Alexsandr?" Richard asked again. "Won't that drive him out of hiding?"

"He's a dangerous man, Richard...I don't want blood on my hands – not his and not somebody else's. The stuff in the papers probably has him more than a little upset right now. The +1 scenario is, I hope, a tool not a weapon."

"Alexsandr? Can I ask you something?" said Ladonna.

"Of course," he answered.

"I know you would not use the +1 scenario unless you had a lot of faith in it. But are you sure the man we're looking for fits the description? Isn't it possible, we're looking in all the wrong directions? I mean we're dealing with a fragile character, aren't we? Suppose this Jacob Lewski is innocent...won't the questioning, the disruption in his life have some kind of damaging effect upon him?"

"I do trust the +1 scenario, Ladonna. And yes, if this is not the man, we should proceed with caution. But, if you weigh the good against the possible side effects, we have to run the risk of disrupting an innocent man's life."

"Let's not forget, if he is our man, he is capable of extreme violence. This Lewski fellow has no record. I doubt seriously if he will suffer any lasting damage. Most people, I find, are usually quite happy to cooperate in a police investigation. We don't know, do we, and if Jacob Lewski has made a complete come around also. He might like his privacy...and that's all there is to it."

"Alexsandr, I had a bad feeling about The Red Flag from the very beginning," said Rachael. "But, for the first time, I can see the possibilities...if it is used constructively. I do have an idea, however. Are you absolutely certain the guy we are looking for has lived and worked in Nohartinit for a long time, as the description suggests? Have you written off the possibility the guy you want did not go to school around here, or grow up in Nohartinit?"

"Rachael, I'm not saying he did. I am saying everything, at this point in the experimental use of the +1 scenario, it appears to be the likely set of circumstances. You have to remember this has never been tried before, the research is incomplete, and there is absolutely nothing else which may lead to a suspect."

"Rachael, if Jacob Lewski is not our man...or Donald Bell, or this Jack Kim Grayborn fellow...we are none the worse for wear," explained Bud. "There is absolutely nothing else to go on. If they have alibis, we will have to dig a little deeper. The idea he is from Nohartinit is mine...just a gut feeling, that's all."

"David remembered nothing of much help. He got clobbered and passed out after hardly catching even a glimpse of the guy. The other victim, of course, is dead," added Ladonna. "I'm inclined to agree with Bud. Even a remote private type is not likely to get upset helping out with a police investigation. And, if this Jacob Lewski fellow is the guy, he'll most likely show something in the way of a reaction that will give him away. Right Bud?"

"Correct," said Bud. "Now, Alexsandr...if I may. One of the reasons I asked everyone here tonight is because I believe in this +1 scenario. I think Alexsandr is on to something that may prove invaluable in the right hands. What I need from each of you is full cooperation...notes, recollections, whatever...so we can present this +1 scenario hypothesis if it proves successful. Richard, Grampy, and Alexsandr are collaborators on this project, and I have offered them every bit of assistance I can. I want the rest of you to do the same. Ladonna...this includes David, when he is up to it. Rachael...Gynna...I want you to help these guys any way you can. We're onto something very big here, and we need to do it right. I have already spoken about it to James and Stephy. And Lalinduh...the librarian you met today...has agreed to help with the research. Alexsandr has, of course, agreed to give credit where credit is due."

"Grampy is working tonight on a sideline," said Alexsandr. "We're trying to piece together a way to bring this man in for treatment...to bring him in under his own power, by his own choice...so nobody gets hurt. I am hoping he is not too resentful of my tapping into his background as a Psychologist."

"What about Chief Renwall, Bud? Do you have his cooperation?" asked Richard. "I can imagine he's anxious to wrap this up."

"That's another problem. He didn't like what the newspapers had to say about his department. He gave us a week to make this +1 scenario work, or he's moving in with his storm troopers."

"Can you do it, Bud?" asked Richard. "I'm branching out, with Alexsandr's permission, in directions of my own. I'd hate to see the +1 scenario discredited before it ever gets off the ground."

"We have to," said Bud. "Chief Renwall is not one to place intellect too high on his list of tools when it comes to police work. It is highly unusual for me to ask this of anyone. I have already spoken to James and Stephy about it, and now I want to ask the rest of you: Will you help us find this Jacob Lewski fellow? Just locate him. Don't put yourselves in any kind of compromising position. Just help us find him, so we can talk to him. Ladonna, I can clear it with your boss. Richard I can clear it for you at school."

"I'll be glad to, Bud...but what can I do?" asked Ladonna.

"We've got a lot of ground to cover. We need people stopping everywhere they can think of asking people if they know this fellow and if the know how we can get in touch with him. That's all. But Nohartinit, in spite of what our people think, is a big place. In theory, if we talk to enough people, we can find this guy in just a day or two. I'll see if I can't get the Chief to whip up some official identification badges or something to help open doors for you. My guys will work the back streets and the red light district. I'll have my snitches and informants working overtime. You guys work the burger joints, the shops, the factories, and the chemical plant, the schools...stuff like that. James and Stephy are going to go out as a team. You and Richard ought to do the same. It will be safer that way, and you are not likely to hit the same place twice by accident. We don't have time for screwups."

"Grampy and I will try to find a way to talk this guy in," said Alexsandr. "I'll still coordinate things here."

Bud checked his watch. "I've got to go," he said. "Gynna...are you ready?"

Gynna said her good-byes. They left.

Richard munched a cookie, and sipped coffee.

Ladonna and Rachael chatted nearby, talking quietly about blue curtains for Ladonna's apartment. Alexsandr sat quietly, lost in contemplation.

"Alexsandr?" said Richard. "How are you going to talk him in?"

"We're thinking about an invitation, Richard. Just place a few flyers in obvious places, inviting him in for treatment."

"Will it work?" Richard grinned. "You can't just invite a murderer to turn himself in, Alexsandr. It'll never work. You'll upset a lot of people if you shake their illusions about Nohartinit."

"A long shot. I don't think our guy has read a newspaper in years," he answered. "Grampy is trying to figure out how to reach a secluded man without making any direct contact. Of course, we won't advertise we want the murderer to turn himself in...we're thinking along the lines of advertising for volunteers for a research project involving single parent offspring. It might draw him in. It might even enlarge our puny list of possible assailants."

"Why would it draw him in, Alexsandr?"

"We'd be betting on a most basic human need, Richard...companionship, someone to talk to."

"Maybe if you guarantee confidentiality and offer some monetary incentive, he might respond."

"I don't think we will have enough time to put it together, though. Chief Renwall gave us a week. I know the man. When he says a week, he means exactly that. He won't budge after the deadline."

"I guess finding the guy is our best shot, Alexsandr."

"If he's out there somewhere in Nohartinit and we can locate him, Bud will have him signed, sealed, and delivered by six o'clock the same evening."

"Suppose it is this Jacob Lewski fellow, Alexsandr? Suppose the +1 scenario proves itself? Then what?"

"Then, Richard, we'll sit down with Grampy and figure out our next move. In the wrong hands, this could be a very dangerous weapon. The success of the +1 scenario will only complicate our lives. We'll have ourselves a moral choice nightmare."

"How are you going to vote, Alexsandr?"

"I'm not sure yet, quite possibly for suppression," he answered. "Anyway, as soon as we wrap this thing up, let's get back to your thesis. I admire your choice in changing everything, Richard. Your grandfather and I did the same thing many times along the way. But if it doesn't come together...it just plain doesn't come together."

"Enough shop talk," interrupted Rachael. "Alexsandr promised to take me out to dinner tonight, and I'm starving. You and Ladonna are welcome to join us, Richard. You probably have not had a well-balanced meal in months."

"I appreciate the offer, Rachael. But I promised Grampy I'd stop by."

"That's a twenty mile drive, Richard," she insisted. "Grampy will forgive you if you're a little late. Besides, it is not good for Ladonna's image to be out alone...a beautiful girl like this unescorted to a fine dinner at a fine restaurant? I insist."

"You're reaching, Rachael," said Richard, cheerfully.

"No...I am." Ladonna reached for his hand, to raise him from the chair. "Don't fight it, Richard," she said, sweetly. She smiled. "We won't take no for an answer. Besides, we have a lot of catching up to do. With all this going on, we have not had any real chance to just sit down and talk. Here's our chance...don't blow it."

The four of them put aside business, and put aside shoptalk, and put the manhunt behind them. Together, they went out, had a grand dinner, and spent several hours relaxing and having plain old-fashioned fun.

By the time Richard started out for Grampy's, it was well past ten. He knew Grampy would still be up, probably working at his desk. That is what he was doing when Richard knocked on the door. Grampy did not get up, but called for him to enter. Richard knew exactly where to find him.

"Grampy...we got some names. It should come together very soon. Some guy by the name of Jacob Lewski seems to be the best bet. Alexsandr tells me you're going to try and pull this guy in under his own power," Richard said. He pulled up a chair and sat in front of Grampy's desk. "How?"

"Lewski? Hmm," mumbled Grampy. "Lewski? That name sure seems to ring a bell. Anyway, in answer to your question, Richard, it is like fishing on the lake, Richard. We just have to put out the right bait at the right time, and we'll hook this guy." In fact, Grampy knew the name Lewski too well.

"If the description is correct, Grampy, you would probably have to be standing in his room before you would get close enough to make anything work."

"Not so fast, Richard. I think there's a way."

"I'm all ears, Grampy."

"I've been going about it all wrong. So I put things in reverse. What is the one point in his whole life this guy was connected with the sensorial reality world?"

"I give up."

"By way of his mother...the love/hate connection. We'll find the mother and she will lead us straight to him. If the description fits, she's probably dead and gone. Buried. Somebody would have to pay the bills to put her away."

"If she's not dead...then what?"

"We'll play my hunch. This guy's mother is dead. She probably overdosed or died of AIDS."

"So now we simply search the death records, find the funeral home, and we follow the money trails from there. This fellow's mother, Monica Lewski, according to Bud, had a long record, and then she suddenly just dropped off the record entirely. A brilliantly simple plan, Grampy. We've only got what...two funeral homes in Nohartinit? Maybe three?"

"Why don't you stay the night, Richard? We'll look into this first thing in the morning." Grampy suddenly seemed preoccupied, as if lost in some ancient recollection.

"Sure, Grampy. If we get an early start, maybe Bud can have this guy by sundown."

"I want to get this guy off the streets, Richard...in the worst way."

"Grampy...for a second there, it sounded like you had a personal interest in getting this guy off the street?"

"No. Nothing personal...purely professional, I assure you." Grampy looked at Richard with tired eyes. He tried to crack a smile, but he seemed just a little too tired to make it all the way. "I have some thinking to do," he said. "You go on to bed. I'll be done in less than an hour. I'll wake you at dawn, and then we can get started."

"Are you okay, Grampy?"

"Just tired, Richard," he replied. "Some old aches and pains are kicking in tonight. We must be in for a weather change."

"Maybe you should rest. You've been pushing pretty hard lately. Whatever it is, Grampy...can't it wait until tomorrow? Maybe you will feel a lot better in the morning."

"No, this cannot wait. Now...go to bed. I need to be alone for a little while."

"Sure," Richard said, meekly. "Sure, Grampy. See you in the morning. Good-night."

"Good night, Richard." Grampy moved slowly back to his desk, and he sat down in his chair. He was hurting sure enough. Bones. Joints. Name it and it hurt right now.

Chapter Nine

An hour later, Grampy got ready for bed. It was becoming more and more a struggle to put on his pajamas each night, and he had recently given some thought to sleeping in the nude. But, this night, he managed once again to put them on. But he was not too overly concerned with such a trivial issue this night. In his thoughts were things from by-gone days. Names. Faces. Events.

"Monica Lewski?" he murmured, as he crawled into bed. He had shut that case file years ago, or so he thought. He remembered the name. He remembered the girl. He remembered her mother. There was so much he knew about Monica Lewski he could never tell anyone. He was tired of the secrets surrounding her, but he knew...and had known for many years...they would probably have to go to the grave with him. But for years now he had lied about it...to himself, to others in by-gone years...now, to Richard.

Grampy tossed and turned, trying, fruitlessly, to position himself comfortably. Finally he settled, pulled bedcovers up to his chin.

This girl, Monica Lewski, had changed his life. He met her the first time when she was barely eight years old. The last time they met, she was not yet nine. It was she that led him to quit Psychology. Their association had been on a purely professional level, in the beginning.

He had never discussed her case with a living soul, not just from concerns about being ridiculed by colleagues, but from other concerns as well. He had been unable, no matter what he tried, to reach the girl. She had been his first...and last...total and complete failure as a Psychologist. He knew somewhere in his dusty collection of boxes in his basement was her case papers, records of all sorts of sordid notes. He recalled what had seemed like mountains of research notes in the case. For an incomplete file, he thought, it is one of the most thorough and completely documented histories I have ever done.

He closed his eyes momentarily. Now, he thought, here she is many years later she - back to haunt him...back from the grave to spread her poison.

One word, of all words he loved to work with, passed through his lips, as he thought back, visualizing this young girl, her wild, glaring eyes ablaze; he remembered her, not as a patient or a client, but something more...his first and last professional encounter with the embodiment of...Evil.

He remembered the bizarre way she slipped in and out of voices, from the flighty eight-year-old girl, to some hoarse and harsh old man, raging on and on about anything and everything. He remembered the time she clawed her way across his desk and tried to bite and rip at his face, lunging at him and snarling like some wild dog. He swore he had seen livid red eyes in the child's sockets during the attack, but he never told a soul; he remembered the child's phenomenal strength, for a girl her size, during this fit of rage. If her mother had not attached herself around the child pinning her arms, he imagined, quite possibly, he would have lost large chunks of flesh that day. Her mother finally subdued the child by using a powerful right cross landing a heavy textbook to the girl's chin, knocking her out cold. He shivered, as the chilling recollections emerged in his thoughts.

It was that day, not long after that session, he turned away from Psychology; he knew, then and there, Psychology held no answer for human beings in severe mental or emotional distress. He knew, then and there, the answers were to be found elsewhere.

But his greatest fear was not that this demon-girl was dead or alive, that her mental presence would possess and torment him, but that this son, Jacob, might have also turned. He was satisfied he had not – not yet – not completely. He had no police record, apparently, so he held out hope the stabbing and the assault on David were just the beginning of a descent. He wondered if the police had covered up other attacks. He knew, in his heart, if Jacob had turned, Nohartinit had not seen the last of him. Unspeakable things were on the horizon. Grampy had no desire to confront Old Horny ever again.

And he wondered about the girl's years between eight and when she had her son?

He was hard put to imagine how her mother maintained control of her. She could not do it when they first met.

Finally, after much discomfort and more painful memories, Grampy fell asleep.

Hours later, Grampy woke before Richard, but he stayed in bed, staring blankly at the ceiling. It had been a restless night. To make matters worse, he ached too much to get out of bed too quickly. It was barely past sunrise, anyway. Rays of light were beginning to cast upon the ceiling.

He and Richard would not be able to search death records for several hours. So he lay there, staring aimlessly at the ceiling, at the brightening light, until he gathered the energy and the will to get up and start another day.

Each passing day now, it seemed the aches got more intense and lingered longer. Some days, he just plain hurt all over, all day long. Not even warmth from the sun could shake the discomfort any more on such days. Grampy had a sneaking suspicion this was going to be one of those days.

"Oh, well," he groaned. "Might as well do it." He sat up, put his bony feet to the floor. He got up. He groaned again, as if somehow it might simplify the task. He tried to stretch, but decided against the effort. "Tremors are bad this morning, too," he mumbled. His hands shook, more than usual. "At least I can still see and hear," he growled.

He struggled to get dressed. He put on brown slacks, a white short sleeve shirt, and, again, his sandals. He was tired of struggling with his regular shoes each morning, so he let the weather guide his choice of footwear. He was glad the weather was pleasant these days.

Grampy ambled into the kitchen, fixed a pot of very strong coffee. Then he went outside to sit on the porch, where he could watch the early morning unfold. The lake was shimmering, and very smooth. And very little wind. The tops of the pines were not even swaying. The sky was brilliant blue and cloudless.

He thought it might be a good time to row out to his favorite spot and catch a few fish. But he knew fishing had to wait. "Business before pleasure," he sighed.

Richard soon joined him on the porch. He brought two cups of coffee with him. He had pulled a change of clothes from the spares he kept in Grampy's hall closet. He wore faded jeans and a blue striped long sleeve shirt, the sleeves of which he rolled up to just below his elbows.

"How are you feeling this morning, Grampy?" he asked, as he handed him the coffee.

"Sit down, Richard. I have a question for you," he said, as he reached for the coffee cup.

"Sure, Grampy."

"This has nothing – yet maybe everything - to do with Bud's work. Have you ever come across a case, in all your research, of a parent restraining an unruly child using street drugs?"

"I've found all sorts of sick stuff, Grampy, but nothing like that. Chaining them to beds. Locking them in closets. Yes. But nothing like that. I guess under the right conditions someone could get away with something like that. It would sure be hard to cover up, wouldn't you think?"

"Unless drugs were as commonplace as soft drinks or sugar," said Grampy. "And nobody saw anything out of the ordinary, perhaps?"

"What ever you are working on, Grampy...it sounds pretty sick to me."

"Oh, it is, Richard. Believe me, it is."

"Can you tell me about it, Grampy?"

"I had one complete and total failure when I was in private practice, Richard. I'm trying to figure out where I screwed up. Tying up loose ends."

"After all these years, Grampy? Why?"

"I just want to know, Richard. That's all. I just want to know."

"I thought you gave all that up for Philosophy and Religion, Grampy."

"The answers are in Religion, the questions are in Philosophy, and the nonsense is in Philodoxy and Psychology," Grampy said, assertively. "But this particular case has been hanging far too long. You are a believer, Richard. I, too, am a believer. This particular patient, Richard, was possessed. I tried my textbooks when there should have been an exorcism. I lost the child to evil, Richard. And I guess I have never been able to live with that. I was young, idealistic, and skeptical. I thought I could play God. I thought my books and all my papered arrogance could save that child."

Richard could see some genuine sadness behind the aging eyes. He sensed something was still unsaid; he knew Grampy was holding something back. He knew Grampy too well to raise questions about his sincerity concerning the possession.

"Grampy...I know you too well to let you get by with this. You're holding out on me. I won't push, Grampy; I have too much respect for you. I will ask you – tell you I guess – you need to level with me." He leaned toward Grampy. "There was something personal somewhere involving this Lewski fellow, right, Grampy?"

"Not exactly," Grampy explained. "I've never told another living soul about that experience with the girl, Richard," said Grampy, with a dry frown. "That girl I lost to evil, Richard, was Jacob Lewski's mother, Monica." He looked Richard square in the eyes. "Brace yourself, Richard. I'll tell you everything. I swear on my wife's grave everything you are about to hear is true."

Grampy sat back, took a deep breath. Richard sat by, attentively, expectantly.

"I had been in private practice about a year, or thereabouts. One day I got a call from a friend in Social Services asking me if I would have a talk with a desperate young mother with what she described as a wild child. I asked a few routine questions, set up an appointment for the following day.

At one o'clock the next day, I returned from lunch to find a woman in her teens with her child standing by my locked door. I opened the door and invited them in. We sat quietly, just the three of us, introduced ourselves. I questioned the mother, and then questioned the child.

Nothing seemed amiss. The child, a thin little eight-year-old girl, seemed friendly enough. She was wearing some kind of pink dress with white lace on it. She looked like a sweet little kid, not a budding monster that had been described to me over the phone. The mother appeared tired, even weary. In later years, the mother connected with the powers and made herself quite a reputation; using the name Milly...she opened a whorehouse down on third; it was known to be infected with all forms of low life. She lived hard and died hard.

My background information told me the girl had attacked her first grade teacher with a pencil, stabbing the poor lady several time on her arms. She had previous episodes of unexplainable behaviors as well. She had thrown a newborn pup down on a sidewalk and stomped on it until the guts came out the mouth. She had set fire to a neighbor's car, after locking their cat inside. She shoved a schoolmate down a flight of steps. These stories the mother supplied me. I asked her if they were, in fact, true. She said they were.

I asked the child why she did those things; she denied ever having done any of them. The mother, of course, merely shook her head, explaining this was just another lie in a long series of lies from the child. The mother said people were trying to get the girl put away, as she explained it, because she was out of control and dangerous. She didn't want any trouble, but the child was all she had. She was getting desperate. She pleaded with me for help.

I was relatively young and inexperienced. I figured I had some kind of textbook case, and if I counseled the girl a few times, she would open up to me. The mother explained to me things seemed to be getting progressively worse, especially in the last week or so. I should have had the girl examined by medical doctors and a psychiatrist, but I didn't want to squander an opportunity to open doors to Social Services and make a name for myself in professional circles. I was a professional nobody at the time. This was the first time I had run across something that was not just ordinary stuff. I sensed something different – exciting – about this child's case.

I asked the mother if she had any control over the girl. She explained she had control until, as she described it, she got weird. I asked her to explain what she meant by weird.

She told me about it: Her eyes, they get glassy and blood shot. She starts growling like some kind of animal. She gets mean...real mean, she throws stuff, hurts people. She said the girl slipped into such mean spells from time to time...just out of nowhere.

She showed me a nasty scar on her right forearm where the child had bitten into her. It had the jagged rip markings more of an animal's bite than that of a human child. She said she clamped down and hung on until she practically had to knock her out to get her to turn loose.

As she was telling me all this, I watched the child. She had the funniest grin on her face…a menacing sort of defiant grin. She glared at me with a resolve that made me shiver. I felt like this frail-looking child was going to rip me to shreds at the first opportunity.

I asked her mother if she was in school. She told me they had expelled her. She was a sincere young woman, as I look back on it, but powerless, it seemed. It was as if the child had some power over her she dared not defy. She was, in effect, intimidated by the child possibly even acutely afraid of the child.

I kept prodding the child to see if I could aggravate her, move her toward something concrete that I could observe first hand. She stared at me with the iciest aura of contempt I had ever experienced. The child had begun to intimidate me as well.

Has she been medicated…anything prescribed? I had asked. I was contemplating suggesting to the mother she make moves toward having the child held for observation at County Memorial's Psychiatric Ward over in Mayberight, but before I could speak, the child began the most gruesome throaty growl…I still can't describe it well. She told me no…no…in a voice that was deep and cold and mean. It was more the voice of a mature – no – an old man than that of a female child. It was as if she had read my thoughts. Then she started hissing and spittle dripped from the corners of her mouth.

The mother sat by, petrified. The girl got up from her chair, walked toward me, leaned over my desk. She hissed in my face, her eyes burning with hate and loathing and contempt.

I stood, pounded my fist on the desk right in front of her. I ordered her to sit down. She did not move in the slightest, as if she had seen or heard nothing. She showed no fear of anything, like she held all the power, barring none. I had not intimidated her in the least.

Then she laughed, a blood-curdling heavy defiant laugh unlike anything I had ever experienced. Then as suddenly as she had turned, she returned to her chair, looked at her mother. In the most gentle, innocent child-like tones, she asked her mother if she could go home.

The mother got up immediately, like a Buck Private jumping to the orders of a General, headed the child toward the door. She looked back at me with pleading eyes. She was a fearful and desperate woman.

She pleaded with me: You have got to do something to help her!

111

I was young, ambitious, filled with high hopes. I knew I had just witnessed an astounding thing. I knew I could lay claim to fame and fortune if I could exploit this experience. In my young and stupid heart, I did not want this child to slip away. I resolved I would do anything in my power to stake my claim to this phenomenal opportunity.

For several weeks I set up the sessions. The child played along. The mother seemed more and more distraught, drawn out, as the time dragged on. The child didn't slip into one of her spells, as her mother called them, until the last session we had...my last session in private practice."

Grampy then told Richard how the girl had clawed her way across the desk, tried to rip into him with barred teeth.

"I swear it, Richard, the child's eyes were blood-red orbs...not human at all. She spoke to me through the voice of Satan himself.

Her mother had to knock her cold with a textbook to get her off of me.

That child was going to kill me...and I was powerless; her strength was simply incredible.

She scooped up the unconscious child, and they left the office.

I knew then and there, I had put my own interests above those of that hapless mother and her demon-possessed child. I left my office that day, never to return.

I prayed endlessly for weeks afterwards to ask God for forgiveness for my foolish and self-centered arrogance. My conscience was eating me alive.

Each day, for the longest time, I searched the streets and back alleys to find that child, to help her in the right way. I needed to repent for the damage done, to make things right. They were nowhere to be found. Mother and child had disappeared. I gave up the search after several hard months.

To this day, I am certain I cost that girl any chance at a good and decent life. As God is my witness, I am responsible for terrible and indecent moral crimes against Monica Lewski and her mother...by way of arrogance alone. I could have saved that child, Richard. As God is my witness, I could have saved her.

I should have turned to Father Wyman instead of my books."

He closed his eyes. He took a deep breath and hissed air between his teeth. He opened his eyes, and looked, guiltily, at Richard. "Somehow, I may have contributed to the outcomes we're fighting against right now."

"No, Grampy. There's no such things as generational possession," said Richard. Then he frowned, almost comically. "Is there?"

"There are bits and pieces that don't add, Richard," he answered. "How could a child like that simply drop from sight and re-emerge years later to have a baby and nothing seems to have happened in between times? Surely, this child would have shown up somewhere…she was a terribly violent child. She could not have escaped the attention of the police or the newspapers for all those years."

"Like it or not, Grampy, there are pockets in the heart of Nohartinit where anything could happen."

"I know…it just seems so unlikely, that's all."

"That's where your question came from, isn't it? You think Monica was drugged all those years? And stashed away, out of trouble somewhere?"

"Stashed away, yes. Out of trouble? I doubt it. Stranger things have happened," he said.

"But, Grampy? If she was truly possessed, would not the demon over-ride the drugs?"

"Not if the drugs were instrumental in using the child for vile and evil purposes."

"This is starting to sound pretty sick, Grampy," said Richard. "You think her mother got her hooked just to control her behavior?"

"Stranger things have happened. I would suspect she kept her locked up at Milly's for all those years."

"We'll never know, will we?"

"What I need to know now is how a child could be so dragged down, so far as to be in full bloom as a super-empty +1 in the space and span of a mere eight years. Some how, some way, if Bud gets this guy, we have to gain access to him. I need to find out what happened."

"Why would the son know anything about the childhood of his mother?"

"He won't, but maybe we can coax him into talking about his own childhood. From that, maybe we can glean enough information to piece things together."

"Shouldn't we warn the others?" asked Richard. "If they're going up against this guy, don't you think they ought to know what they are up against?"

"We don't know, anything," said Grampy. "Not a thing. It is, at this point, guesswork and pure speculation. They have been warned he may be very unstable and dangerous. Are you going to run around and warn them against a demon with red eyes, claws, and fangs?"

"I see your point. What have I gotten myself into, Grampy?" Richard sighed. "A few days ago, all I wanted was some insight for my thesis. Now I find myself caught up in the middle of a king-size mess, involving murder, attempted murder, demonic possession, the complete disappearance of a woman and her child, and an unresolved Social Services referral that is older than I am and, to top it all,...no thesis." Richard chuckled, somewhat frustrated.

"Relax," urged Grampy. "Roll with it, Richard. Stranger things have happened."

"Yeah," agreed Richard reluctantly, conveying his willingness to accept the mess for what it was. "Strange how life takes you places, isn't it? Stranger things have happened, I guess. But not to me."

"Look at it this way, Richard. If my guess is right...and I'm fairly certain at this point...we could be a few steps closer to affirming the +1 scenario, even the +1 super-empty."

"And?"

"No one, hopefully, would ever let a +1 child slip through the cracks again...never. We could spot and be ready for them before they are even born." Grampy smiled. "Suffer in silence for a while, Richard. You are sitting on the cutting edge of new science. If we vote to save and publish The Red Flag, you'll be able to write your own ticket from now on."

"I don't know what to think of it any more, Grampy."

"Tomorrow will tell us a lot, Richard. If we find the address today, Bud will have him very soon. I hope Bud lets us visit with the guy once he is in custody."

"It won't be Bud's option, will it?"

"No. But I'd bet he can arrange it."

Grampy asked Richard if he would get him a refill of coffee, explaining he was in for a bad and uncomfortable day. Richard did so, without hesitation.

"It gets worse every day, doesn't it, Grampy?" asked Richard, when he returned with the coffee.

"I'm old now. I have finally accepted it," he replied.

"Are you up to the trip into Nohartinit? I can go alone."

"I will go. I have to keep moving, Richard. If I don't I have the funniest feeling my joints will freeze up, and I'll start wasting away."

Richard checked his watch. It was about time to leave for town. Grampy wanted to sit just a while longer.

"You know something, Grampy?"

"What?"

"If your hunch is right, and Bud gets this guy, we ought to be back on the lake within two days."

"I'd like that...I'd like that a lot," he said.

Chapter Ten

They made the drive into Nohartinit, and picked up Ladonna at Alexsandr's house. Richard told Alexsandr of their first stop, and he agreed it sounded like a good idea. They found Monica Lewski's death certificate; it listed her cause of death as a drug overdose. From that, they traced the funeral home. In less than half-an-hour, they had the address they needed. They went immediately to the Police Station, and tried to locate Bud. He was out, but the Desk Sergeant paged him, and he called back within minutes.

Richard gave him the address, after explaining how they got it. He told Richard he was coming in, and he asked him to sit tight just a few minutes longer.

When Bud arrived, he invited the three of them into his office. He closed the door. He asked them to be seated.

He sat behind his desk, sorted through phone messages, and then he looked up and smiled.

"Good work," he said. "I put the word out to call back James and Stephy. I pulled back the street cops. I have the place under surveillance. We'll have the guy very soon."

"What about the other two, Bud...Donald Bell and this Jack Kim Grayborn fellow?" asked Ladonna.

"Good, strong alibis," he said. "You guys were right about one thing. Jack Kim Grayborn has it together. And, yes, he not only packs his flock to church every Sunday, he's an Associate Pastor."

"And Donald Bell?"

"Works hard, long hours. He seems to be a late bloomer, apparently. He's recently gotten engaged, plans to be married in a few months. Nice guy. He invited me to the wedding. Wears a cross on a chain around his neck."

"So it looks like Jacob Lewski is our man, Bud?" asked Grampy.

"Our best shot," he answered.

"Alexsandr will be pleased," said Ladonna. "Can we tell him?"

"Sure."

"Now what? Wait and see?"

"That's about it. I've got my best men on it. I'll personally bring him in."

"Bud, I have to ask. Can we...myself, Grampy, and Alexsandr talk to this guy when you bring him in?"

"Let me get him in, questioned, booked, if we have sufficient evidence or a confession. Maybe I can work something out with the

Public Defender's Office. It would be highly irregular, I think, and I would not bet on any kind of cooperation once the lawyers get involved. This will be a capital case, and you can bet they won't do anything that might appear to compromise their position. They'll go through the motions of defending the guy. But they'll decide his fate long before he goes to trial. You may have to kiss off this otherwise golden opportunity."

"Can you sway the lawyers, Bud?" asked Ladonna, innocently.

"Shit! Are you kidding me?" Ladonna blushed, and she cast her eyes downward. He apologized almost immediately. He had embarrassed her. "No offense, intended, Ladonna," he explained. "I didn't mean to embarrass you. Cops and defense attorneys have sort of a hate/hate relationship. Besides, this is a political matter now. As soon as Chief Renwall knows we have brought in our guy, he'll be dealing with every lawyer and judge in town to put this guy away, whether he is guilty or not. I hope to hell you guys are right about this Lewski fellow...he's a dead duck. If your description is right, he's poor, a loner, and kind of weird, friendless. He's dead, folks. The perfect fall guy. Chief Renwall is on the hot seat, and this guy is going down. You can't stop that now."

"I won't pretend the corruption isn't there, Bud," said Grampy. "But this would be an excellent opportunity in so many ways. Can't something be worked out...you know...before the politicians take over?"

"If the man is guilty, Grampy...I have a moral obligation to get him out of circulation. I can't do that if I accommodate you. You do understand the dilemma?"

"It isn't right." Ladonna protested. "We don't know the +1 thing works...not yet."

"These guys don't care what's right or wrong, Ladonna. They have to have their killer. And they have to put him away. For his sake – and yours – I hope this +1 scenario is the real thing. I, for one, don't want to see an innocent man fry."

"We have to have access to him, Bud," insisted Richard.

"Let me get him first, Richard. We'll cross that bridge when we get to it."

"That's not good enough, Bud," said Grampy adamantly.

"Damn it," Bud barked. "You brought me the guy on a silver platter...what the hell do you want from me?"

"Nothing personal, Bud...this +1 scenario has a human dimension to it now," said Richard. "It isn't just words any more. We have got to be able to prove, one way or another, that it works...or doesn't work.

We have to be able to back up the ideas with facts. We need access to this fellow to do that. Just bringing him in, running him through the motions, are not good enough."

"Bud?" Grampy queried.

"Yes?"

"Do you have any hard evidence yet?"

"No. Technically, we don't even have a suspect. If we don't get a confession, you guys will have all the access you need...if he will go for it. That you will have to work out among yourselves." He smiled, weakly.

"You can sit there and pretend nothing is happening here?" asked Ladonna, showing more than just some low-keyed disdain for the process.

"My job is to catch the killer. What happens after that is out of my hands. Without a confession, we can't hold him. And that is one call I can make. We'll bring him in for questioning. What comes down after that is anybody's guess," Bud explained. "I don't feed people to the grinders. I suggest you sit back and wait. I will keep you closely informed. That's all I've got to offer at this point." He smiled, weakly. "Hey, if the guy confesses, you have what you need, right?"

Someone knocked on the door, opened it, and peered in.

"That fax you were waiting for is coming in, Bud," said the intruder, a handsome young cop in a pressed uniform. He looked like a rookie, fresh out of the academy. He looked at Ladonna and gave her a wide, approving smile.

"I have to go," Bud said. "Excuse me. I will keep you informed. Can I reach you through Alexsandr?"

"Certainly," said Richard. " We'll be going now."

"Ladonna, before you go I want you to know something," said Bud.

"What's that?"

"I will do the right thing."

"I know you will, Bud," she replied. "Thank you."

That said, Bud went about his business, and the three of them left the building, chatting among themselves, like contestants on their way to a debating contest. They had mixed feelings.

"Grampy, what now?" asked Ladonna as she paused to be sure he could navigate the steps in front of them.

"Wait and see. They may be able to question him, but if he says nothing, they can't do much."

"They'll probably keep him under surveillance for a while, hoping he will slip up."

"Grampy, you spent some time testifying in court, didn't you?" asked Richard. "Can they stack the deck like that?"

"I used to get paid handsomely to give so-called expert testimony," he answered, as he took the steps slowly. "One side hires their whore, the other side hires their whore. The most convincing whore wins." He smiled dryly. "I used to play the game...I was actually very good at it...in these parts...I was one of the best Psychologists that money could buy."

"Did you ever work for Chief Renwall?" asked Ladonna.

"No. That's not how it works. Usually the Prosecutor or the Defense Attorney would tell me what he needed, and I would shape my testimony to fit the needs. They'd coach me before I testified, so I'd sound sincere, convincing, and truly concerned about Truth, Justice, and the American Way."

"That's awful," said Ladonna, sincerely. "I can't believe I'm hearing this."

"I was young and ambitious and arrogant," Grampy replied, as he navigated the last step. "I had the image these guys some times needed. I sounded cock-sure every time I spoke. I did a lot of things I'm not proud of. I did what I thought I had to do to get results, for some rather strange reasons now and then."

"You sold your soul to the highest bidder," Ladonna said, harshly. "How could you, Grampy?" She stopped walking. "Here I'm thinking you are a fine, upstanding, and righteous man anyone would be proud to know. Now I hear this?" She was visibly upset. Richard tried to console her. She pulled away. "No, I have every right to be upset," she demanded.

Grampy stopped. He looked at Ladonna, his old eyes bright and clear. "That you do, Ladonna, but don't judge me too harshly, young lady," he warned. He shook a quivering bony finger at her. "Think what you will, but judge not, lest ye be judged." He motioned to a bench nearby. "Sit," he ordered. "Before anything gets out of hand, sit. You need to hear this, Ladonna. You, too, Richard."

"I'm disappointed, Grampy," said Ladonna. "I feel...ah...betrayed or something."

"You will listen to me, please hear me out," insisted Grampy. "Hear me out...then think of me what you will."

Richard looked at Ladonna, hunched his shoulders. "Ah...okay, Grampy," he said. He motioned with a movement of his head to play along. Ladonna walked to the bench and sat down. Richard sat beside her. Grampy positioned himself on the end.

"Things are not always what they seem," Grampy began. "Nohartinit has come a long way since my younger days. I've seen a lot of changes take place. I've seen the town grow. It is huge now compared to what it used to be. When I was a little kid, and the chemical plant came in things changed very rapidly. A lot of people flooded in, and many of them stayed, bought homes here. They raised their families here.

Before the chemical plant, Nohartinit was just a town...a small town with small people, small ways. There was the university...not much like it was when people cared, mind you. A couple of rooms, I think. The town was basically stuck together with clapboards and rough-cut timber. There were a few cops, a Police Chief, a few city guys who ran things.

Some towns start out good and decent and they flourish and pass along certain community values to the young. Nohartinit was not like that.

Alexsandr and I both were born here, and we both grew up here. Alexsandr doesn't like to talk about how it was. He always dreamed of how it could be. I don't mind talking about the old days.

In the old days, before my time, Main was lined with brothels and saloons, back in the days of board sidewalks, muddy trails for roads. Prostitution and illicit booze kept the town alive. The local government guys were nothing but gangsters, a bunch of crooks. The cops were on the take. The Police Chief worked for the mobsters. Justice was dispensed with a gun or a rope, and nobody asked any questions.

But when the chemical plant came in, it brought people with families, for the most part good and decent working class people. The two forces would inevitably collide. It took two generations to clean up this town. Remnants of the old bunch...the power brokers...remain. There are controlling powers in Nohartinit; their influence and their presence is so strong at times you can feel the evil stirrings behind their activities.

Nohartinit is run behind closed doors in smoke-filled rooms, just like other cities this size. That's why there is an evil and corrupt underbelly. In my day, it was clearly understood one had to choose sides. That dividing line is still with us, but it is not so obvious any more.

When Bud talks about drugs and prostitution, he knows, as I know, there's nothing he can do about it. He goes through the motions, patiently taking one day at a time, hoping...sometimes against hope...he will have the chance to do his part to put a crack in the underbelly.

When I testified in court, I sometimes got a chance to put a crack in that underbelly. I'm not saying it was right what I did, but one-by-one, I worked with people who took down the thugs, one case at a time. Some times, yes, we took them down with underhanded...even corrupted methods...but we took them down. We often had to fight fire with fire. You can't take for granted what you have here...many good and decent people did some lowdown stuff and gave up a lot to pave the way for you. Some times, I had to work with one foot on each side of that dividing line. And, yes, I made a lot of money doing what I did. But I've poured tons of it back into the effort. I took a lot of tainted money, but I used it as a weapon, turned it back on those from whence it came.

Guys like Bud and ordinary people like you two can now play by the rules and still get things done because of what took place here in Nohartinit a hundred, fifty, even fifteen years ago...before either of you were out of grade school. You're probably of the first generation in Nohartinit to get a taste for real civilization. God knows my generation didn't have a clue what it was all about until it was too late."

Richard and Ladonna sat quietly, neither knowing what to say.

"Don't judge the people of my time too harshly, Ladonna," he whispered. "Above all else, don't take any of this for granted." He looked around slowly. He sighed, forlornly. Tears welled up in his eyes. "It doesn't look like much, I know. But for God's sake, don't let it slip away; a lot of good people have paid dearly for this grubby patch of ground. The graveyard outside of town is full of unacknowledged heroes."

"I think we just got a history lesson of the highest order," said Richard, sheepishly. Ladonna cracked a shy smile.

"Grampy," she said. "I don't know what to say. I feel about two inches tall right now."

"Say nothing," he answered. "It is the paradox of history...to past generations you are indebted for everything you have, and, yet, you owe those who came before you absolutely nothing...not even a well-earned thank you. We did the best we could, just like those who came before us did. It is your responsibility to do as we did...do whatever it takes to preserve the good and do what you can, no matter how trivial it may seem, to improve on it. Go to your graves, when the time comes, knowing, in your hearts, you did your best."

After a long silence, Grampy stood. "Let's go," he said. "I want to talk to Alexsandr before we head home, Richard. I have an idea. I think I have a way we can get to this guy."

They escorted Grampy to the car. He seemed tired, worn down, like he needed a good long nap.

The drive to Alexsandr's took just a few minutes. Alexsandr was sitting on his porch. They joined him there, as Richard went inside to get Grampy a cushion for the porch chair.

"Bud's dropped Donald Bell and this Jack Kim Grayborn from his list. He will probably have Jacob Lewski in custody by nightfall," Richard said.

"Good," said Alexsandr.

"Bud said Chief Renwall and his buddies are going to fry the guy, whether he did it or not," Ladonna added, matter-of-factly.

"Chief Renwall won't let him get away," agreed Alexsandr. "He's got to have his hide."

"Bud also said there's probably no way we will be able to get to him once the lawyers get involved," Grampy said.

"That won't do," said Alexsandr. "We have to have access to him."

"I have a way, Alexsandr." Grampy leaned forward as Richard slipped the cushion behind his lower back.

"I'm all ears, Grampy. We have to get his story."

"Remember our expert testimony days, Alexsandr?"

"I'd rather not," he answered, sarcastically.

"Well, Alexsandr. How much of General Perkins' money have you got left?"

"Most of it, nearly the entire fifty thousand."

"What's your old buddy Heinz up to these days, Alexsandr?"

"Retired...to Mayberight," said Alexsandr. "Are you thinking what I think you're thinking, Grampy?"

"It is for a good cause, Alexsandr."

Richard and Ladonna listened, but understood nothing at this point.

"Let's do it, Alexsandr?" said Grampy, hopefully. "Do you think you can talk him into it?"

Alexsandr stood. "Let's give it a shot, Grampy...for old time's sake." He went indoors to make a phone call.

"Okay, Grampy? What's going on?" asked Ladonna.

"Heinz is a lawyer...a very good one. We used to work together. We'll get Heinz in town to represent Jacob Lewski...he'll get a fair trial, and we will gain something akin to unobstructed access."

"Fighting fire with fire, Grampy?" asked Richard.

"Chipping away at the underbelly," he said. He smiled widely. "I may be old. I may creak, and I may have trouble getting around. But you have to chip when you can chip."

"It will let Bud steer clear, right, Grampy?" asked Richard.

"Sure will."

"It will keep the man from being blindsided, right, Grampy?" asked Ladonna.

"Sure will."

"You've got a beautifully devious mind, Grampy," said Richard, as he cracked a smile.

Grampy's eyes twinkled. "If you're going to run with rats, you have to think like rats," he said, coldly. "You two stick with me, and I'll show you how to fight the good fight."

Chapter Eleven

Jacob Lewski, wearing his usual gray slacks and light blue shirt, was eating his plain hamburger on his way home from work, when Bud stopped him, not far from his room. Bud, wearing his usual suit and tie, presented his badge, identified himself, and then he put his badge away.

"I need to ask you a few questions, Mister Lewski. Would you mind coming down to the station with me?" Bud wanted him in the station building, just in case. Alexsandr had told him it would be a long shot, but there was a chance he would tell all within a short time after being picked up. Bud hoped Alexsandr was right.

"What's this about, Officer?"

Bud said only they needed to talk.

Jacob put his hamburger back in the bag.

"Can I bring this along? My supper," he explained.

"Sure," said Bud.

Jacob tucked the bag under his arm, treating it with the care and attention one might give to a bag full of cash.

"My car is this way. You can finish eating along the way. I appreciate your cooperation."

They walked to Bud's car. Across the street, Officer Orville Detrick started his car. He radioed the dispatcher, to confirm the pickup of Jacob Lewski. When Bud pulled away from the curb, Orville drove into traffic behind Bud's car. He followed them to the station. Keeping his distance, he followed them into the building.

"Am I under arrest?" Jacob asked, as Bud led him toward his office.

"I just need to talk to you, Mister Lewski. You may have some information we need."

"Me?" Jacob queried. "You must have the wrong fellow. I just go to work. I go home. I go to the park."

Bud opened his office door, asked Jacob to be seated. He followed him into the room, and he sat behind his desk. The description from Alexsandr was on the desk in front of him. In a few minutes Orville entered. Bud identified him as Officer Detrick. He was a tall, muscular fellow with a crew cut. He wore a dark suit, a white shirt, and dark brown tie. He had a file folder with him that held some photographs.

"I want you to look at some photographs, to help identify some people," said Orville.

"What is this about?" asked Jacob again.

He handed Jacob two photographs, one of the stabbing victim and one of David Wilson, with his face bloodied and swollen. Jacob looked at them.

"Do you know these guys? Does any of this look familiar, Mister Lewski?"

"Should I know them?"

"You tell me."

Jacob handed the photographs back to Orville.

"Pretty disgusting, if you ask me."

"Do you know why we asked you down here, Mister Lewski?" said Bud.

"I go to work. I go home. No. I don't know what you want. What do you want from me?"

"You don't get out much, do you, Mister Lewski?"

"I go to work. I go home. Most days, I go to the local park after work and I go to bed at night."

Orville handed the photographs back to Jacob.

"We think you killed this guy and beat the crap out of the other one, Mister Lewski," he said, bluntly. "We're going to keep you here 'til hell freezes over if we have to. You're going to tell us what happened. And why you did this?"

"I go to work. I go home. I don't know anything about killing anybody. And I don't go around beating up on people."

"Where do you work, Mister Lewski?" asked Bud. He moved to change the tone of the questioning, hoping for some cooperation at the least. He did not detect the slightest sign of nervousness or stress in Jacob's demeanor. He just sat there, unmoved, and he answered the questions, plainly, simply, without a fuss. Bud glanced momentarily at the description, to guide his questions.

"I'm a grill man at Paddy's Place."

"The burger joint downtown?"

"Yes."

"How long have you worked there?"

"A long time now."

"You live alone, right?"

"Yes. I do."

"Can you tell us where you were on April Fifteenth, between eight o'clock in the evening and midnight?" asked Orville.

"I go to work. I go home. I go to the park. At eight o'clock any night I would be home in bed, asleep, most likely."

"Do you have any hobbies, Mister Lewski? Do you watch television? Anything like that?" Bud asked.

"No. What's that got to do with anything?" asked Jacob.

"Actually, Mister Lewski," said Bud, trying to move him in any way at all. "I'm trying to see if you're the kind of guy who could take a knife to a perfect stranger and not bat an eye."

"I lead a very dull life," said Jacob. "I go to work. I go home. I go to the park."

"Do you have a girlfriend?"

"No."

"Do you have any friends who might have been with you April Fifteenth, between eight in the evening and midnight? You need an alibi, Mister Lewski."

"I don't have any friends. Does that mean I don't have an alibi?"

"Something like that. It means you had the opportunity to do these things. It is up to you to prove where you were at the time of the incidences."

"How'd you hurt your hand, Mister Lewski?" asked Orville. "Doesn't that kind of make things difficult for you from time to time?"

"This?" he answered, holding it for them to see very clearly. "I was born with this nearly worthless, ugly thing." He demonstrated the limited movement. "Looks kind of like a cow's hoof, doesn't it?"

"That's a nasty scar on your forearm, too. How'd you come about that? Looks like you came out on the wrong end of a dog fight with a mighty big dog."

"This thing," he replied, as he ran his fingers around the jagged perimeter of the scar. "I'd tell you, but you wouldn't believe it," he said.

"Try me?" said Orville.

"My mother bit me," he answered, with a smirk.

"Yeah, right," said Orville, feeling like he had just been set up.

"I'll bet the kids in school when you were young made things pretty hard on you because of that hand, didn't they?" asked Bud.

"My mother was a addict. I got it from her. A birth defect."

Now, we're getting somewhere, thought Bud. He tried to push him.

"I know all about your mother, Mister Lewski. But it is you I'm interested in. Monica could not have been a very good mother. Maybe you have a lot of hate welled up inside you because of your mother? I've seen her record...she was a drunk, a whore, a doper, a petty criminal. Did you hate her? Did you build up enough hate you had to get even with somebody...even some stranger? Was that it, Mister Lewski? You just wanted to strike out at somebody? Anybody?" Bud was fishing for a motive.

"Listen...I've been flipping burgers ever since I was old enough to get a job. I quit school to flip burgers. I didn't give a damn about my mother then...and I don't give a damn now. She didn't give a damn about me, either. She was just too weird. All I ever wanted in this life was to flip burgers...and be left alone. Until now, I got from this life just what I wanted from it. For the most part, I don't know and I don't care what goes on outside my front door."

"You don't care about too much at all, do you?" asked Bud.

"You wouldn't even get up in the morning if you didn't have to, would you, Mister Lewski?" added Orville.

Jacob said nothing. He sat quietly, more than willing, it seemed, just to let them keep talking. Bud knew, from experience, they were getting nowhere at all; they were just wasting their time.

"Excuse us for a minute, Mister Lewski." Bud motioned for Orville to join him in the hall outside the office. "We'll be right back. Can I get you anything?"

"Can I have some water...room temperature?"

They stepped into the hall, out of Jacob's hearing range.

"How are we going to move this guy, Orville?" asked Bud. "He's solid as a rock. This is not going to take us anywhere."

"Renwall wants this guy by the balls, Bud. We have to come up with something."

"Orville, go back in there. Take him some water. I've got to make a phone call. Chitchat, shoot the bull...whatever. Buy me some time."

"Sure, Bud. What's up?"

"I'm not sure, Orville. Just do it. I'll be right back."

Bud called Alexsandr.

"Alexsandr? We've got Jacob Lewski at the station. Orville is talking to him now. The long shot didn't pan out. I've got to have an edge, Alexsandr. This guy isn't moving one inch in any direction. I might as well be talking to the walls."

Alexsandr thought for a moment. He gave Bud instructions. Bud listened attentively, taking mental notes.

"Are you sure it will work, Alexsandr? I don't want to lose this guy."

Alexsandr explained his ideas.

"Alexsandr? That's pretty cold-blooded stuff."

"If he's the guy, he'll open up. Push hard but stay calm...almost indifferent...throughout the interrogation. Don't stop until you get him moving...even if it takes all night. Hit him with what's real, Bud. Burst his bubble. Trust me."

"You're the boss, Alexsandr. Oh, by the way, Alexsandr, he fits the description to the letter so far."

"Call me if...make that when...he cracks, Bud."

"Sure, Alexsandr. Bye." Bud hung up the phone, took a deep breath. He gathered his thoughts. When he was ready to shift into a mode that was un-natural for him, he went back into the office. He closed the door behind him. He sat behind his desk, propped his feet up as if he was settling in for the night. I hate these facades, he thought. I'm a lousy actor.

He sat there, saying nothing, studying Jacob Lewski. He saw nothing extraordinary about the man. Nothing except the hoof-hand. He got up from his desk. "Just a few more questions, Mister Lewski, then you will be free to go." He opened the office door, asked Orville to step outside with him again.

"We're going for the jugular vein, Orville. No matter what you hear, play along, okay. It is going to be intense...don't let up until we get what we need, okay? We have to push hard but stay detached, like you are bored stiff and don't really give a damn. No matter what, stay detached and calm. Just ask questions, don't bait him. Let him do the talking. Follow my lead, okay? I will talk mostly about sex, realities, and the facts nobody cares about Jacob Lewski." He instructed Orville to go back in. "I'll just be a minute." He stalled for a while, and then went back into the office.

"I'll take over from here, Orville," he said. "Show him the pictures again." Orville handed him the pictures. Bud told Orville to be seated. "You'll want to hear this," he said. He took a tape recorder from his desk, and laid it out in full view. He turned it on.

Bud looked Jacob squarely in the eyes. He poised himself, decided on his proper voice and intonation, and then he spoke. "Jacob...I need to ask you something," he said, carefully speaking as if he really did not care one way or another. "When was the last time you were butt fucked?" Before Jacob could say anything, Bud hit him with more questions and comments. "You can tell me...nobody cares...you can talk freely. Nobody cares...not me, not Orville, not your mother...nobody. Not a living soul in the whole wide world cares, Jacob. How old were you? Eight? Ten? Twelve?"

"I'm not queer," Jacob answered.

"You didn't answer my question. I just want to know. Did you like it?"

Orville moved in. He hoped to confuse him, maybe hit him with too much too fast.

"Not queer? Who was the last woman you were with, Mister Lewski? Your mother, maybe?"

"Did you do your mother?" Bud pitched. "She gave it away, to anyone and everyone, didn't she? Did you get some of it, too?"

"Did your mother pimp you to feed her habits? You can tell us, Mister Lewski. Nobody cares. Your secrets are safe with us."

Orville looked at Bud like he thought he was crazy. Bud motioned for him to keep the questions moving in.

"Is that it, Jacob...did you proposition these guys...then try to kill them when they told you to get lost?" asked Orville, imitating Bud's disinterested style. Orville knew it did not happen that way, and he had no idea what Bud was up to, but he played along. "You can tell me, Mister Lewski. They told you to get lost, didn't they? What's real is you needed somebody, didn't you, but nobody cares, do they, Mister Lewski?" Orville picked up the pattern very quickly, but he was having a little trouble keeping his distance, disengaging.

Bud knew he had to burst the bubble.

"Why did you kill that guy?" he jabbed.

No response, Bud noticed. Not a blink. No squirming. No sweating. No heavy breathing. Nothing.

"Here's what's real. You know we're going to get you for it, Mister Lewski," said Orville. "Why not just make things easy...let the situation decide for you? Get real, Mister Lewski. You are not going to get away with it. You might as well tell us what happened."

They used up over an hour with sustained but restrained pushing; by repeatedly attacking his lack of sexuality and reinforcing the idea nobody cares, just as Alexsandr had recommended, they hoped to come up with something. Through it all, Jacob never raised his voice, and he never seemed to get upset. They were just about ready to call it quits and turn him loose, when he decided he was tired of holding back. Inadvertently, Orville had burst the bubble.

Jacob had listened and listened as they threw everything they could imagine his way. Bud had called in a rookie patrolman, and he was about to have him take Jacob back home, when Jacob decided he had heard enough. Jacob thought they were on to him, and he did not want the hassles of dragging things on any longer. He let the situation decide for him. Who cares, he thought, as he began his tale.

"You have it all wrong," Jacob began, coldly. "You guys are way off the mark. Calm down. You are right, Officer Detrick. The situation does dictate the inevitable. I'll tell you everything." He looked at the patrolman standing in the doorway waiting for Bud's instructions. Jacob asked him to stay, explaining to him he might do something even though nobody else would. The patrolmen looked at Bud with a questioning frown on his face. Bud sent the patrolman back to his duties. He closed the door.

"Don't waste our time with this I go to work. I go home shit, okay?" said Orville, impatiently. "What's real is I want to go home...soon."

"Oh, no...no. I'll tell you everything. You won't believe me, but I'll tell you anyway. Nobody ever believed me." He looked puzzled. "Do you have to arrest me before I tell you all this? I know how you guys work by technicalities."

"We can do that. If you will be honest with me," said Orville. "I'll believe you."

"Would you like an attorney present, Mister Lewski?"

"No. I won't need an attorney."

"I am placing you under arrest, Mister Lewski; to be charged with murder and attempted murder," Bud said; he then read him his rights.

"Do you understand your rights, Mister Lewski?"

"Oh, yes. Is it official now...I am under arrest?"

"Yes, it is official," said Orville. "You will be in our custody, and we will have court papers by tomorrow morning. You will have some papers to sign tomorrow. Does it matter?"

"I can't do anything about it, can I?"

"No," said Orville.

"I guess I have no choice. I'll tell you everything."

"Will handcuffs be necessary, Mister Lewski?"

"No...no. You won't need them."

"One last question?" said Jacob. "Will they kill me?"

"Murder is a capital offense," said Bud. "That will be up to a jury to decide."

"I guess it doesn't matter, does it?" said Jacob.

"Before you begin, Mister Lewski, will you tell me why you killed this one guy and tried to kill the other?" asked Orville. He knew he had to hear it from the man's own lips.

"You did kill him, didn't you? And you did attack this other guy, didn't you?" Bud asked.

"I did. I sure did. You'll find the knife at Paddy's. The pipe I threw in the drain by the curb."

"Why? You didn't even know them, did you?"

"I knew them. They were customers."

"Customers?" quizzed Bud. "Are you telling me the men went to Paddy's and they bought hamburgers...so you killed them?"

"No. Not customers at Paddy's. I would never do anything to hurt Paddy's," he said. "Do you ever eat there? I don't recognize either of you."

"You said customers. What kind of customers, Mister Lewski?" asked Orville, redirecting him for the first time in over an hour.

"Milly's...down on Third Street. They were using those kids," he said.

"Milly's?" Orville was about to say something, but Bud motioned frantically for him to be quiet. He had him talking finally, and he did not want anything to stop him.

"And you guys just turn the other way. It isn't right. Somebody had to do something. I don't care about myself...it is way too late for that. But the kids...you people should be ashamed of yourselves."

"Orville, make a note to bring in David Wilson, if he can make it. I want to confirm he was there. If he can't come in, I want a statement."

"So that's why you tried to kill these guys, Mister Lewski? They went to Milly's, so you killed one and tried to kill another for going there?"

"I did that. Yes."

"Have you killed any of Milly's other customers, Mister Lewski? Anybody we don't know about?"

For the first time, he smiled. He looked straight at Bud. "Had any good car wrecks lately?" he said. "A hole in the brake line...a slow leak. Worked beautifully. I punched it with a knife. The guy was a drunk...it was just a matter of time anyway."

Then Jacob told his story, slowly, deliberately, and without showing any emotional attachment to it at all. Bud let him talk, and he did not dare interrupt him, even though he seemed to ramble at first; with nothing else to go on, any thing he had to say would come in handy...anything. He had never let on to Jacob they had nothing on him. As they listened, they watched each other, as Jacob described his life, his grandmother, his mother, and his ideas about cleaning up the red light district. He talked on and on, seldom changing his tone, seldom showing any signs of emotion. He talked about many strange things. Many times he stopped and told them the same thing: "I know you won't believe me, but..."

Bud and Orville were both exhausted by the time Jacob Lewski was handcuffed and escorted from the office to a waiting patrol car. Bud had prepared himself for an emotional or otherwise violent outburst, but Jacob Lewski never broke down but simply started talking, and he told them everything, instead. He told them a whole lot more than they had wanted to hear. But Bud had obtained information he had needed for a long time, and it brought a lot of loose ends to a neat and tight closure. Bud was glad he got everything on tape.

After fifteen years on the force, Bud thought he had a stomach for just about anything. This evening, Jacob Lewski had proven him wrong. They were both somewhat stunned by what they had just been through. Jacob had seemingly covered the entire spectrum, from incest and bestiality, to heroin addiction and backroom abortions. He spoke of children being bought and sold. He even described, in putrid detail, an acid bath, something Alexsandr had not heard of in years.

"They'll get a kick out of this guy at County Memorial," said Orville, summing up the experience. "We can get the knife from Paddy's in the morning, and search the drain for the pipe. If the stuff is really there, that is. We'll get a statement from David Wilson. Snoop around Milly's...if we have to. Let's wrap this up. Man, Renwall will be pissed when he finds out what we've got here."

"There's no political capital in exploiting some loony from never land, is there?"

"Such is life," joked Orville. Bud grinned.

When it was all over, when the preliminary paperwork was done, and they saw to it Jacob Lewski was safely on his way, under heavy guard, to the Psychiatric Wing at County Memorial in Mayberight, Orville cornered Bud as he was heading out the door, heading home to go to bed. Orville carried his suit coat over his shoulder, hooking it by a finger, and he had his shirtsleeves rolled up. He carried a paper cup full of thick coffee. They were both worn out, sweaty, and still somewhat bewildered.

"I've got a splitting headache, Bud. What did we just do in there? You have to tell me, man?" Orville insisted. "Man, this is Nohartinit...armpit of the world, USA. But that stuff...right here...under our noses, Bud?"

"That was some of the most bizarre stuff I've ever heard," said Bud. "No question the guy is nuts. How much of what he said was real do you think? I think our guy has been reading some pretty flaky stuff, Orville."

Orville grinned. "Real? None of it, man. At least, I hope not! It would be convenient if he did kill those guys and we can prove it. Other than that, it sounds to me like this guy has been a stoner since he was in diapers. His mother...right...with red eyeballs, howling, and growling like a mad dog, a man's voice as deep as the Grand Canyon...claw marks on the doors. Taking huge chunks of flesh out of her Johns? That part about her own mother keeping her locked up for use by her special customers who liked things rough? And the men and women in masks beating the hell out of everything and everybody with clubs and ax handles and stuff...busting his grandmother's head into bits and pieces. Setting fire to the place. Whew! What a nut case!" He shook his head in disbelief. "And what's the thing about Milly's? Why would he kill people for going into a used bookstore? Why would he imagine such things taking place in a book store?"

"Before you joined the force, Orville...a long time before then, Milly's was one of the better known and disreputable brothels in town. Maybe some weird stuff did happen there. I didn't have the heart to tell him it was shut down when he was maybe fifteen or so. The bookstore just kept the name. Do you think it has been that long since he first checked himself out of reality and locked himself inside the strange world of his? Why would he have waited all these years to cut loose? What a fruitcake!"

Orville did not have an answer. But he did have something else on his mind. "How did you know what to do and say, Bud...you have to tell me, man? I have not been a cop as long as you, of course, but I have never seen such an odd way of handling a suspect. How did you know how to break through?"

Bud mumbled. "I'm not too sure myself, Orville. I had a gut feeling it would work." He untied his tie, stuffed it in his coat pocket. He unbuttoned his top button. He rubbed his eyes. "All I can tell you right now, Orville, is one plus one does not always equal one." That said, he headed out the door, content in the knowledge he had one last item to take care of and his day was done.

"Alexsandr...you're going to love this guy," he mumbled, as he walked toward his car.

He pulled the tape from his shirt pocket. He would duplicate it, give a copy to Alexsandr, and return the original in the morning.

He put the tape back in his pocket. He got into his car, started the engine, and headed for home.

A few blocks down the road, he realized he had a big problem on his hands.

His joy subsided. "And, on the other hand, you are going to hate his guts." Bud knew he had, inadvertently, opened a can of worms, with possible devastating consequences.

Chapter Twelve

Bud woke the next morning feeling refreshed yet still somewhat bewildered and perplexed by his encounter with Jacob Lewski. He had never been that closely involved with someone who was, he judged, truly insane. It had been, to say the least, a stirring experience. He could not recall, in his fifteen years in Nohartinit, ever having dealt with an insane person.

Now that he had time to think about it, in actuality, Bud now realized, the encounter had opened more doors than it had closed. Renwall had his killer, a feat he could now exploit in the press. But Jacob Lewski could prove to be the undoing of many good people. Alexsandr was among them.

Of all the people in this dustpan of a city, thought Bud, why this Lewski guy...damn...the irony of it. The simple, tragic, blood-sucking irony.

Bud got dressed. He clothed himself in his brown suit with a very light blue shirt, and a plain blue tie. He wondered if he, too, would go down along with the rest. He also knew he had to devise a plan, some way to keep from taking a dive. He wanted no one to get hurt, but he knew it was an inevitable consequence of the arrest of Jacob Lewski.

His first stop was at Alexsandr's to deliver the duplicate tape. Alexsandr understood, implicitly, the source of the tape could not be divulged to anyone. It was, and it had to be, a secret between them, at least for the time being. He arrived to find Alexsandr puttering in his garden.

"I've got it, Alexsandr," Bud said, as he handed over the tape. "I think you will find this very interesting, to put it mildly."

"What do you think, Bud?" asked Alexsandr, as he tucked the tape in his pants pocket.

"When you hear this stuff, Alexsandr, I think you'll have a whole new set of problems you will have to deal with. Of all the people in Nohartinit, this guy is going to be more troublesome than a Ted Bundy would be."

Together they started walking toward the front porch.

"Are they going to railroad him?"

"I'm not too concerned about that, Alexsandr. But if the stuff on this tape ever gets leaked to the press, they'll have a heyday at his expense. But there's more to it than that."

"I see," said Alexsandr. "I don't know what position it will put you in, Bud...I've asked Heinz to represent Mister Lewski. He'll be here in a couple of hours. He's going to stay with me a few days to look things over."

"Thanks for the warning, Alexsandr," he answered. "How is Heinz these days...and how in the world did you ever pull him out of retirement to handle this? He used to make my life miserable, but this is one time I hope he can pull the stops on this one."

"I called in a few markers...and fronted him five thousand dollars in cash."

Bud laughed.

"Don't ask where the money came from, okay?"

"Oh, I won't, Alexsandr. I think the General would approve, however. But you never heard me say that, did you?"

"For the record, what is your role in all this, Bud?"

"I merely investigated a murder, Alexsandr. I need a lot of distance. You need to impress on Grampy, Richard, and Ladonna I had nothing whatsoever to do with the +1 scenario. Someone would probably throw it all out of proportion and discredit the method. And tell Heinz I do not wish to deal with him in any but a professional capacity until all this blows over. This could get very messy, Alexsandr. You better hope he's good at suppressing evidence...if this whole tape can be considered evidence."

"Why, Bud?" asked Alexsandr, as they turned the corner of the house. They headed toward the front steps.

Bud stopped. Alexsandr stopped.

"What is it, Bud?"

"You understand it is my job to put this guy away."

"Of course."

"You understand...one professional to another...I had to tape everything because that was all we had to go on? Orville Detrick heard it all."

"I understand? Get to the point, Bud...what's the problem?"

"The problem, Alexsandr, is Milly's. I may be a recent resident in Nohartinit compared to many other people here, but Milly's will play a central role in everything. Monica Lewski and her mother will resurface also. I know you and Grampy and Heinz and a few others do not want that story told."

"Damn," Alexsandr growled. "Maybe we better sit down. I'm too old for these kind of complications." They walked up the steps, and they seated themselves. "How much do you know, Bud?"

"I'm an investigator, Alexsandr. There's nobody better in these parts, except that Findfello guy down by the County Line. Nobody can beat that guy. I'm as good at my work as you are at yours. Before I went into this kind of work, Alexsandr, I studied history. I love history. I know an awful lot about what happened at Milly's, Alexsandr. What I didn't know, Jacob Lewski did. And he talked, plainly. In great detail."

"What's it mean?"

"I know enough to put somebody away for a long time, Alexsandr. You know there is no statute of limitation on murder."

"You understand why we did what we did?"

"Of course, Alexsandr. Taken in the context of the time, I understand completely. I, personally, would call it a public service. But my opinion doesn't mean much, does it, Alexsandr?" Bud lowered his voice. "Tell me about the kids?"

"No. I'm not sure it would serve anyone to bring that up."

"Listen...I see what's happening to the kids these days...I see stuff in this forsaken town that'll make you want to puke. You can't shock me, Alexsandr. But maybe you can put it all in a right perspective."

"Let me tell you this much, Bud. We found six girls and a boy that might. The oldest of the girls was around nine...hardly more than a baby. We found one of them, probably about six or seven, in a bed, beaten black and blue, stale blood all over the child's face, teeth missing, face swollen. One little girl we found right in the middle of a photo session...they had her standing nude on a small platform with about a half-dozen drunken, smelly old trashy men gathered around her like slobbering wolves...posing her, fondling her, fondling themselves...and taking pictures."

"Anything else?"

"We found a room not much bigger than a closet with a strong door on it...no windows, a huge lock on the door...sort of like a cage. Urine stains were all over the floor and piles of human feces were everywhere...the smell was gagging. A bowl of some kind of slop was in one corner. We found expended syringes on the floor. The kids were scared to death to talk about that room, Bud. We found marks made by desperate little fingers where the kids had apparently been trying to claw out of that hellhole." Alexsandr looked at him, his old eyes painfully alert. "You know the powers behind it all will not allow any kind of public examination of Milly's or any of their other operations, Bud. What you just heard might get people killed if it ever goes public. I'll die before I admit to having told you anything!"

"I understand," he replied, sympathetically. "What did you do with the kids?"

"As God is my witness, you will never know, Bud...never. That's the best-kept secret in Nohartinit's history. I'll burn in hell before I'll disturb those kids again...and I'll never, not ever, pry into their lives."

"Your final word, Alexsandr?"

"As God is my witness!" he answered. "Bud...tell me something? Have I just stepped on a Bouncing Betty?"

"If the contents of that tape go public in a trial, Alexsandr, Betty's going to blow you apart...a lot of good people could go down hard. I might go down as well. I wish I had never met Jacob Lewski."

"Okay, Bud. The implications are clear. What are you telling me? Why are you here?"

"Alexsandr, I can't take this guy down without taking you guys down with him, unless you can find a way to wipe out everything he knows about what happened at Milly's. He was there, Alexsandr. Right smack in the middle of everything. He was that boy you found. He gave names, Alexsandr. You got careless, and used your real names in calling to one another during the raid. If I can't take him down, Alexsandr, the +1 scenario might as well go in the trash. To save it, we have to set him free. If we set him free, the credibility of the +1 scenario goes with him. It just isn't in me to set a murderer free."

"You've got the original tape?"

"Yes. It has not been transcribed yet."

"Can you misplace it for a day or two?"

"That's no problem," he answered. "What about Orville? I don't think I can misplace him."

"He doesn't know anything about Milly's, does he?"

"Only what I've told him, which is next to nothing," Bud said. "I doubt he attached much importance to anything Lewski said. He won't bother looking any deeper. I can run him around gathering evidence against Lewski. After that, he has a full case load to keep him busy."

"What about Jacob Lewski?"

"Ah, those guys at County Memorial will test him and retest him for days on end. He's out of our hair for quite a while. But Alexsandr, we have to figure out what to do. I can hide the tape for a while, but there's no way of knowing what he will say or do at County Memorial."

"I'll get with Heinz. I'll call Grampy. We'll listen to the tape, and we'll take it from there. Can you stall Renwall?"

"I'll stall him with generalities, ho-hum stuff. I can buy us a few days."

"Is there any reason you can't just bury everything surrounding the Monica Lewski business altogether?"

"Alexsandr, I can't do that. The man going to prison was the son who saw his mother exploited and abused, who saw justice perverted. He saw his own grandmother murdered in the name of good. In the name of good, the system now will probably kill him. He did the same thing you guys did...except it was now and not then. It doesn't add, Alexsandr."

"Listen, Bud...you're probably the only person who has even looked at the grandmother's case in what...close to two decades. Just look the other way, Bud. Let me think about this. Can you be persuaded to think about dropping the whole business? I'll call you at home tonight, okay?"

"Sure, Alexsandr, I'll think about dropping it, for about two seconds," he sighed. "Alexsandr, before I go, I have to ask you one very important question. Which one of you killed Monica Lewski's mother? I've eliminated you and Grampy and Heinz...I've eliminated all the men involved. Who was she, Alexsandr? Who is this woman who killed Milly Lewski?"

"We'll talk later, Bud."

"Not good enough, Alexsandr. Do you know?"

"We'll talk later, Bud. End of conversation."

"No, Alexsandr," he insisted. "This is not quite the end of the conversation. I've got a deal for you, Alexsandr. For right now, just think about it: I'll trade you Jacob Lewski and your +1 scenario for the killer of Monica Lewski's mother. Think about it, Alexsandr."

"You son-of-a-bitch," said Alexsandr, harshly.

"Look at it from my perspective, Alexsandr. I clean up my cold file. I get two killers off the streets, and you get your freedom, your grand +1 scenario – untainted – and I fulfill my promises to General Perkins. Don't look so shocked. Isn't that what this is all about, Alexsandr...the triumph of good over evil...making sure the good guys win?"

"The good guys won some ground...years ago, Bud. Let it be."

"I can't do that, Alexsandr. That woman was murdered. Her grandson watched this mystery woman beat her to death. You know what he told me, Alexsandr? Referring to the police, he said you guys just turn the other way; you don't do anything about it. He said nobody believed him, Alexsandr. Nobody. Funny, isn't it...I want justice for Jacob Lewski...two ways, Alexsandr. Your loyalty to your friends can't change that. I don't care who the old bitch was or what she was. She was a human being, just like Jacob,...just like the rest of us."

"Hmm," grumbled Alexsandr. He looked squarely into Bud's dark eyes with a cold and penetrating stare. "Sure, Bud...you just keep thinking that way; you don't know shit about Monica Lewski or her mother. Now, get out of here, before I lose my temper."

"I'll call you, Alexsandr. You can count on it," Bud said, as he walked to his car. Before he got in, he looked back toward Alexsandr. "I can't let it go, Alexsandr. You better remember that. You're going to have to cut some sleazy deals...they might as well be with me."

"Go now," Alexsandr insisted.

"Isn't it time you practice what you preach, Alexsandr? I can probably get you immunity in exchange for testimony. Good has to prevail, Alexsandr...and you know it."

BOOK TWO

Chapter Thirteen

Richard called Lalinduh at the library, to confirm their date. She was pleasant, as usual, and she told him his grandfather was there as they spoke.

"Going through the old newspapers again," she said. "Doesn't he ever just stop and enjoy being retired?"

"To him, going through old newspapers is the highest form of entertainment known to man," explained Richard. "I drove him in this morning, but he didn't say what he was going to do once he got here. Now, I know."

Lalinduh chuckled. "Six o'clock, then?" Her huge brown eyes shimmered.

Richard confirmed the address, and then agreed to pick her up at six.

Meanwhile, across town, Orville Detrick was out talking to people, gathering evidence against Jacob Lewski. Much to his surprise and much to his relief, the knife was at Paddy's and a borrowed guy from the water department retrieved the pipe from the storm drain. His next stop was at the hospital, to get a statement from David Wilson. He wondered if he was still there. His injuries had not been severe. He hoped he would not have to chase him around town to catch up to him. He had other business to take care of, and he did not want to waste his day running down a statement.

Back at the library, Grampy searched the newspapers, looking for stories surrounding the death of Monica Lewski's mother, a.k.a., Milly. His search had two purposes this day. First, he was looking for anything that might have implicated anyone. Second, he wanted to see if there had been witnesses to the events of that day, other than Monica's son. None, as he remembered it, ever came forward, either out of fear and intimidation or from lack of interest. Monica was not there that night. It had been written up, he recalled, as a simple disturbance at a cathouse. Two paragraphs. Maybe three.

Finding next to nothing in the old newspapers, he returned the heavy volumes to Lalinduh.

"Thank you, Lalinduh," he said.

"What's up?" she asked. "Seems like I've been dragging out these particular volumes right and left lately."

"Oh? Some sudden burst of interest in the period?"

"Mister Detrick, from the Police Department, was in yesterday. Some old guy who said he lived in Mayberight was in earlier."

"This old guy from Mayberight...did he have wavy white hair and a bushy white moustache by any chance? Walked with a slight limp?"

"Yeah, that's the guy. I take it you know him?"

"Yes. I guess you could say that," Grampy looked at Lalinduh, and he smiled. Heinz was in town. "I guess, at one time or another, you meet a lot of people, don't you, Lalinduh?"

"Oh, yes."

"Have you ever met an ex-reporter by the name of Ralph Whalen? He's probably well up in years now."

"Whalen? Hmm. Can you describe him? If I heard his voice, I could pinpoint him in a matter of seconds."

"Never met him. He used to work for the local paper."

"Maybe he's the old guy with the funny-looking cane...it has some kind of carved head on it."

"That may be him. Can you tell me anything about him? Any idea where he lives these days?"

"In town, I guess. He never checks out any books. He just passes through now and then, looking at the art prints and the local paintings. I doubt if he gets out much," she added. "He has a terrible time walking, even when he uses the cane. Kind of like his legs were crushed along the way somewhere. Between you and me, he doesn't look well."

Grampy had already checked the phone book for a local listing. He had already checked with the newspaper. No one there had heard from him in many years. They had indicated he had moved away many years back. Whereabouts unknown.

"Thank you, Lalinduh. You and Richard have a good evening. He's a swell guy."

She smiled. "Has he talked about me? I'm kind of nervous, I guess."

"Don't be. He is, too. Yes, he has talked about you. A lot," Grampy lied. "For the last couple of days...a lot. I hope he doesn't overdo things to try to impress you. He gets a little clumsy when he overdoes things. He hasn't had a date in months...stays too busy with his studies. Just show him a good time, and you'll do fine."

"Grampy?" she said, somewhat astonished. She blushed.

"Did I say something wrong?"

She looked hard at this frail old man standing in front of her. She realized things did not mean the same thing now as when he was younger...much younger. "No...no," she assured him. She changed the subject quickly. "No books today?"

"No. I have to meet an old friend," he said. "It could be a busy weekend." Grampy bid her good bye. He had a lot to think about, with Heinz in town and this Detrick fellow looking into past events. I don't like the way things are shaping up, he thought, as he headed for the exit. I have a bad feeling about this. What is this Detrick guy up to? Who is this Detrick guy?

Once outside, Grampy looked around him. It was a warm day, and things seemed kind of slow in Nohartinit. But it was a good day for a walk. Alexsandr's house was just a few blocks away. Grampy decided the walk might do him good, keep a few joints loose.

He walked a block, sat on a cement-based bus stop bench, beside a couple of ragged-looking teenage boys. Their jeans were torn, and their tee shirts were dirty. They both had long, unwashed hair. One was trying to grow a moustache but his whiskers looked more like dirt than whiskers.

"Hey, man," said one of them as he seated himself. "Where you headin'?" Grampy noticed right away the boy desperately needed a bath.

"Nowhere. Just resting," said Grampy. "I don't get around too well these days."

"It must be a bitch gettin' friggin' old, huh?" said the other.

"Yes," answered Grampy. "Yes, it is."

"My grandpa's getting' real friggin' old," said the larger of the two. "He lives in the nursin' home on the other side of town. He can't even get out of the friggin' bed any more."

"Do you visit him?"

"Yeah, man. I do. I love the friggin' stories he tells, man." His enthusiasm was authentic. "Covered wagons, gangsters, the Depression, wars, and all that shit. I don't know how much of that shit is true, man...but I love it, I really friggin' love it! Bitchin' stories, man. Them old folks can talk some heavy shit."

Hmm...I'll bet they can, thought Grampy. "It is a good thing that you visit your Grandpa," he said. He looked at the other fellow. "How about you? Do you visit your grandpa?"

"Nah, I was just a kid when he died," he replied. "But my Grandma tells stories...scary stuff about demons and witches and junk. She's batty, though. Swears that stuff is true. Says we used to have one of them things with red eyes and wolf teeth and claws instead of hands...right here in Nohartinit...way back when."

"He ain't friggin...that old lady can talk some shit that'll make your skin crawl, man." He laughed. He punched his buddy, playfully. "Your Grandma was the original friggin' stoner, man...'cause she's toasted...weird as hell and friggin' toasted. I heard her say it, man. She said she seen that red-eyed monster, but nobody wouldn't never believe her."

143

"That is certainly a strange story," said Grampy. "This monster sounds like something you would have to see to believe, I guess." Grampy seized the opportunity. "What's her name, son? I just might know your Grandma."

"Alba Beecham. They call her Beechie for short. A little bitty old shit about this high." He held his right arm to his chest, hand extended. "She lives over by the creek."

"Sorry...don't know her," said Grampy. "Did she ever mention anyone else who might have seen this monster?"

"Yeah...she says my Grandpa had a big scar on his arm to prove it," the fellow said. "He had a big scar, sure enough...you can see it in the picture of him she keeps in her room. But it wasn't from no friggin' red-eyed monster. My mom says he was wounded in the war. She said Grandpa never said nothin' about no monster."

The bus pulled up. The squeal and the throaty hiss of air brakes and the flapping open of the doors ended the conversation. The boys took change for the fare from their pockets.

"Hey, take it easy, Buddy," one said, as he boarded the bus.

"If you see any red-eyed monsters, give me a buzz," said the other, with a huge grin.

The driver took their money. "Is the sick-looking old guy getting on?" he asked, as he took off his hat and wiped sweat from his forehead.

"Nah! He's just friggin' restin', man."

"Nice old guy, huh?" said the bigger one to the other.

"Man...I don't never want to get friggin' old," said the other.

"Me neither...no friggin' way."

The driver closed the door, signaled with his flasher, and then pulled into traffic. Grampy watched the boys as they walked toward the rear of the crowded bus to find seats. The bus pulled away, leaving behind a thick black cloud of stinky exhaust fumes. Grampy stood to finish his walk to Alexsandr's. He had a strange little grin creeping across his lips. "Hmm," he whispered, as he digested the conversation. "I'm not alone in this...maybe, just maybe, there is a way I can seal that case file once and for all." He walked on, steadily plodding along. He was thinking.

Grampy found Alexsandr and Heinz sitting on Alexsandr's porch, sipping hot coffee. Alexsandr always had a hunch if you drank hot fluids on a hot day, you would stay cooler. He never argued the point. Rachael, once again, had gone shopping with Ladonna; a friend had become a grandparent for the third time, and she wanted to find a cuddle toy for the baby. Grampy looked at the two men, thinking to himself if Alexsandr had Heinz's hair and moustache, he would, indeed, look like Santa Claus. Heinz had laid his cane by his side. It was a plain but obviously very expensive cane. Mostly for show, thought Grampy.

"We've got a problem, Grampy," said Heinz, after a very brief hello.

Grampy sat on the top step of the porch. "So, what's new? Every time the three of us have even been in the same place at the same time, we've had a problem...or made one in short order."

Heinz chuckled. Alexsandr was in no mood for levity.

"Bud knows everything, Grampy. The whole damn story behind Milly's death," said Alexsandr. "I don't know how he did it, but he's narrowed his list of suspects to the women only."

"Good God Almighty! What does he want?"

"He wants to make a deal, Grampy. He said he would trade Jacob Lewski and the +1 scenario for the name of the murderer. He offered immunity if I will testify. You know I can't do it."

"If you don't testify?"

"Jacob Lewski saw everything, Grampy. This investigator got it all on tape. Names.; some pretty good descriptions. A second man was with Bud at the interrogation..."

"Detrick?" interjected Grampy.

"How'd you know?" said Heinz. He twitched his moustache.

"Never mind. Detrick has been doing some independent snooping; I was at the library this morning. He's been going through old newspaper accounts."

"And?"

"Nothing there...I did find the name of the guy who covered the story. A fellow named Ralph Whalen. They cut his story down to a couple of paragraphs but still gave him a by-line. But he's gone and left no trail."

"Okay. I saw that story. Nothing there. Maybe he knows something. We'll find him if we need to," said Heinz. "Anything else?"

"What did Jacob Lewski have to say?" asked Grampy. He was not about to mention the demonic possession aspect. Not yet.

"The tape is a killer piece of work," said Heinz. "Detrick has heard it all."

"There's a copy that Bud is holding back, buying us some time," added Alexsandr. "I have a copy."

"Editing is out of the question. And...there's no telling what they're hearing in the Psych Ward at County Memorial."

"What are you going to do, Heinz? We can't just sit here and let Bud do this thing, can we?" asked Grampy.

"If we give him what he wants, Grampy...he'll deal with the right people. Jacob Lewski will take the fall for his crimes, Bud will be a hero for cleaning out his cold file, we'll salvage the +1 scenario, and everybody...with one exception...will live happily ever after. Bud knows we were there, Grampy. He just doesn't know who killed Milly."

"I won't tell him, Alexsandr," replied Grampy. He looked at Heinz. "I won't do it."

"Grampy?" said Heinz.

"What?" he snapped. "I won't do it, Heinz. Don't force the issue."

"Grampy...listen to reason," pleaded Heinz. "We're three old men...we had our day. We did what we could. In our time and our place, we did what we thought was the right thing to do. Those days are gone, Grampy. What was the right thing to do then is, and would be, wrong now. We did that, Grampy. We did that much. It is time to step aside. I'm going to suggest nothing right now. Let it be and wait. Look at our options, yes. But say nothing. Make no deals. I still have to meet with my client, Mister Lewski. Don't lose your nerve and don't do anything until you get my go-ahead."

"If you don't mind a cliché, Grampy...we won that battle, but we're going to lose this war; I'm lost, Grampy. Bud is not going to give up," said Alexsandr. "And now...this Detrick guy?"

"Call in some markers, Heinz...God knows you've engineered every slimy deal this town has ever known."

Heinz nodded his head, signifying surrender. "We're old, Grampy. None of the old bunch has any power any more. We're way past our prime. Open your eyes, Grampy. I couldn't pull strings these days if I had to...the old bunch is out of business or dead and gone."

"I knew when I got up this morning, I was going to have a bad day," grumbled Grampy. "What about Renwall, Heinz...got anything on him?"

"Sorry. Rude he is. Unrefined he is. Corrupted by the powers that be, he is, but vulnerable? I don't know how he's done it all these years, Grampy...he's so clean...in spite of what we know to be true...he squeaks like a chalkboard and smells like a new car."

"Alexsandr?" pleaded Grampy.

"You know I can't say anything, Grampy."

"Heinz?" pleaded Grampy.

"We're hanging onto a pledge we made a half-century back. I can raise a good but hopeless defense; there's no statute of limitations on murder, and that tape will kill us. To defend what we did, I'd be shooting way above the heads of a young jury, Grampy. Nobody today will justify what we did back then."

"Maybe we can buy the judge?" suggested Grampy. He knew he was grabbing at straws. "Or pack the jury?"

Heinz moaned. He hissed air out between his teeth. "I don't want to go down, Grampy. I don't care what you think of me...I don't want to go down. That was never in the plan, was it? And there's no way in hell you'll buy Judge Lambert...he's the first honest and honorable judge to sit in this town since it was founded. You don't have enough money to sway Lambert, Grampy. He simply cannot be bought."

"To hell with the deal!" said Grampy, angrily. "Alexsandr...help me out here!"

Alexsandr, now worried and nervous, was not sure what to do. "Can we get through to the District Attorney? Or anybody on the prosecution staff?"

"Young blood, Alexsandr," said Heinz.

"Young blood or no, people still love money."

"Can we reach Bud?" Grampy asked.

"We'll dealing with a man who is dedicated, as we were, to doing the right thing, Grampy. I don't think we can reach him," said Alexsandr.

Grampy looked straight at Heinz. "Okay...tell it like it is, Heinz."

"We have an option. If we hand over a killer...not the killer but a killer...then Elbudro will not put the tape or us or the +1 scenario on public display through a trial. If we make the right deal, maybe we can settle everything in the judge's chamber and never have any of this see daylight. We can salvage our reputations, save the +1 scenario, and, quite possibly, use it to take another chip or two from the old establishment. All we have to do now is find us a patsy."

"The graveyard outside of town is full of unrecognized heroes," replied Grampy. "It can't hurt to elevate one of them to martyrdom."

"There's got to be a bachelor out there somewhere," Heinz agreed. "No need to damage innocent survivors."

"Didn't you say Jacob Lewski saw everything?" asked Grampy.

"Yes. And?" answered Alexsandr.

"Why can't we dump it on him?" replied Grampy. "He says he saw it...we were there, we surrender that much and take our lumps...we say he did it? What's wrong with that, Heinz?"

"He's killed one, assaulted another. Who wouldn't buy into the idea he's killed before?"

"His own Grandmother?"

"Stranger things have happened," said Heinz. "The man is obviously deranged. If I can get him to talk about his red-eyed boogie woman in front of a jury, we could sell them anything from that point onward. Who is to say he hasn't been that way for decades?"

Grampy knew he had to fake it now. "Red-eyed boogie woman?" he muttered.

"He went on and on about his mother, Grampy. Red eyes. Claws. Howling and growling. Crazy stuff."

"If we dump on him, why would we not say anything until now? I sure some one would want to know," asked Alexsandr.

"Nobody cared, Alexsandr," answered Heinz. "I could put it in the time and place. Alexsandr. The newspaper squelched the story. The powers covered their tracks. We got what we wanted...they shut down Milly's. Everybody got what he or she wanted. So, in the heat of the moment, we let it go." He twitched his moustache. "There's only one problem...other than this vigilante stuff is hard to justify...a big one," said Heinz. "We were carrying the clubs, not the kids. We're not going to convince anybody that when we went charging in like assault troops this kid, unlike any of the others, gathered the presence of mind to use the situation. And then convince them he used the chaos to waste his Grandmother? It won't fly, guys. And how are we going to explain he lay dormant all those years between murders? It won't fly."

"Why not? He hated his Grandmother for what she did to his mother...motive, right?" suggested Alexsandr.

"He was there...opportunity," added Grampy.

"Is there any way to coerce this guy...as nuts as he is?" asked Heinz. "Can we get a confession? He's dead meat anyway."

"If we could do that, it would defuse everything," said Alexsandr. "Bud would have his killer. We'd smell like roses. The +1 scenario would glow. The powers would never get involved."

"Heinz, do you think you could negotiate something with Bud?"

"Elbudro? He and I never did see anything eye-to-eye. Can you arrange a private session? Just the four of us?"

"He refuses to meet you any way but as professionals. I think he knows enough he wants to stay distant. I don't think you can move him, Heinz. Could anyone have moved us...back then? He's the contemporary version of what we once were," replied Alexsandr. "But he gets to play by some rules."

"I know the guy. At least I used to. I used to get under his skin in court. At heart, I think he's a decent fellow. If that's the case, Alexsandr...maybe he'll go for something if we can convince him there's good to come from making such a deal."

"We are overlooking one possibility," said Grampy. "Maybe he just wants to solve the case...just for the sake of solving it."

"And Detrick? He just turns his head? I don't think so," replied Heinz. "He's probably bucking for a promotion."

"Okay, Heinz. Suppose we look at something else. Hear me out before you interrupt, okay?" said Grampy. "Suppose we come up with an unknown entity...something so far fetched it reaches into credibility by the intensity of the absurdity of it all?" Grampy's tremors began acting up. He appeared nervous, although he was in complete control.

"Grampy...I see where you're going. Do you expect me to face a jury and convince them some red-eyed boogie woman with fangs and claws killed Milly?" Heinz shook his head in disbelief.

Alexsandr laughed.

"I'm serious, Heinz."

"And just where and how are you going to come up with this boogie woman?"

"You're losing it, Grampy; those tremors have gone to your brain," said Alexsandr. "This is serious stuff. We can't afford to play games. There's too much at stake here."

"Could you do it, Heinz?" Grampy demanded. He set his bony jaw, to signal no nonsense. His bright eyes glared.

"Damn right I could...I could hang juries with that kind of crap from now 'til doomsday. Make it convincing enough, and nothing would ever even reach the courtroom...that I could guarantee."

"Just what would you need to make it convincing enough, Heinz?" asked Grampy.

"In the olden days, I'd just say we hire the best whore we can, they'll hire their best whore. You know the drill, Grampy." He twitched his moustache. "But a red-eyed boogie woman...you'd need credible witnesses, a few photographs might help. The testimony of a crazy man isn't good enough. But I could build on it. I would have to present enough credible stuff to remove any possibility of the prosecution establishing proof beyond a reasonable doubt. In a case like this, if I can slap 'em hard enough to create the illusion of a reasonable doubt, their case will never make it to trial. It takes a preponderance of the evidence to prove a felony. And it must lead to a verdict vested in a belief the defendant is guilty beyond a shadow of a doubt. If they can't get a confession, they'd have no case."

"You're saying if enough credible people back up the red-eyed boogie woman story, the case will never go to trial even if Bud identifies the right person?"

"Yes. That's what I'm saying. I don't think they could gather any physical evidence after all these years. Of course, it would help if there were no eyewitnesses. So far, all Elbudro has to go on is what this loony said."

"Gentlemen," said Grampy, confidently. "Fate has just knocked upon our door."

Alexsandr looked at Heinz. Heinz shrugged his aged shoulders. "Ah, man," moaned Heinz. He twitched his moustache. "I'm getting too old for this shit. I should have stayed retired."

"Okay, Grampy, what's your plan?" asked Alexsandr.

"Heinz...we need the best private investigator money can buy. Can you get him?"

"You have money?" replied Heinz. "This guy is pretty expensive."

"We can get it, right Alexsandr?"

Alexsandr nodded in agreement. Alexsandr held up three fingers.

"Would three thousand up front bring him in?" asked Grampy.

"You bet," said Heinz. "Make it four and he'll be here by sundown."

Alexsandr agreed, by a nod.

"Heinz call your man. Cash in hand when he gets here. If he can make it by tonight have him meet us at my house. Gentlemen, be at my house at six o'clock tonight. Bring the tape with you. Better yet, I'll take it with me. I need to hear it," Grampy said. He got up. "I need to call Richard to take me home." He started toward the door to make the phone call. "Be there. Six o'clock sharp."

After he went indoors, out of hearing range, Alexsandr looked at Heinz. He shook his head, as if he had just bumped into a telephone pole. "He's losing it, Heinz. What are we going to do now?"

"Humor him," Heinz said. "What else can we do?" He stretched, moaning as he did so. "I don't get it."

"Get what?" answered Alexsandr.

"Leave it to you guys to play Sherlock Holmes...to solve a murder and you track down the one guy in the whole city...hell, the whole damn state for that matter...who can fry us all. I just don't get it. I hope this damned experiment of yours was worth it, Alexsandr." He reached for his cane, and then, using it for leverage, he stood.

"Where you going?"

"I'm going to call my man. You get the tape for Grampy."

"Then what?"

"Then I'm going to take a nap, Alexsandr. Maybe when I wake up I will discover this whole thing is just a dream...just a lousy stinking dream." He headed for the door, mumbling, rehearsing: "Your Honor, I'd like to call my next witness...the red-eyed boogie woman! The lady over there with claws and fangs and red eyeballs. Damn. I should have stayed retired...I'm getting too old for this shit."

Chapter Fourteen

Grampy located Richard, as he expected to, at the library talking to Lalinduh. In minutes, Richard picked him up from Alexsandr's and was driving him toward home.

"What's up, Grampy?"

"In a couple of hours, Richard, I'm going to begin a process of closure...the Monica Lewski case."

Grampy then told him of his chance encounter with the boys at the bus stop. "This woman, Alba Beecham...she saw what I saw, Richard. I'm not alone any more. I hope you're in for the long haul because I'm about to show you stuff that will shock and maybe frighten you."

"God, yes!" He answered, excitedly. "This is for real, Grampy?"

"More real that you can imagine, Richard." He handed Richard the tape. "Jacob Lewski described it in detail on this tape somewhere also."

Richard looked curiously at the tape. "You can back it up, then?"

"After I have a chance to listen to the tape you can take it with you. I have a name, too. A reporter named Ralph Whalen had a story chopped up which I believe also involved her. I think he knows, too. Heinz has called in an investigator...I'm going to have him run down the leads...at last, Richard, I don't have to hide what I know."

Richard slowed the car, then pulled to the side of the road, not far from the Interstate. He put the car in park, and left the engine running.

"This is fantastic, Grampy," said Richard. "But what can I do to help? They're still going to think you're nuts. Me, too, I guess. What the hell?"

"Oh, you're not going to help, Richard. You're going to build a thesis like none that has ever been put before a panel."

"You must be relieved after all these years?"

"Oh, yes. That I am." Grampy then looked into Richard's eyes. "See this."

"The wound? I've seen it a thousand times, Grampy."

"Suppose I tell you that Alba Beecham's husband has one just like it? The boy I talked to mentioned a photograph of her husband that clearly shows what she describes as a bite mark. What might that tell you?"

"You're telling me what, Grampy?"

"It was a bite, Richard...not some war injury." He gazed upon a hesitant young face. Bewildered, he thought.

"You're telling me a little girl could take out a chunk of meat that big, Grampy?

"If you help me dig out the file from my stuff in the basement, I'll show you a photograph when it was fresh. The date on the picture will no way reconcile with the war, Richard. It will reconcile with the time I had sessions with Monica Lewski."

"Then what?"

"I'd hope Mister Beecham's photograph is dated, too. They used to be dated, you know."

"Does anyone else know about any of this?" Richard asked. "The wound...the bite...whatever the hell you want to call it. Are you telling me not even Alexsandr knows this?"

"Help me find the file. I'll have you take it back with you. Read it, protect it. Let's go. I have a long day ahead of me."

Richard put the car in gear, pulled off the shoulder. He headed for the Interstate.

"How's Lalinduh?" asked Grampy, as Richard merged into traffic on the Interstate.

"Just fine," said Richard, as he cracked a satisfied little smile. "I think I like her, Grampy."

"She likes you, Richard," he replied. "But watch yourself...she's got a lively streak buried behind the facade. She's...uh...experienced. She was nervous this morning...excited. Asking me what she ought to wear, stuff like that."

"You think I'll do okay? I haven't had a date in so long I don't know what to do any more."

"Just be yourself, Richard. You'll be fine."

"Grampy...how come nothing ever developed when Monica Lewski was running wild?" he asked. "If several other people knew about this stuff, how come nothing ever came to the surface? Why has it taken all these years for the pieces to fit together?"

"Well, Richard. Look at it. Look at the real story and you tell me?"

"Do you think this newspaper guy had the story and it was crunched?"

"I think so; but not just the story but him too," he said. "We will never know if we can't find him. He could well be dead and gone by now."

"I can see why a newspaper would not want to run a story like that...credibility and all that stuff?"

"You've got it all wrong, Richard. The newspaper was...and still is...owned by the powers. It runs nothing that may draw attention to their mischief. I have a feeling not only did they crunch the story, they crunched the reporter, too."

"You're saying the powers are behind what happened to Monica Lewski?"

"That is the part I have not figured out completely...let's just say they had a lot to do with it."

"You're telling me these powers you always talk about can conjure up a demon if they need one?"

"No," he replied, softly. "They can make one any time they want to. There is a difference."

What in the world have I stepped into this time? He wondered about it. "Make a demon, Grampy?"

"She was a vessel, Richard."

"Would you explain that, please?"

"They took a little girl, stripped her of everything that made her human."

"The +1 super empty?"

"They probably had her working customers in a brothel at a very young age...maybe long before I set eyes upon her. What they didn't count on was a power stronger than they ever dreamed possible took over their handiwork."

"Possession?"

"But you said the mother pleaded for you to help her? Surely, she would have known."

"I'm sure she did. I'm sure she was a working girl a long time before I met her. She was acting, Richard. Playing a part to get what she wanted. She used me...a good excuse, if you will, to keep the girl out of school, keep her busy, so to speak. To keep people from asking too many questions. I was such an arrogant and pompous ass I never thought for a moment that might be the case. I played right into her hands."

"So that's what you were driving at when you asked me about using street drugs to restrain an unruly child?"

"I think the little girl fought like hell to hold onto her human side. They probably used drugs, kept her under lock and key. She probably never saw daylight until her services were in demand."

"That's awful, Grampy. Sick...really sick."

"It gets worse, Richard. She gets pregnant just about as soon as she comes of age. Rather than abort the baby, a boy, they see another opportunity to tailor-make another worker...probably worth ten times what the mother is because of the aversion to homosexuality in these parts. They probably made a fortune off the boy. Now, many years after a quirk of Fate frees him from his bondage, the boy strikes back...the human side...as perverse as it is...stews for years on end then breaks free in the only way it knows how."

"Jacob Lewski?"

"Jacob Lewski, trapped in an awful and unspeakably degrading childhood, strikes back."

"Nobody is going to believe you...you know that don't you?"

"No. For a lot of reasons they won't. That's where you come in. They'll never believe me, but here's your chance, Richard, to put another crack in that underbelly...you might as well start now. You'll be fighting it all your life."

"You set me up didn't you?"

"Not exactly."

"Tell me something, Grampy."

"What?"

"What have you got in store for Ladonna?"

"Oh, she's got a hell of a fight on her hands...and I had very little to do with it. Be patient, Richard. You'll both do the right thing when the time comes. You'll see. Like I said, you two stick with me, and I'll show you how to fight the good fight."

Richard smiled, weakly. "Are we going to have to run with the rats to do it?"

"I hope not. But you will have to think like the rats to do it right."

"Great...just great. I can hardly wait," he said, sarcastically.

In a few more minutes they would pull up in front of Grampy's house. They did not speak too much for the last few miles. They were both, in their own ways, lost in thought. By the time they pulled into the driveway, Richard had thought things through.

"Grampy?" he asked, as he parked the car and turned off the engine. "If you had photographic proof, your records, and stuff why did you stay silent all this time?"

"Honest to God, Richard...I thought I would get laughed out of town. I never told a soul. I guess I was afraid to go forward with what I knew. I was too damned arrogant to put my budding reputation at risk."

"Do you have any regrets?"

"As I said before...I might have saved that girl," Grampy replied. "For that I can never forgive myself. However, there is a bright side."

"I'm afraid I don't see it, Grampy."

They walked side-by-side toward the porch.

"If things go right, you'll be able to take on the task...armed with the things I didn't have...witnesses, photographs, a recording I hope will shed a lot of light on this matter. If that newspaper man can be found, maybe he will have enough to really build a very convincing case." Grampy smiled. "Enough valid documentation to take on the powers and maybe, just maybe, kick their collective assess right out of the county."

They walked up the steps, opened the front door, and stepped inside. Grampy lost no time heading for the basement. He opened the basement door, turned on the light.

"This way, Richard...watch these steps."

Grampy moved slowly, as if each step was a separate and pain-filled experience. Richard followed close behind.

"Over there, in the corner. Under the canvas tarp."

Richard moved toward the grubby tarp, pulled it back.

Two small stacks of old cardboard boxes were exposed.

Grampy moved closer to the boxes.

"They're kind of arranged in alphabetical order. Open the boxes, check the tabs on the file folders."

One-by-one Richard went through the contents of the boxes until he found the one he was looking for. He thumbed through the folders. He pulled one out.

"Here we go, Grampy. Monica Lewski." He blew some dust off of it. "That's a thick file, Grampy."

"That it is. I thought, at the time, I was as thorough as I could ever be."

Richard thumbed through it quickly.

"Bring it upstairs to my desk, Richard. We'll take a quick look, for your benefit. Then you take it with you. Get back to me tomorrow and I'll have the tape for you."

Richard handed him the tape.

"Otherwise I might forget and take it with me. You have not heard it yet?"

"No."

After painfully going back up the steps, Grampy led the way to his desk.

"Put it down, open it, and spread the contents. I want you to see the photograph in particular."

Richard found the photograph. It was well preserved.

"Damn, Grampy. How the hell did you get this picture?"

"I held the camera out in front of myself and snapped it. Hurt like hell, Richard. But look past the wound. It is not the wound that is important...look at the date. I put my desk calendar in the picture to document things. I thought I was so damn smart in those days! Look on the edge of the photograph."

"Damn, Grampy."

"Credible?"

"I'd say. That had to hurt! You lost a lot of blood, didn't you?"

"I packed that hole with everything I could find right after I took that picture. I thought I would bleed to death before I could get to the hospital. I was practically unconscious when I got there. It seemed like it took forever to get to help."

"Now...look through the papers when you get some time."

"I sure will, Grampy."

"Okay, now...to change the subject...do you need any money for tonight?"

"I've got a few bucks, Grampy."

"No. You have to impress this girl, Richard. Here," he insisted, reaching for his wallet. He thumbed through some bills and handed him eighty dollars in twenties. "Spoil her...if you can still spoil a girl for that kind of money." He grinned, and he then made a clicking sound with his lips and teeth. "I think she likes you a lot. Don't take that for granted. Lalinduh is a swell girl." He then gathered the papers and put them back in the folder. "Take this. I don't want you to think I throwing you out, but Alexsandr and Heinz are coming over. I don't want them to get wind of this folder's contents. Guard it with your life, Richard. There's power here. Real power."

"Can I copy some of this stuff...for compilation purposes?"

"Sure. It belongs to you now...I failed when I should have shown some guts, Richard. Don't you do the same, okay? I'm counting on you to do the right thing."

Richard tucked the folder under his arm.

"I'll show myself out, Grampy. I'll get back to you tomorrow."

"Remember...show her a good time."

"Right, Grampy."

With that, Richard left the house. Grampy sat behind his desk, to think things over. He scribbled two names on a note pad:

Alba Beecham.

Ralph Whalen.

Underneath the names he wrote:

Have the guy find them. Gather information. Borrow or photograph Beecham photograph. Get the full story from Whalen, if he will talk.

Then, from his desk drawer, he withdrew a diary. He opened to the next available page, dated it, and then he made his latest entry:

I shall ramble today. It has been a bad day for me, and I'm disinclined to discipline my writing. I will write generally and, as always, to Richard. In what order I cannot say. Today, I have decided, I will close a few chapters in my life and try, if possible, to cleanse my soul.

Things have turned. After all these years, I can finally expose the depth of corruption from which sprang forth this tragic character, Monica Lewski.

I am saddened, indeed, by the turn of events recently. It now seems probable there were other people in Nohartinit who knew this story. Blinded by my arrogance, my self-interest, I thought I was the only living soul to witness the ferociousness of authentic demonic possession. My arrogance, my drive, my self-interest seems to have been not only instrumental in the eventual destruction of this child, but also may have, inadvertently, contributed to the unfolding of other recent events, through the heart, mind, and soul (what is left of it) of her son, Jacob.

I have given my complete file on the Monica Lewski case to my grandson Richard.

I have trusted to him the great burden of doing what is right. He will put together the Monica Lewski tragedy with material I will supply.

Through this information about this tragedy I am, in fact, depending on his good character and his sincere desire to do good to put into the public's eye the depth of corruption that has plagued this city for decades now.

Richard does not yet understand the powers that practically own this city. I have warned him he will have to fight them all his life. It is a sad legacy we older folks have handed down, but we did the best we could.

Alexsandr and Heinz are coming here tonight. We are going to plot and plan a way to save our butts. This police investigation of our past so-called crimes is getting out of hand. We have been implicated in the Milly's debacle, and this investigator, Bud Elbudro, has proposed a deal with Alexsandr. I so wish Elbudro had let his cold file be, but it is too late for regrets. We must outfox this fellow, if we are to save our good names and reputations.

Alexsandr, of course, will say nothing. How could he? I will not either; I would rather die than betray my dear friends. Heinz will probably not get involved unless he has no choices left, and I am not sure the rest of us can trust him now.

He will save himself at any cost, I think.

We know, Alexsandr, Heinz, myself, and others, we all know we did what we had to do to serve and preserve good. The powers were weakened by our efforts.

We cannot and we do not lay claim to a victory. They are too strong and too many for us to have defeated by our seemingly feeble efforts.

We are faced with the awesome realization that by our efforts we have defeated ourselves. The people of Nohartinit still have no established and pervasive public morality that veers toward the good. We have not succeeded in moving the peoples' hearts and minds to the good, but, by doing what we could, we have placed ourselves in the position wherein we cannot hope for these new generations to understand, much less forgive, the things we had to do to bring them the little safety and the security they do have.

We are doomed. If anyone cared, we would be seen, once we are dead and gone, as tragic heroes of a by-gone era. But it will not happen. We will, and we all know it but deny it to ourselves and to each other, we are going to be called to account for our actions. We will not be able to face our new generations and convince them that past days were different, calling for different ways of doing things.

They will no doubt call us vile names. They will think we are barbarians. What do they know? They know only the way of rules and regulations and they spend very little time thinking about what it took to bring even these things into being. They have them, they use them, and they are satisfied. They do not care who brought them the little peace and security they now enjoy, nor are they interested in the price those people paid.

Our only hope, this old bunch soon to be gone, is to be judged by a few living souls, a tiny few of whom might, God willing, put everything in a right and proper perspective and see us not as butchers and vigilantes but as soldiers. We put on the full armor of God, and they will hate us, denounce us, and probably break us for it. We have, at stake, our lives as we have lived them; we tried to do right things. Nobody, save perhaps a minimum few, will care.

We will, all of us, go into the ground, disgraced in the eyes of the people we have served.

I am old; I deny it no longer. I hurt. My bones. My joints. It is testing to even get up in the morning. I will soon meet my Maker. May God forgive me for my many sins. May God see that my intentions were honorable, after they lay me down, when I stand before Him.

My latest checkup was not good. I am old. Worn out. Seventy-four years I have plod this Earth; I am tired. I have not told my grandson I am leaving soon. I have chosen, instead, to fight to my last breath. He,

Richard, will be a worthy ally. The powers will, I hope, hate him, too. If he does the right thing with what he has, they will hate him, as they will hate me even though I will be in the ground.

Grampy paused for a moment. He had to think about something. He knew where his next entries were going, but he was not sure...not yet...whether to implicate the killer of Monica Lewski's mother. He knew what it could do. To Alexsandr. To Rachael. To Heinz. To all of them. Richard. Ladonna.

I know what lies ahead of me, he wrote. He rubbed his eyes. They were burning, welling with tears. Then he continued his entries:

I shall die soon. My body shall go back to dust. So be it. It has been a wonderful journey, this thing called life. I am too worn out to fight the inevitable any more.

I am torn, at this stage, between what is right and proper and what is best left unsaid. I do not know which way to turn. If I stall off my final confession, I will surely face the Master with sorrow in my heart. I cannot face the Master if I hide human frailty behind the cloak of righteousness. He, and none other, can make that call.

I must trust my grandson, to whom this diary goes when I am gone, to do the right thing. It is, I guess, not a simple matter of propriety that I must confess what I know. It is, because of all things, imperative, I let the good among us do their choosing; they must decide, when I am gone, if I did, in fact, do the right thing, by giving up a secret heretofore known but to a few and God Almighty, Himself.

I shall, in coming days, bare my soul in these pages, that future generation may learn something about duty and honor and loyalty to human institutions; these new generations of people must make their own decisions about such things.

May God forgive me if I have chosen wrongly, but I give up, to my grandson Richard, the name of the killer of Milly Lewski. Milly Lewski was a most vile and vicious and mean-spirited human being, Her death was a turning point for the good people of Nohartinit.

It is, before I name the one, my intention to make clear my position on this issue. The person I am handing over to the wolves is an honorable and sincere person, a messenger, I think, from the world outside our comprehension or understanding.

It is said the angels which watch over the little ones look upon the face of God every day.

Richard, please forgive this transgression, but you have to make the call. Monica Lewski's mother, Milly, was killed by none other than Rachael Simon.

What you do with this information is up to you. I am too far into the situation to make a clean call on this.

Before you rush to judgment, discern good. Rachael has dedicated her life to helping children, as you know. She has worked with children as far back as anyone can remember, long before the Milly's debacle, she was doing what she could.

She has always loved children.

Hundreds of children in Nohartinit have benefited, either directly or indirectly, by her selflessness and her dedication to children's causes.

I cannot count the numbers of changes in Nohartinit in behalf of children that have sprung from her presence and involvement.

She knew, as did Alexsandr, Heinz, myself, and others, Milly exploited children for profit, in unspeakable ways, through her brothel. You can imagine, I guess, what went on in her establishment. The depths of depravity as you might fabricate them in your worst nightmare would probably pale in comparison to the realities of what went on behind closed doors in that place.

We put a stop to it. We shut it down.

One evening, late, we gathered among ourselves, and decided the time had come to shut her down. We armed ourselves, men and women alike, with ax handles and baseball bats, and put masks over our faces, and attacked the place.

Our plan was to free the children and literally destroy the place. We never planned to kill anyone, but we did not guard against the possibility. We wanted an end to the exploitation, to shut her down forever.

I won't try to whitewash what Rachael did. The Commandment is: Thou Shall Not Murder.

She killed.

Once inside the building, Rachael confronted Milly and, raging at what she perceived as the embodiment of evil, she began to strike out at her, wildly and ferociously. I, myself, was sickened by what I saw inside the place. I can only imagine what went through Rachael's mind. She, literally, would kill for the children. She would still, I think.

This night, she unleashed energy and power no one could have guessed a woman of her size could muster. Her love for children fed her unrestrained fury.

She bashed Milly's head in with an ax handle.

161

She had not let up her attack until most of Milly's head was an oozing mass of blood, brain, and hair.

We found her standing over the body, blood-splattered and exhausted, and frozen in her tracks, crying out time after time: "Die bitch! Die bitch!"

She was panting and gasping for air, chanting hysterically, and seemingly hypnotized by her handiwork. We had to pry the bloody ax handle from her hands and forcefully remove her from the premises. She fought us like a wildcat, demanding to be let alone to watch the blood flow from Milly's body. She had, as you people say these days, flipped out and no one was around to rein in her fury until it was too late.

We were trashing the place, and, in the chaos, it was everyone for himself. People, young and old, men, women, and, of course, the children, were frantically running everywhere, yelling and screaming, and the sounds of destruction rebounded off the walls.

We were convinced we did the right thing in human eyes...and we, human animals that we are, hid it all these years from everyone but the Almighty.

Richard, we have discussed the discernment of good, you and I. Have we, you and me and the rest of them, got the right to make that call?

We did, my dear grandson. We made the call. You have no conceptual understanding of how corrupt Nohartinit was back in those days.

We've paid a heavy price ever since.

Richard, you have to call it from now on, I can't do it for you. The powers are your problem now. Fight them hard when ever and where ever you can.

God bless you and guide you. Please forgive me, Richard, and pray for me when I am gone. We did it for the children.

With all my love, Grampy.

Grampy closed his diary.

He was not sure if he would return to it this day. He put it back in the drawer. It is time, he thought. I have to hear the tape.

"I'm not sure I want to do this," he murmured. "Oh, well. Here we go."

He walked slowly into his den, and he put the tape into his tape player. "At least I get to seal my Fate in stereo," he whispered. He then turned the tape player on, and he sat back in his favorite overstuffed chair, to listen.

Chapter Fifteen

"Good God, Almighty!" hissed Grampy as the tape came to the end. "May God have mercy on our souls!"

Chapter Sixteen

Six o'clock rolled around. Grampy was waiting on his porch when Alexsandr, Heinz, and another man drove up. Grampy was looking out at the lake, wishing for fishing instead of fighting for his own survival.

The man with them was a tall, muscular fellow, with a buzz cut, wearing jeans, a sweatshirt and tennis shoes. He looked like a recruit fresh out of Basic Training. He looked to Grampy he might be lucky to be scraping twenty-five, more likely just past legal drinking age; you've got to be kidding, he thought, as they approached.

Heinz introduced the young man, after they climbed the steps to the porch. Normally, Grampy would have stood up for a proper introduction, but he was not up to it.

"Skug Findfello," said Heinz. "This is Grampy."

He extended his hand, and Grampy shook hands with him. "Have a seat," said Grampy. "Nothing personal, but you look kind of young to be a Private Investigator."

Skug smiled. "Oh, no. I'm not licensed yet. I'm sitting in for my father. He'll be in tomorrow. He couldn't make the trip on such short notice. He asked me to stand in until he gets here."

"Stand in?" asked Grampy. "We're not shooting a movie here." He looked at Heinz, thinking: what kind of nonsense is this?

"It is okay, Grampy," said Heinz. "Skug is very capable, in spite of his youth. I've worked with Skug and his father many times."

Grampy looked at Alexsandr for approval.

Alexsandr shrugged.

"Okay," said Grampy. "Sit down young fellow. Here's what we have to do." Grampy handed him the handwritten note. "These people...you need to find them and get their stories. And any documentation they might have to back up their stories. This one lady Alba Beecham...they call her Beechie...lives in Nohartinit somewhere near the creek. This other one...Ralph Whalen...was a reporter for the local newspaper, until he retired maybe ten years ago. He dropped out of sight. He may be crippled, has a real hard time getting around. He likes art...prints, local stuff...any kind of paintings. He might carry an ornate cane with some kind of head carved on it. That's all I have to go on right now. One other thing, you might check the old folks home for collaborating stories. You never know. Get the stories on tape, if you can."

"That's it?"

"That's all there is," replied Grampy.

"Hmm," Skug said. He tucked the note in his jeans pocket. "What stories am I looking for?"

Grampy grinned. He looked at Alexsandr and then at Heinz. "You didn't tell him?"

"Oh, no, Grampy. He knows absolutely nothing. I might have to work with him again," replied Heinz cheerfully. He twitched his moustache. "You do the telling."

"Okay, young man," replied Grampy, seriously. "A few things, call them conditions, okay? First we need absolute secrecy. This stays among us, okay?"

"Okay. Heinz will vouch for me."

"I will."

"We're going to need a copy of Mrs. Beecham's photograph of her husband. It shows a big scar on his forearm. She keeps it somewhere in her house."

"Okay. I can do that," Skug said, confidently. "The stories?"

"We're looking for a monster...a woman with red eyes, fangs like a wolf, and claws instead of hands."

Skug laughed. "Okay," he said, playfully. "Your dime." He noticed quickly he was the only one among them who found it amusing. When he realized they were serious, he apologized. "Good God...you're serious?" he said. "This is for real?"

He looked at Heinz for confirmation. Heinz nodded his head ever so slightly.

"You're not just pulling my leg? You really want me to find a red-eyed monster woman?"

"Yeah," snipped Heinz. "We're serious, Skug."

"Good God...Dad's going to shit his drawers when he hears this!"

"You're not going to back out, are you?" asked Grampy.

"No...no. Hell no."

"And one last thing...anything you find comes straight to me. And when you're done, you never heard of me or seen anything concerning this monster."

Alexsandr spoke up. "We'll give you fifty bucks apiece, pocket money, for any original document or photograph you can get. No fakes; this is, believe it or not, very important stuff."

"Any questions?"

"Can I keep any souvenirs?"

"Absolutely not."

"Another question?" asked Skug.

"Sure?"

"What's this for?"

"My grandson is a writer, that is, wants to be a writer...he heard the story from some kids; he wants to write the tale and get rich and famous and all that. Maybe he can put Nohartinit on a real map," Grampy answered, off the top of his head. "He's all I have...money is no object, if you're wondering why you are being paid so well just to find a story or two let's just say I want to see the boy succeed."

"We all have a stake in this boy," said Heinz.

"Sounds like a lucky guy," said Skug. "I'll see what I can do. Will I get to meet him? I've never had much dealings with writers."

"Some other time, perhaps," said Grampy. "He's got a date tonight. Maybe another time."

"Has his girl got a sister by any chance?" replied Skug, lightheartedly.

"Yeah," said Heinz. "She's got red eyes, claws and fangs...I can set you up if you want?" He chuckled.

Skug laughed. "Sounds like I'm going to meet her, anyway, right?" he said.

"Can I ask you something?" mumbled Grampy.

"Sure. Anything at all."

"Where the hell did you get a name like Skug?"

"The kids in school tagged me. 'Skinny, knot-headed, ugly guy'. I just kept it. No great mystery there."

"Sounds to me like you were not well liked?" said Alexsandr, with a dry grin.

"I really couldn't tell you, Alexsandr, because I never really gave a damn what any of them thought. I've been working with my Dad since I was about sixteen...I knew what I was going to be and where I was going to be before most of those kids had their first driver's license. They didn't bother me. There was too much distance between us."

Grampy looked at Skug. I'm beginning to like this kid, he thought. "Tell me something, Skug? How long before I might be able to see something?" he asked.

"I'll have something in the next day or two. Dad will be here tomorrow. Don't worry, Grampy. We do good work. One last question: Is there anything out there to collaborate the stories? Time is money. Stories are easy to get. Proof...of something like this? That's something else entirely different."

"Hey, if you find proof, you have proof, right?" said Heinz. He twitched his moustache. "Just don't come back with claws and red eyeballs, okay?"

Skug laughed.

"And no fangs...I hate fangs," joked Alexsandr.

They all had a good laugh. The Grampy explained the situation. "We're not expecting miracles, Skug. Just find what you can," answered Grampy. "Other than this one old woman's story, there may be nothing at all. That's what we're paying you to find out, isn't it. Just keep an open mind...stranger things have happened."

Skug nodded. Then smiled widely. "Hey, if I find this red-eyed monster woman...I'll bring her here on a silver platter. If I even smell the possibility of something real, you couldn't hogtie me with bridge cable until I get to the bottom of it." He looked at his watch. "Heinz, can you take me back to my motel now. I've got some things I have to do."

Skug shook Grampy's hand. "It'll be a pleasure working for you," he said.

"You want me to wait until I hear from you?"

"I'll have something soon," he said. "Me and my Dad...we don't mess around, Grampy. We're good. But how much is enough? When do we pull the plug?"

Heinz chuckled. "Skug...if you find this red-eyed monster, trust your instincts. I'm sure you will figure out when enough is enough."

Skug laughed, as did Alexsandr and Grampy. He and Heinz turned to go.

"I'm telling you, Heinz. Dad's going to shit his pants when he hears this."

"I'd love to see his face when you come dragging this red-eyed monster bitch into your motel room!" joked Heinz.

"Ready?" asked Skug.

"Ready. Anything new? How much longer before you get your license? How's your Dad? Everything okay?"

They were about to start down the steps, when Grampy spoke. "One last thing before you go, Skug. Keep your inquiries discreet. Some of the older folks around here don't like strangers snooping into local stuff. Going around Nohartinit talking about she-monsters isn't going to win you many friends."

Alexsandr tapped Grampy gently on his shoulder. "Are you doing okay?" he whispered. He motioned for the others to go ahead. They started down the steps.

"Fine," he said. "I'm still alive, Alexsandr."

Whispering again, he said, "Take care of yourself, Grampy. I'll be in touch." He shook his head. "This is the most hair-brained idea you've ever had, Grampy."

"Do you think this kid will come up with anything useful?"

"Who knows," answered Alexsandr. "What have we got to lose, Grampy? We're reaching into the barrel this time, Grampy…this one tops them all."

Alexsandr then went down the steps, got into the car, and they, together, drove away.

Grampy watched them go. "What have we got to lose, Alexsandr?" Then he spoke his answer into thin air. "Everything, Alexsandr. Everything."

Grampy was relieved, in a way, however, with all of the joking going on, it was obvious Heinz and Alexsandr had no idea about what really happened to Monica Lewski. This would make his job that much easier. "I sure hope that kid doesn't get hurt. I kind of like him."

Meanwhile, back in Nohartinit, Richard tapped on the door of Lalinduh's apartment, Number Three, Pine Ridge Apartments. She opened it, and smiled. She invited him in. Wearing just a white slip, she asked him to be seated on the sofa while she finished dressing.

"Sorry I'm late," he said. "I got caught up in some paperwork."

"No problem. I'm running late, too," she said, with a healthy smile. "I'll be ready in just a minute." She moved to a bedroom. She peeked out from the open bedroom door. "What should I wear? Have you planned the evening…or are we going to wing it?"

"Just pick something you feel comfortable in," said Richard. "Be yourself."

"Are you going to take me to dinner?"

"Sure. What time do you usually eat? Early? Late? What are you in the mood for, anyway? Something fancy? Something so-so? Any preference?"

"I'm not up to fancy tonight," she said. "Make it casual. Let's just have fun…just plain old-fashioned fun."

She picked out a simple blue shift and put on a delicate necklace, but then she decided against it.

She came back into the living room, to find Richard walking around, looking the place over.

"You look nice," he said.

"I live a simple life, as you can see. I try to keep things uncomplicated."

"I guessed as much…no TV, no stereo, no pets. That's a good thing, Lalinduh. These days, I would give anything for a simple, uncomplicated life."

"Been pretty busy?"

"Oh, yes. Very busy."

"How's the thesis coming? Seems like you've been working on it forever."

"How'd you know about the thesis?"

"Grampy told me."

"That figures."

She moved closer, wrapped her arms around his neck. She looked deep into his eyes.

Imitating some sultry voice she had heard somewhere, she explained, "He told me to show you a good time."

But she could not keep it up.

She backed away, laughing shyly. Her huge brown eyes flashed playfully. "Sorry, I can't keep a straight face and do that."

Richard was left standing, speechless.

Then he joined the laughter. "It did seem a little out of character, Lalinduh, although Grampy also says you are...uh...experienced?"

"I like you," she said. She reached for his hand. "Come on...I think we're going to have a lot of fun tonight."

They joined hands, and moved toward the door.

Richard opened the door, and stepped aside to let Lalinduh go through first. He followed her out, and closed the door behind him.

"My car or yours?" she asked.

"Pick one, and we're gone."

Chapter Seventeen

This afternoon Alexsandr and Heinz came by. The investigator was with them. I visited with the investigator, a young man who calls himself SKUG. He is off to investigate the stories surrounding this creature I believe to have been Monica Lewski. He seems like a nice young fellow. I sure hope he doesn't get too far toward the powers in his investigative work. His father, of whom he seems to be quite proud, will join him tomorrow. I will feel a lot better with an experienced person working with this youngster.

Alexsandr and Heinz do not seem to attach any credibility to the monster-woman story, and this serves everybody quite well at this time.

I have turned over all my records to Richard, including the old but all-important photograph. He is convinced now that something happened, and my own explanation is about as clear as anything he has to go by.

It is my feeling he will start compiling his data very soon.

If the investigator does what I think he will Richard's job will be a little easier. Soon, however, I will have to expand on the numbers of people who know what Monica Lewski was all about. Our attack on Milly's has come back to haunt us. Alexsandr is protected against testifying against Rachael. I guess, if it all comes down to it, we will simply take the Fifth or go Presidential and lose our memories until all this blows over.

I have a funny feeling Bud is not going to let this rest. I have no idea what Detrick is up to, and I doubt he has either the skill or the ability to make sense of everything.

This investigating team is not likely to stay involved, even if they find what I hope they do. They have no reason to. And if I know Heinz, he has something by which to gain their complete cooperation if he has to.

My biggest problem right now is whether to expose the information or keep it under wraps...perhaps even destroy it, right along with the +1 scenario. I hope we can convince the District Attorney we can cast a lot of doubt against anything Bud might come up with. Maybe everyone will agree to leave it alone and let bygones be bygones.

I cannot, personally, see why anyone would want to go after Rachael, if we ever get the chance to put everything in a right perspective. I don't think we will have that opportunity because I find it hard to believe Bud would seriously consider it. Yet, as he says, there is no statute of limitations on murder. All he stands to gain is to clear his cold case. Nobody really cares about Milly's death any more. Nobody. Bud, himself, referred to it as a public service.

How strange it is, how times change. But people do not change too much. If Rachael killed an enemy in combat, no one would say a word. But we were in a war, of sorts, a war against wrong things, evil things.

All of us have gone on to build good and decent lives. We have a city that is by far less corrupt than it was when we started out to clean it up. Surely, that must count for something. But, more than that, I hope that Rachael comes through this not too badly damaged. I doubt if Alexsandr has said anything to her yet.

For many years now I have known Rachael. She is a kind and gentle woman who loves children. She has spent host of her life...and that is a long time now...helping children in any way she could.

Not many people know Rachael deep inside where it really counts. She has had a good life with Alexsandr. They had two children, only one of whom survived the early years. They lost a daughter to polio many years ago. Their son, Jeffery, grew up healthy, married Sarah McKee, from Mayberight. Rachael's granddaughter, Ladonna, is an absolute gem.

In time, people may find out what we are planning right now. Again, we will have to face the choices...to preserve what is good or surrender to powers that would destroy us all. Not a one of us will deny we regretted...even mourned...the death of that awful woman, Milly Lewski.

But mostly, our hearts and our minds were set on freeing the children she had held in unspeakable bondage. We found six girls, the oldest of whom was maybe nine at the most, and we found a boy in his early teens...with no clue or hint he was, as time has shown us, Milly's own grandson, Jacob. The children were dispersed among waiting families we had brought in from all surrounding communities. They were to be moved away, just as the slaves were moved away in like times; their whereabouts, most of them to this day, we do not know. We got the children into safe and loving hands, and we never pried into matters after that. In some ways, I guess, our raid was a success. Milly was out of business and her establishment gone forever, and we saved the children. How Jacob fell away I will never know.

Did we do anything more right or more wrong than those who operated the underground railroads of yesteryear? Of course, we had a casualty. So what?

I believe in my old heart, Rachael is one of the very few of the originals involved in what we called the clean-up campaign to have never surrendered her soul to what we did there. Understandably, she never prided herself on having done her part. How could she? But I know she has never again assaulted the values lines without them being first unmistakably and clearly defined. She, of all the originals, has admitted she did not do right, but merely served right...she did the right thing in the wrong way.

I never agreed with her assessment, and she has never deviated from it.

One thing I would like to do in this life before I go is to find one of those children and just say hello. I am curious. I think I am entitled to that curiosity.

None of us knows if we got to the children before their souls were permanently ruined. I pray God, Jacob Lewski is not typical of what Milly and the powers did to those children. If he is, our years of silence, our years of private anguish have been in vain. We will have failed. Perhaps, now that I think of it, we may be better off not knowing what became of those children. Without knowing, all of us, what few are left of the originals, can at least die in some kind of peace when our times come. I can go to my grave knowing, at least, somewhere is a child who, because I cared, got a second chance.

Soon, I will invent this mythical creature that may save us from the hangman. I don't think I will name this creature Monica...because that child has a special place in my life. I will get with Richard and Alexsandr and Heinz and invent a name.

I guess now all we can do is wait. I hate to wait for our investigators to uncover what I already know. I am curious just how many people knew about this child.

Monica still troubles me...where was she the night we raided Milly's? Milly died, if I remember right, about the time Jacob would have been fifteen. That would have put Monica somewhere around thirty when she died. Yet our man Jacob says he buried his mother just a few years ago...he is still paying off the bill for her funeral?

There's something wrong here! There is something very wrong here!

Grampy put down his pen. He shut his diary. He ripped a piece of paper from a note pad, and drew a time line and did some basic math. He figured and refigured.

"They're all liars," he hissed. He wadded up the notepaper, and he threw it away. "Why would a prostitute ever tell the truth about her age?"

He opened his diary again.

Having broken away for a few moments to do some calculations, I have come up with a most disturbing conclusion. The chronology makes sense. Monica was not present the night of the raid on Milly's. Her son was there. So where was Monica? Here's what I think happened:

I believe Jacob's birth certificate is authentic, except the girl giving birth was not Monica Lewski. It was someone who took her name, gave birth to a boy. Whoever this mystery woman is, she kept the identity, which explains, in part, why Monica never showed up again...but by surrogacy. I believe Monica gave birth in the brothel.

I believe Monica was kept around long enough to nurse the baby, to assure his good health for future purposes.

It is noted Jacob has a huge scar on his forearm that he says was a bite from his mother. I believe this to be true...except the chunk was taken out of him when he was a very small baby or, perhaps, a toddler. I would guess, fearing for the baby's life after being bitten severely by his mother, Milly did not kill her daughter, Monica, but simply handed the boy over to a new woman, who, for practical purposes was his real mother. As Jacob grew, the wound would become more pronounced, taking on the appearance of a wound to a full size man. Milly probably kept Monica around until her usefulness...or her rage...made it necessary to dispose of her. There is no question Jacob saw his mother, for he described precisely what I saw. Yet, I would guess he was probably but a small child at the time.

From what I can gather, Jacob never had anything to do with his mother, and quit school at his first opportunity. He said he took on debt to bury her, and saw her buried. Because she was headed for a pauper's grave, Jacob probably never laid eyes upon the body, but merely assumed, from her identity, it was she. He has, I guess, spent his money and has paid dearly for a burial for a woman he probably never in his lifetime even met. His mother, Monica, probably lived but three or four years beyond his birth.

It is my guess there is absolutely no legitimate paper trail of Monica Lewski in existence, except what rests in my own notebooks. To accommodate the powers, for all the world knew, Monica Lewski was never born, thus she never lived, and thus she never died.

She probably ended up in a shallow grave somewhere...where, in all probability, she will sleep for eternity without so much as a marker bearing her name.

It is safe to assume the case file for Monica Lewski could have been closed many, many years ago.

I believe also, my bite mark and that of Jacob Lewski will not match very closely...they will be from the same source, but not of anything near the approximate same age for Monica. She was smaller and younger when I was bitten. The character of the scar in the Beecham photograph will be close to that of my own, which tells me that Mister Beecham used the child, through Milly, for his entertainment and pleasure. That his wife claims to have seen the monster tells me she dragged him out of Milly's at a most inopportune time.

That the daughter says it is a war wound means she probably knows the truth...or at least part of it.

At this time, I'd almost guarantee our investigating team would come back from the Beecham residence empty handed.

Still hanging in all of this is the reporter Ralph Whalen. Will he talk? There are two possibilities, neither of which is very good. First, if Lalinduh is right and this badly crippled old man she described is Mister Whalen he will not talk. I have a feeling, from the nature of the condition his legs appeared to be in, he got too close to the powers and they persuaded him to lose his story. The other prospect is that he is dead and gone...and his information is gone with him.

I am surprised the powers have let us live as long as we have. I have to wonder why. Is it is a sad thing the bunch of us must move toward speculation instead of facts. I have facts, even the photograph, but that is not enough. If the investigators do not turn up anything, we may have a very hard time formulating some kind of strategy.

Maybe, if the investigators come up with nothing, we will, after all, have to find us a bachelor in the cemetery, name him as a member of the originals and dump everything on his grave. I get so tired of having to trash good people to fight the powers!

They are still very much an influence behind the scenes in Nohartinit. At times, I am like Bud in that I am tired, sick-to-death tired of seeing lives wasted and squandered to feed the powers. I, too, often wonder if the good guys are winning or just barely hanging in. What to do?

I'm going to sleep on it. Maybe it has to be left to God to get a breakthrough. I will pray tonight and see what tomorrow brings. I will pray for Rachael.

No more entries this day: Grampy.

Chapter Eighteen

"I love Saturday mornings, don't you?" said Lalinduh, as she rolled over, and gently stroked Richard's face. Her voice was dry and raspy and calm. Her huge brown eyes were bloodshot but lively. "Wake up." He was somewhere caught between sleep and awareness. He opened his eyes. Lalinduh was inches from his face, smiling, her dark, bloodshot eyes shining. Her breath smelled like beer.

"Wow!...what happened?" He looked around. She shone against an exceptionally bright blue sky. The rising sun hurt his eyes. He saw huge pines everywhere. He sat up. "Where are we?" he mumbled.

"Outdoors...in the middle of the woods somewhere...I don't remember exactly where."

Richard sat up, propping himself up with stiff arms. He found himself sitting in a rolling field of high green grass splattered here and there with bright yellow wildflowers, surrounded on all sides by tall pines. "Wow." Scattered on the ground around them were what seemed to be maybe a couple of dozen clear glass beer bottles...all of them apparently empty.

"How'd we get here?"

"I don't remember?"

"Ah...Lalinduh?"

"Hmm?"

"Where's the car?"

"I don't remember. Out there...somewhere, past the pines?"

He uncovered himself, exposing his bare chest to the morning sun. "Where'd the blanket come from?"

"No idea. It is safe to assume we brought it with us."

"You don't talk much first thing in the morning, do you, Lalinduh?"

"Nope." She snuggled close by his side and kissed him. She pulled the blue thermal blanket toward her. "Hold me...I'm cold."

He put an unsteady arm around her waist, and held her tightly. She moved it a little lower. He let it rest there. He looked around, squinting in the sunlight. His head hurt like he had been hit with a sledgehammer.

"Much better," she said. "You unzipped me last night." She motioned to the back of her dress.

He zipped it. "Not a very big zipper, is it?"

"I put it in myself, makes the thing easier to put on...and take off."

It occurred to him, somewhat hazily and numbly but occurred to him anyway, he had no shirt on. "Lalinduh?"

"Hmm?"

"Do you see my shirt anywhere?"

"Nope. I looked around a little bit. My bra and panties are gone...my shoes, too," she said.

"You know what?"

"What?"

"I don't have a clue where we are." Richard smiled. He held her just a little bit tighter. "But, you know what?"

"What?"

"I had a great time getting here!"

"You sure did," said Lalinduh. "I guess we could just stay here a while until we figure out where we are."

"My shoes are gone, too," said Richard. He stuck his bare feet out from under the blanket and wiggled his toes. "Oh, well...it feels good to go barefooted now and then."

Lalinduh repositioned herself to fit between his legs and back herself up against his bare chest. Richard put both arms around her waist this time, placing his right hand on top of his left. She slowly slid his hands a little lower.

"Yeah, let's just stay here a while until we figure out what to do."

"When the time comes," she said, dryly. "We'll just follow the clothing trail and find our way back home. But...I'm in no rush. I don't think I could walk a straight line if I had to."

"I'm not in any great rush either," he answered. "Where ever we are, I kind of like it here."

"Me, too," She agreed. "But I'd give a twenty for a drink of water right now. I love the beer, but I hate the hangover."

He looked at the beer bottles they had obviously thrown around them. "Tell me we didn't drink two cases of beer? That's not humanly possible."

"I think we left most of one in the car. I think we did, anyway."

"Yeah. Yeah, that's what we did. I remember now...we brought the unopened one with us. But...where are we."

"Hmm...looks like we pressed down a lot of grass last night," said Lalinduh.

"Hmm. We covered a lot of territory, so to speak?"

"That we did. You're quite the explorer," she joked. "I've got to have some water. Come on. Let's see if we can find a creek or something." She stood, stretched, and then extended a hand toward Richard. She grumbled playfully as she helped him get up.

She wrapped the blanket around her shoulders.

"Which way, Lalinduh? Best guess?" She looked like an Indian, he thought. With her dark hair and dark eyes, with the blue blanket draped over her shoulders, she did, in fact, look like an Indian girl heading out for an early morning stroll.

"Geez...umm...that way?" She pointed toward the rising sun.

"East it is."

Side by side, they walked for a few minutes. They did not seem to be heading anywhere except into more pines, more tall grass, more rolling hills.

They stopped near a large pine so Lalinduh could pick a sticker out of her foot. Richard borrowed the trunk of one to pee on. They walked on, she limping ever so slightly. They walked for about fifteen minutes and still saw nothing but more trees up ahead of them. Another fifteen minutes later, they stopped again.

"Maybe if we are real quiet we can hear something...cars, a creek...cows...anything," suggested Richard. They listened intently, but heard nothing that would guide them back to civilization, just wind through the trees and a couple of birds calling in the distance. They had not seen the first sign of any clothing or any more empty beer bottles, and they definitely concluded they were not heading out the way they came in.

"Well, we tried east," said Lalinduh. "No point in going back. Pick one. North? Or South? We have to hit a road sooner or later."

"If nothing else, maybe an old logging road or something?"

"Anything flat would be nice right now," said Lalinduh. "My feet are kind of sensitive. I wouldn't mind walking on some pavement for a while. This soil is pretty gritty, like walking on rough sandpaper."

"Ah, what the heck...head southward," said Richard.

They walked and talked, rested a few times. Finally, from a distance, they heard what sounded like a car, or maybe a pickup truck. They headed toward what they hoped would be a highway, but they were more than willing to settle for a paved road of any kind. They had still not come across a creek, and Lalinduh was playfully complaining now.

"I have got to get a drink! Water. Beer. Pop. I don't care...as long as it is wet."

"Hang on, Lalinduh," said Richard, playfully. "Help is a'comin' soon."

She laughed. Then she stopped. She motioned for him to be quiet. "Listen," she whispered. "Do you hear that?"

"What?"

"Shh!"

"Voices?"

Richard nodded. "I hear it now...somebody sounds pretty mad."

"Over this way," said Lalinduh, as she started walking cautiously toward the source of the voices. Twenty yards away, they saw the land dropped off quickly, where it looked like a road had been cut. As they got closer, the intensity of apparent argument was clear. "I don't recognize the voices...not from here, anyway," she said. Her huge brown eyes glowed expectantly.

"Maybe we better not walk in on them," said Richard, cautiously. "Let's kind of sneak up and check it out first. No telling what's going on down there."

They got low to the ground.

"You wait here while I check it out," said Richard; she refused. "Leave the blanket," he said. They crawled cautiously to the precipice and peered over, and their eyes came to rest on several men in very expensive looking black suits. One of them looked like a stereotypical mobster...black suit, black shirt, and white tie. You have got to be kidding, thought Richard. Two of the men were arguing fiercely, while a third held another man at gunpoint.

Richard motioned for Lalinduh to move back, very quietly. "I know where we are now. Come on," he whispered. As soon as they were far enough away to run without being seen, Richard grabbed her hand, and pulled her up. "Come on...quickly. Say nothing. Run like hell and don't look back." She snatched up the blanket.

They had no sooner started running, than a shot echoed through the trees.

"That's one hell of an argument they must be having," panted Lalinduh as she ran. "I hope they didn't see us!"

Richard just kept running and towing her along, the blue blanket flapping like a flag. They came upon a slight depression and dove for it. A second shot echoed through the trees.

"Lay flat. Don't look up. Give them time to get the hell out of there."

"What's going on?" Lalinduh asked, as she huffed and puffed. Her huge brown eyes glared at him, as if demanding some answers very quickly. "Who are those people down there?"

"Shhh...quietly. Speak softly."

"Well?" she demanded.

"Just like in the movies, Lalinduh. A couple of guys in fancy suits, holding a gun on another guy? They have this huge black car...I think we almost walked into an mob execution or a drug deal gone wrong."

"Damn," she whispered. "What the hell are we going to do now?"

A third shot echoed through the trees.

"Listen I know where we are. That's not a road down there; it is an old rifle range that hasn't been used in years. I used to go there with my Dad."

"Can you get us home?"

"Yes, I can. But we're not going anywhere until those guys are gone, and I get a chance to see what's happened."

"You're going back over there? To see what happened? Three shots...that's what happened."

"As soon as the coast is clear, I'm going to see what happened."

She grabbed his arm and squeezed it hard. "No you're not...you're the first decent guy I've dated in Nohartinit. Listen, you! I think I love you...don't do this to me! You can't just trot down there and check out their handiwork...they're mob people...drug dealers...or whatever, for God's sake! I won't let you!"

"Keep your voice down!" he snapped, but still managing to keep his voice down. "And let go of my arm...you're about to break it in half."

"Richard?"

"What?"

"Don't do it, okay...tell the cops what we saw or heard...or whatever. Don't go back down there."

"Did you mean it? You think you love me?"

"Yes. I mean it," she whispered. "So?"

He kissed her. "Me, too...I think I love you, also; let's build on that, okay?"

"Sure."

"But right now, I have to take a look. They should be gone if we give them a half-hour or so. Let's just stay here...try to relax."

He started back toward the old rifle range, after waiting patiently for what seemed quite a while.

"I'm going with you. If they're going to kill the first decent guy I've ever been in love with, they might as well kill me, too. Damn it all...we're not the hero type, Richard."

"We have to see what happened...don't you get it?"

"Shit...let's go."

They moved cautiously, staying low, hiding behind trees and small ridges, like two wayward soldiers on a mission of some urgency. When they got close to the precipice, they crawled very slowly to the edge to look over. There were no sounds at all. No talking. No car engine running. Nothing. They crept closer and peered down into the range.

179

"There...there...over there," whispered Lalinduh nervously. "Just like in the movies...they just shoved the body into that little ditch. Can you see it?"

"Good God...look at that blood trail."

"Oh, shit," Lalinduh said. "I think I'm going to puke...there's a second body, Richard. There...not far from the other...I see a leg sticking over the side of the ditch."

"Damn!" he answered. "I have to get down there." He started to move. She grabbed his arm.

"What the hell for...you think they left them without making sure they're dead? Let's get out of here...let the cops handle this."

"We can't do that. I have to see who these guys are."

"What does it matter who they are? Let the cops do it...listen to me."

"No. I have to see."

"Why not the cops, damn it? What the hell is wrong with you?"

"The cops won't do it. Are you coming...or staying here. It'll just take a minute." He started to walk around the perimeter, and, belatedly, Lalinduh decided to join him.

"Wait for me," she pleaded quietly. She ran to catch up. "Can we make this fast? I want to go home."

"We can see what we need to see from the edge over there. Then, we're out of here. Fast."

The eased their way to the vantage point above the ditch where the bodies had been dumped. They crept to the edge and looked down into the ditch.

The bodies were less than twenty feet away, almost straight down. There was blood in pools and blood trails showing where the bodies had been dragged.

"Look...the old guy...they shot him twice. The other guy hardly has any head left."

They had casually tossed the old man's cane on top of his body.

"Oh, God...look at the cane, Richard...see it."

"Yeah...some kind of dragon head or something."

Lalinduh began to sob and she pulled back. She leaned against a nearby tree and threw up, until she got the dry heaves. Richard stood by her side, but was unable to comfort her.

Finally, she straightened up. She turned to look at Richard. He saw something akin to terror in her eyes as well as an enveloping sadness. She was pale. Her huge brown eyes burned.

"Are you okay? Talk to me, Lalinduh. Talk to me!" He held her by the shoulders and forced her to face him.

"That's the old guy who used to come to the library, Richard...the one Grampy was asking about...some kind of reporter or something," she sobbed. "He was a sweet old man, Richard. What the hell is going on here?"

"I don't know what's going on...come on...we have to get out of here."

"What's going on here, Richard? Why would somebody shoot a harmless old crippled man like that?"

"I don't know...but we damn sure can't stick around here to find out."

"Hold me...damn you. Hold me...and get me the hell out of here! Now!" Richard embraced her, and she sobbed on his shoulder.

"You can't get hysterical on me now, okay? Let's go."

They walked away from the precipice.

Richard explained they were about four miles away from Grampy's, if they took an overland, direct route. He also knew of a creek not too far away.

"The creek is just a few minutes away, Lalinduh. We'll get you something to drink, soak our feet, wash up...in a couple of hours we'll be at Grampy's."

She was agreeable.

"The lake should be in sight in an hour or so. Maybe we can catch a ride at the lake. We'll tell Grampy everything we saw and maybe he'll know what to do."

"Hmm...I didn't think we came this far out the Interstate. That means the car is on Dawson Road somewhere, doesn't it."

"Most likely."

"Wouldn't that be a lot closer? Why don't we head that way?"

"Dawson is a very long road...we could search for hours out that way," Richard said. "Let's get you to some water, we'll head for Grampy's. He'll drive us to Dawson Road to get the car. We can get something to eat and maybe a long hot bath while we are there."

"Why would they kill that nice old man?"

"If he's had dealings with those guys, I don't think he's exactly what you could call a nice old man, Lalinduh."

"Let's get going, Richard. I don't want to spend the night in these woods again."

"Okay. Stay with me," he said.

"The sooner we get there, the better. My feet are killing me. I just saw two murdered men. I'm hungry as a bear. The sooner we get out of here the better."

They started walking, at a slow and steady pace. It was starting to warm up quite a bit, and they both knew they had a long walk ahead of them.

"One thing for sure," said Lalinduh.

"What's that?"

"We'll probably both be sober again by the time we get to Grampy's."

Chapter Nineteen

They were hot, tired, sweaty, dirty, and grimy by the time they got to Grampy's. They found him sitting on the front porch, looking out at his lake. He had the longing look of a child held back from recess for misbehaving. They had rounded the corner of his house, and almost immediately, Richard told him, as they ascended the steps, "Grampy...we've got a problem."

"You don't need to restate the obvious," Grampy said, as he stood to greet them, "You two look like hell. The last I heard, you two were going out to dinner; the steakhouse must be getting kind of rough these days." He insisted they come in, get cleaned up, and refresh themselves, before he heard their tale. "You two smell rather...ah...rough. And you look like street brawlers."

"Grampy...we lost our car, some of our clothes, our shoes, and then cut our feet up running in the woods, damn near got dehydrated and starved to death...and we saw two guys who have been murdered," said Lalinduh. She was so tired she just wanted to go to sleep in a steamy bath. "It is a long story...can I have some water?"

He hustled them indoors, insisting they could talk as soon as they get cleaned up and refreshed. "I'm not sure about clothes that will fit you, Lalinduh," he said. "We'll find something. Go now. We can talk as soon as you get cleaned up."

Grampy pulled Richard to one side after directing Lalinduh toward the bathroom. "That must have been quite a date?" His tone told Richard he was at once pleased and somewhat confused. "What's this she's babbling about...a murder?"

"An execution, Grampy. Out at the old rifle range. Just like in the movies...guys in black suits, a long black car. They shot one guy once and one guy twice, rolled them in a ditch. Then they left."

"Did anybody see you?"

"No. I'm sure of it."

The he insisted that Richard say no more until he got cleaned up. "What ever happened to you two, I'm sure will not change in the next half an hour. Clean yourselves, eat something, and drink something. Then we'll talk."

Grampy did not like the sound of it. Many years back there had been a turf war, and it got pretty messy. He had not expected to ever hear of such ever again. He had hoped those days were gone.

The powers had been behind the scenes, operating out of sight and out of mind for a long time. Either they had been witness to an isolated settlement between drug dealers or there was another mob war about to erupt. Grampy was not as upset as Richard and Lalinduh seemed to be. He already knew what they had just discovered: The powers were alive and well in and around Nohartinit.

He was thankful the kids were okay. He returned to his chair on the porch, to wait for them. We don't need any complications right now, he thought. He knew what he was going to say before they ever told him the tale: Forget about it; forget you ever saw anything. You didn't see anything; run your mouths and you'll end up dead.

He looked out at his beloved lake. It was calm and inviting; it was just choppy enough to sparkle under the bright afternoon sun. The sky was bright blue and puffy white clouds with grayish flat underbellies floated very high. The pines had been swaying with the wind most of the morning, but it was starting to die down.

He looked at his beloved gray skiff, tied in the usual place. It bobbed up and down, but not too much. He remembered catching a huge trout on just such a day, an hour or so before sundown, but that was a long time ago.

He wondered if he might talk the two of them into going fishing with him later.

Lalinduh was the first to join him on the porch. She had showered, scrubbed really well, and washed her hair. She was barefooted. She carried a glass of water, from which she sipped intermittently. She wore the same dress. Grampy insisted that she check the hall closet and find something clean to wear.

"Throw that dress in the washing machine...in the room just off the kitchen. We'll hang it up out back. In this weather, it'll be dry in a matter of a few minutes. In the meanwhile, put on something else...Richard keeps extra clothes here, in the hall closet. They'll be a little large, but they're clean."

She complied, and returned to the porch in just a few minutes, wearing a blue shirt with the sleeves rolled up, a pair of baggy brown pants, with the cuffs rolled up.

Richard joined them not long after.

"Okay, you two," said Grampy, when he had them together, sitting nearby. "Tell me what you saw."

They took turns explaining various things. Then Lalinduh told him about the old crippled man with the cane.

"They shot him twice, Grampy. Once in the midsection and once in the back of his head."

"And the other guy?"

"Through the back of the head. Blew his face off just about," said Richard.

"I've seen this kind of stuff before," Grampy explained. "The guy they shot through the head was probably one of them who tried to pull a fast one. They probably shot him first, to scare the old guy...to make him sweat, to make him tell them what they wanted to know. The old guy was not one of them...but was a threat to them; he probably had some information or something. They shot him in the gut first...a very painful wound...then they let him suffer a couple of minutes then executed him."

"How awful...how cruel," said Lalinduh, weakly and sadly, "That old guy couldn't hurt a fly."

"Probably not," Grampy said. "But whatever he knew could have done a lot of damage to these other people. He probably didn't talk, if this is the guy I was looking for."

"How do you know this, Grampy?" asked Lalinduh. She wiped tears from her eyes.

"Remember how you thought his legs might have been crushed or something?"

"Yes."

"They used to work people over like that...take heavy pipes and pound the bones in their legs until they broke them up enough to cripple their victims for life. This way they bought their cooperation without having to dispose of a body. If they liked the guy, they'd drop him off in the street in front of the clinic when they were done with them. Otherwise they usually just dropped them in a back alley to suffer and die." Grampy looked at both of them, and shook his head. "They're cold and vicious...you must never let on you ever saw anything...no cops, no phone calls...nothing. Everything you saw must end right here and right now."

"That isn't right, Grampy," said Lalinduh.

"Right? Listen...listen well, both of you," he scolded. "You're up against powers you don't understand. If they even thought you knew anything, they'd break your legs, too, or you'd end up in a dumpster somewhere."

"But Grampy...we can't just turn our backs on this...Lalinduh's right. We have to do something."

"Don't be stupid, Richard," Grampy barked. "You've got no idea what you'd be dealing with. It is no business of yours. These people own half of Nohartinit, you idiots...cops, lawyers, the Mayor, the Councilmen, the newspaper publisher...you name them...they own them. Why in God's name do you think Nohartinit is loaded to the gills with drugs? Why are the whorehouses still open on the backside of Main? I'll tell you why...because nobody can touch them, that's why. Nobody."

"They can't or they won't, Grampy?" asked Richard.

"Nobody cares any more, Richard. That's what it is all about. Nobody cares. Those who don't work for the powers do not care what goes on as long as they get to buy their beers, their hamburgers, and their television sets. Do you think anything would change if you two ended up in the old rifle range right beside the other two? You'd be written off as a pair of frustrated lovers...a murder-suicide."

"Okay, Grampy. I get the message," said Lalinduh.

"And you, Richard?"

"Me, too," he replied. "Now what?" He looked at Lalinduh as if he expected some answer from her.

"One thing for sure," she said. She grinned slyly. "I won't have to use my stock line about how much fun I had on our date."

Richard chuckled. Then Richard looked at Grampy. "Now what?"

"Kids still drive out to the old range to drink and party. They'll discover the bodies, and call in the police. It'll be over and done with in a couple of days. It probably will not even make the news. I hate to seem so casual about it...or callous, as you choose to see it. You ask me: Now what? I want you two to do me a favor. I won't take no for an answer."

"Sure, Grampy," said Richard. "Name it."

"Take me fishing. I don't want to go alone."

Chapter Twenty

"What do you think about this case, Dad?" asked Skug, as they opened the door to the ratty motel room. His Dad stepped inside, and he followed close behind. Taller than his son, equally muscular, he had longer hair, more penetrating eyes, and a face which looked like it could have been carved out of sandstone by some careless amateur stonecutter. "God...I hate this town," he said.

"Why would anybody want to live in this dump, Dad? Even the air stinks."

"Nohartinit is nasty, isn't it? Anyway...what have you got so far, son?" he answered, as he tossed his suitcase on one of the beds. He took off his coat, loosened his tie. "Sorry I'm running so late, son."

"That's okay, Dad. Here's what I've got. I talked to this lady, Alba Beecham, yesterday, and she was wide open about it, Dad. She showed me her husband's picture, told me the story. She didn't fill in too many details, however. Kind of like she was hiding key details. She let me tape our conversation and was kind enough to let me take the picture out of the frame and take a few photos of it." He took the tape and several photos out of his shirt pocket, and he handed them to him.

"She was sincere?" He studied the close shot of the scar. "She swears this was a bite?"

"Absolutely."

"Any leads on the newspaper fellow?"

"At the newspaper office – got there just before closing yesterday...I told them I was a writer for one of those UFO weekly tabloids, I had heard rumors, and I joked about the monster. I explained someone had told me Ralph Whalen knew something about the story. I also asked at the old folks home if they knew him or anything about the story...nobody provided any information. It looks like this Alba Beecham woman is the only source of information. Nobody's heard from Ralph Whalen in years, apparently. They seem to think he moved far away from Nohartinit. They told me I was the third person this week looking for him. They didn't have any names for me."

"Hmm?" he mumbled. "What gives?"

"Seems our man has suddenly become very popular, Dad."

"Who did you talk to at the newspaper office?"

"The little guys and the publisher, who just happened to be there, too. The publisher was the only one who remembered Ralph Whalen very well. Said he had a terrible accident and retired and moved away soon after."

"At the old folks home?"

"Anybody who could talk to me did. Lots of them wanted to talk. I got back late. They told some very colorful stories but nothing about our monster woman. I left this room number just in case somebody remembered something."

"Well, son? What do you think?"

"I think there's something to it, Dad. These guys didn't pay four grand just for a story from an old woman they could have easily gotten for themselves."

"Anything else?"

"Yeah, Dad. The wound in the photograph...I saw another one quite similar to it...on the forearm of one of the guys who hired us. The one they call Grampy."

"Did Heinz have anything for you?"

"No. He acted like the whole thing was a big joke. But he did go along with it."

"An expensive joke, wouldn't you say? What story did this Grampy fellow give you?"

"He said his grandson was writing a story about this red-eyed monster woman. He wants to be a writer...and use this story to make a big name for himself. Heinz went along with this."

"Are you thinking what I'm thinking, son?"

"Heinz is running another scam?"

"Yep. I think so."

"Well, we'll keep looking. If we can, we'll give them what they paid for, right Dad?"

"As always."

"Why in the world would Heinz want a red-eyed monster woman?" asked Skug. He sat on the foot of the other bed and took his shoes off. He rubbed his feet.

"He doesn't, son. He wants the newspaperman. He can't find him. For some reason, he's using this Beecham lady to cover the fact he wants to locate this fellow...Ralph Whalen. Heinz wants him and two other people want him as well."

"The scars, then? A coincidence?"

"Most likely. Surely you don't think some red-eyed monster woman took a bite out of these two fellows, do you?"

"Maybe she did and this Ralph Whalen fellow knows something about it."

"Possible...but highly unlikely. I don't think three people in the whole state much less in Nohartinit are looking for this red-eyed monster woman. It has to be this Whalen fellow. He's evidently got something a lot of people also want. Probably information of some sort."

"Tomorrow we start the search for Mister Whalen?"

"That's what they're paying us for...let's find the guy so we can get out of this slimy town. It shouldn't take long."

"Dad, can I ask you something?"

"Sure." He reclined, crossed his legs at the ankles, and propped himself up against the headboard, carefully placing a pillow behind the small of his back. He reached for the remote to the television.

"How long have you known Heinz?"

"Fifteen, maybe twenty years. Why?"

"Has he ever tried to scam you when he was working one of his own scams?"

"No. Not until now...if that's what he's up to."

"What gives? Why wouldn't he just come right out and say he needed to find this newspaperman?"

He clicked on the television and began a search for news. "That part bothers me, son. Heinz is a scoundrel, and a good one. He's had years of practice at it. What I don't understand is what is important enough about this whole business to drag Heinz back to this hellhole of a town?"

"Do you know Alexsandr Simon?"

"We met years ago...he and Heinz worked a scam to frame some cheap hood. I don't remember too much about him. Why?"

"He was there when I talked to Grampy. He was there when I met up with Heinz. He's got a part in this somewhere."

"Hmm...and here I thought this would just be another boring find 'em and go home deal. This one, son, might even be fun. There's something out of the ordinary going on for sure; it would take something extraordinary to drag Heinz out of retirement."

"Maybe we ought to visit Heinz some time tomorrow...can you talk the truth out of him, Dad?"

"Maybe if we had a clear picture of exactly what's going on, it might help us. But talk the truth out of Heinz? That's a tall order; he's a lawyer, for God's sake. Let's think about that. Right now, I just want to rest. It has been a long day."

Chapter Twenty-One

Diary of Prof. Alexsandr Simon, PhD, cont'd.

I am at a loss, facing the possibilities of the future. My dear Rachael has no idea yet what lies in store if Grampy, Heinz, and myself do not find a way to break the clutches of our investigator friend, Bud.

He has narrowed his search for Milly's killer to the women who were with us, and it will not take long for him to zero in on Rachael.

We are, in desperation, reaching into the improbable hoping we can distort the unlikely so much it not only seems probable but also, indeed, likely. Heinz has said if we can come up with this creation of Grampy's...a she-demon...and back it with enough substantial documentation, he can get all possible charges dropped by spoiling the District Attorney's ability to establish guilt beyond a shadow of a doubt. I must say, Grampy's plan is bold, imaginative, and so far outside the lines of feasibility it just might fly. Heinz seems to think it will, under the right conditions.

I think if we can create this she-demon, using the +1 scenario...two parts extra-dimensional reality and one part sensorial reality $(1+1=1)$ we can pull it off.

We have affectionately nicknamed Grampy's unworldly creation The Red-Eyed Boogie woman.

She is an ugly creature...red eyes, fangs, claws instead of hands. She growls, and speaks in a very gruff old man's voice. She has a bite preference to the forearms of her victims, and she rips the flesh right to the bone when she bites. Jacob Lewski furnished the description in his confession tape. We are just going to exploit it...we hope we can, anyway.

Grampy seems to think he can put the package together.

I don't know how much time we have before Bud comes to arrest Rachael for the murder of Mildred Lewski. We may have only a few days.

I hope we can close Bud's case for him, without having to go to trial. He is a man of firm convictions. But, as some astute philosopher once observed, convictions are the enemy of truth. Bud wants a killer, and we are going to give him one.

I have not told Rachael anything. Not yet. I know her too well to allow her access to Bud's search right now. She would, I believe, surrender herself. Although she will deny it, she is a valuable asset in this community and she has done some wondrous things for the children of this and outlying communities over the last few decades. I am presuming to make the call here...the good she has done far outweighs the price we all had to pay to develop our city into a quasi-civilized place in which to live.

We fought hard to save the children over the years. We did our best and gave our best years in their behalf. God, alone, should judge us in this regard.

I see, with each passing day, how values crumble. The city we live in is no different than the state, or the nation for that matter, in this regard. Nobody seems to be able to distinguish right from wrong any more. Those of us who took it upon ourselves to serve the good, the right, and the decent seem to be dying off. When we, of the old crowd, are dead and gone what will remain? What kind of city...indeed what kind of nation...will the children inherit?

I have to wonder how justice can be served when Rachael could pay dearly for the death of a whore who traded in human flesh...children at that...in a nation that sees nothing inherently wrong in aborting unborn babies by the millions. I can see no sense and certainly no good in such violence against the unborn. I see even less sense in punishing someone for doing their part to save children from wholesale exploitation in an unholy and ungodly house of prostitution.

The supreme irony in all of this can be seen in the luck of the draw. Two men, of exceptional character will be Rachael's most formidable adversaries.

Judge Lambert will follow the letter of the law; he is an honest, dedicated professional. Bud Elbudro, the investigator, will not back off. He, too, is honest and dedicated. They are good men. They will, in their own minds, do the right thing.

The best we can hope for, I think, is the judge will temper justice with mercy. I think Bud, if given an out, will take it; he has been fighting the powers for too long not to side, if only in spirit, with a fellow fighter. The one consoling thought in all this is Judge Lambert will hold the prosecution people to a rigid standard of proof. We are, in fact, counting on this. Heinz intends to cloud the prosecution's case with our Red-Eyed Boogie woman scenario.

God go with Grampy...he is our last best chance to salvage our good intentions. I don't have any idea how he plans to pull this off...this Red-Eyed Boogie woman stuff...but he seems sincere. I have to admit to myself it is possible...for I have a lot of faith in the man. I know, in my heart, he would not take such an offbeat route toward saving Rachael unless he was sincerely convinced it would work.

I shall pray tonight...for Rachael, for Grampy...and, God forgive me if I am wrong for doing it,...for the emergence and life-like existence of this non-entity...the Red-Eyed Boogie woman.

To be continued:

Prof.AlexsandrSimon, Ph.D.

Chapter Twenty-Two

Hear my prayers this night, oh Lord. You know me as Grampy. I humble myself before You, oh Lord! I ask forgiveness for my sins. Lord please show mercy on me!

My days are numbered. I know in my heart, oh Lord, my worldly adventure is about to end. My soul is Yours whenever You are ready for it.

But I need to ask You a favor, Lord. I have one more task before me, and, Lord, I ask You to give me a few more days. Then do with me what You will.

My doctor told me I would most likely know when my time drew near. I know it is near. But Lord, I have unfinished business. Bear with me...and, if it be Your will, give me a few more days!

The powers, Lord, are at it again. I'm too old, too weak, and too fragile to head back into the war. I'd just be in the way. All of the originals would be in the way.

But there's new blood, Lord...Richard, Ladonna, Stephy, James...and, of course, Lalinduh Lord. I feel good about this unusual kid, Skug. I need time to arm them, Lord.

They'll put on Your full armor, Lord...I know in my diseased heart they will. I ask You to walk with them, work through them, guide them, and give them wisdom, strong backs, and vibrant minds that they may always discern good and defend it...to keep Your good name and good works alive in this demon-infested city.

And Lord, I have a special request before I go...there's this man, Bud Elbudro,...a soldier in Your ranks...touch him, Lord. He's just a man of flesh and bone...just like the rest of us...but he's trapped in the awful politics of our times. His job requires that he do right things, but it also requires him to destroy the life of Rachael Simon...You know her, I'm sure. He is in one of those all-too-common human messes where only the impossible is his best option. I hope and pray, Lord...he gives his mess to you. If he doesn't give it to You, Lord, would You take it from him?

Oh, Lord...hear me cry! We did the best we knew how to do! Right or wrong, we did it...and we cannot erase any of it.

Hear me, Lord. We never intended to kill anyone...we wanted to save the children!

You and You alone know if any of the children were saved, whether our efforts paid off or were in vain. If it is not too much to ask Dear

Lord…I'd like to know, before I leave, those children…at least some of them…were saved.

As usual, Lord, I thank You for all the blessings You have bestowed upon myself and my grandson, Richard, and I thank You for all the prayers You have answered.

This diary is my closet, Lord. Hear me. Have mercy upon me.

And Lord, there must be thousands out there who are suffering tonight…sick ones, lost ones, weary ones, those, like me, facing the prospects of eminent death, some trying to cope with heartbreaks, pain, or substantial losses.

And the kids, Lord…I know there are a bunch of them out there crying desperately in the dark. If it be Your will, Lord…save them.

I give You my pain and my suffering in union with the pain and the suffering of Your beloved Son, Lord…in their behalf.

I know I have suffered far less than my beloved Savior Jesus did…it is, and I ask only that it be considered in context, what little I can give to put my soul at ease.

I will be in Your arms soon. Hear my cries, oh Lord.

And, one last thing, Lord.

I thank You for wonderful time fishing with my grandson and his girlfriend Lalinduh.

If they are intended in the wisdom of Your plan to marry, bless them and keep them Lord.

I ask these things in the name of Jesus Christ.

In the name of the Father, the Son, and the Holy Spirit I pray…Amen.

Your humble servant. Grampy.

Chapter Twenty-Three

Skug and his Dad woke early, and got dressed. It was a Sunday, and they were not too sure just how much they could get accomplished, but they were ready to plan their day when the phone rang.

"Hello?" said Skug. He paused a few moments. "Yes, I'm Skug Findfello. Who's calling please?"

"You don't know me," said the female voice on the other end of the line.

"What can I do for you?"

She sounded like she was probably in her early forties or thereabouts. She spoke with certain, smooth and deliberate tones.

"You spoke with a friend of mine Friday night."

"I spoke to a lot of people. Could you be a little more specific?"

"At the nursing home. You were asking about the red-eyed monster story. You left this number just in case anybody remembered anything."

"Oh, yes. I was there. I had a wonderful time. I hit a blind alley, but I had a wonderful time. Is that why you're calling? I hope I didn't upset your friend or anything. I assure you that was not my intention."

"Can we meet somewhere?"

"Sure. For what purpose might I ask?"

"I have information for you, Mister Findfello, I have seen this monster you're looking for."

"Might I ask your name?"

"I will not give it."

"Okay. Where can we meet? When can we meet?"

"Do you know the city, Mister Findfello?"

"Not well. I'm not from around here. Could you perhaps meet me at my room here at the motel? We could speak in absolute privacy. I just want the story. I don't want to embarrass anyone, I assure you."

"I have the information, obviously. In about half-an-hour?"

"How will I recognize you?"

"I'll be in jeans and a white sweat shirt."

"I'll be waiting. I'll leave the door open for you. Thank you for calling." Skug hung up the phone. He looked at his Dad. "We're in, Dad. You're going to have to get lost for a couple of hours."

"What is it, Skug?"

"The woman wouldn't give her name. She says she has seen our red-eyed monster woman. She'll be here in about half-an-hour."

"Hmm," he mumbled. He picked up his suit coat and put it on. He adjusted his tie. "If you ask me, somebody dumped a few gallons of acid in the city's water supply."

"Give me two hours, okay?"

"Sure." He started for the door.

"Bring back a couple of donuts, okay?"

"Coffee?"

"Lots."

"Okay...see you in a couple of hours." He opened the door, peered out, and then he opened it completely. "Looks like a good day for a get-lost walk in hell town." With that, he started walking. He left the door open.

I knew it, thought Skug, as he used the remote to turn on the television set and flipped channels for some news. I had a gut feeling about this monster thing. He sat back, and watched most of a news show before she arrived.

She walked up to the door, wearing, as she had said she would, jeans and a white sweatshirt. She stood about five and a half feet tall, had shoulder-length auburn hair. She had strange-looking blue eyes. She was slender and walked like an athlete. He guessed she was just past forty.

He clicked off the television.

"Mister Findfellow?" she asked, as she stood before him. She extended her well-cared-for hand.

"Call me Skug. Please come in. Be seated."

She entered, looked around the room. Skug dragged up a chair, and she seated herself.

He pulled up another chair, and sat nearby.

"Before we get started, be honest with me," she said. "I want you to level with me. You're not with the tabloids, are you?"

"Of course not. I just say that so people will feel at ease talking to me. I'm a private investigator who was hired by a writer to find out about this monster woman tale. He's a busy man, and he didn't have time to come to Nohartinit and check it out himself. This guy pays me very well; he can afford it. He has to stay anonymous."

"What's he going to do with the story?"

"He's thinking about a film script. It would, you have to admit, make a great B movie." She seemed perfectly at ease with his story. "Now...you be honest with me. Why won't you give me your name? I can understand your not wanting to be embarrassed or even ridiculed for the story. I have to call you something, don't I? It would make our talk a little easier."

"Call me Mary."

"Is that your real name?"

"No."

"Okay, Mary it is. I assure you no names will ever go public. I'm not even sure my employer will be able to use anything you tell me. I can't pay you anything for your story, either."

"Do I need to sign a release or anything?"

"No. This is strictly informal and strictly voluntary. I won't influence anything you might have to say. You are free to go at any time. I would like to tape our conversation if it is okay with you."

"I want to tell my story. My friend says you can be trusted. She is usually right about such things. She has always been an excellent judge of character."

Skug opened his suitcase and took out a small tape recorder. He placed it nearby and turned it on.

"Okay, Mary. Talk to me. Anything you want to say is fine."

"Turn that off for a minute, please."

He turned off the tape recorder. "Is there a problem?"

"No problem...just a question before we begin: Do you have any idea what you're dealing with?"

"I'm not sure I understand the question."

"This is a true story, Mister Findfello."

"I'm sure it is, Mary. I don't question your integrity. As a matter of fact, Mary, one other person has come forward."

"No. I mean it, Mister Findfello."

"Look," he said. He opened the suitcase again and took out the close up of the scar on Mister Beecham's forearm. He handed it to her. "You see that? Do you know what that is?"

She seemed relieved. Slowly she pulled up her left sleeve to expose a massive scar. "There was such a creature...but it was not a woman. It was a child."

He reached for his camera. "May I?"

"Not my face, okay? No one must know I talked to you."

"Could you kind of hold your arm across your front...so I can get good light?"

"I'll cooperate, Mister Findfello," she said, as she posed her arm for him. "Just one thing...if the story gets told, please try to convince your employer to stay faithful to real events."

He took several pictures. "I can't control that," he answered. "I will try."

She lowered her sleeve to cover the scar. "You can turn that thing back on now. I'm ready to talk."

Richard Cox

"You seem to be especially calm about this...why?"

"Why? Do you ever listen to that little voice in your head, Mister Findfello? The little voice that sits inside your brain and overrides your own conscious thinking?"

"Not often enough," Skug replied.

"It tells me the time has come to tell what I know. It isn't just a coincidence you came along when you did, Mister Findfello."

"Oh?" he said, as he turned the recorder on. "I'll think about that." He sat back in his chair, motioned toward the recorder. "All yours, Mary. Any time."

"I was unofficially adopted when I was ten years old," she began. "A year before that a series of events took place which changed my life forever. Nohartinit was a very different city back then. It was a vile and corrupt place...full of saloons and brothels and evil people and human misery."

Skug listened patiently; he was determined, no matter what, not to interrupt her.

"I never knew my real parents. From what I know of them, they were as vile and corrupt as any of them. They sold me into prostitution when I was but four or five years old, and they subsequently disappeared altogether. There were other children who had met the same fate as myself."

He turned off the recorder. Good God, thought Skug: What have I gotten myself into now? He interrupted. He changed his mind. "Mary? You don't have to do this," he said.

"Oh, but I do," she replied. She was calm and collected. "I have to. My little voice will never forgive me if I don't."

"Continue." He turned it on again.

"There was a special room in the brothel where they kept a teenage girl, maybe fourteen or so, locked up. She was known as Crazy Girl, and from time to time, I could hear her violent tantrums through the door of that special room. We were warned never to go into that room under threat of painful punishment if we disobeyed. One day, foolishly, I sneaked the key to the room and let myself in. I found the girl cowered in a corner, trying to hide an obvious late-term pregnancy. She had her head slouched downward, as if staring at the floor to hide her shame. What happened next I have kept to myself all these years; only now have I come forward with the story.

I spoke to her. She slowly raised her head. She transformed right before my eyes...into a hellish demon...her eyes were like fire, she grew fangs, and claws emerged where her hands had been. I was terrified. I cowered in an opposite corner and screamed for help. This thing lunged

198

at me, and I fought with all my might…it was incredibly strong. It ripped a huge gash in my arm. A man rushed in, a customer I guess, and fought frantically to save me. He, too, was bitten. Two bouncers who clubbed this thing into submission finally took down this demon, and they dragged it away.

The Crazy Girl was never seen again, and the room stayed locked.

My wound was treated in a back room, and I was severely beaten for my misadventure. They threatened my life if I ever told a living soul about what had happened in that room."

She paused. She motioned for Skug to turn off the tape recorder.

"No more, Mister Findfello, Make of it what you will. I'm not nuts, Mister Findfello. I am quite sane. If you can find that customer, you will know I am telling you the truth."

He handed her the Beecham photograph again. "I think maybe we have found him, Mary…unfortunately, he's been dead for years."

"Hmm," she said, softly. "If it was him, he will surely burn in Hell!"

"For my own curiosity, Mary…you don't look like you've been through that kind of degradation. You're too composed, too seemingly together. How did you break away?"

"That's a totally different story altogether, Mister Findfello, a story of death and destruction and resurrection. I chose not to tell it. I'll be going now." She stood, extended her hand again. "Tell me something, Mister Findfello? Have you ever come face-to-face with the devil himself?"

"No."

"Do you believe it is possible?"

"I do now. Will I ever see you again?"

In the doorway, she turned and faced him. "No. Never. Between you and me, Mister Findfello…we have never laid eyes upon each other. I have a good life now. I want it to stay that way. Don't try to find me, okay?"

"Your secrets are safe with me, Mary. Good luck to you."

"You, too, Mister Findfello." With not another word said, she walked away. She went to her car that she had parked around the corner from the motel, got in, and she started the engine. She drove to a nearby convenience store, took off her wig, took out her tinted contact lenses, and removed her false nails. She threw them in a dumpster. Then, without looking back, she got back into the car, and she drove away.

In just a few minutes, Skug's Dad came back to the room. He handed Skug two large cups of coffee and a small bag containing donuts. "That didn't take long. I've got the license plate number if we

199

need it. She drives a late model brownish Honda. She parked around back."

"You've been watching all this time?"

"No. Just long enough. I just sat in the car and moved with her. She dumped her costume in a dumpster at the convenience store halfway around the block. Do we need to run the tag?"

"Costume?"

"She went to a lot of trouble not to have anyone recognize her...wig, tinted contacts, phony fingernails."

"We don't need any more from her, Dad. I would never ask more from this mystery lady than what she has already given us. Have you ever heard of an unofficial adoption?"

"Interesting discussion, I take it?"

"Very...and sad," Skug said. "I can understand her desire to keep things secreted away."

"Do you believe her?"

"You've got to hear this tape, Dad. This woman has literally been to hell and back; she just summed up what has probably been a lifetime of anguish and suffering in just a few short minutes." He rewound the tape in the recorder. "Listen to her voice, Dad. This lady has found inner peace."

"Well? Is this red-eyed monster woman for real, son?" He sat on the bed, then reclined and stretched his legs out.

"It was not a woman, Dad," he sighed, somewhat sadly. "It was a child. A girl about fourteen or so. Listen to the tape, Dad. You tell me."

"Play it, Skug. Let's see what we've got here."

"There's one more thing, Dad. She, too, has a scar...where this creature ripped into her. I got some pictures. There's a remote chance she and Mister Beecham were old...ah...acquaintances."

"You're saying this monster woman...child...is for real? You know what I think? I think they're putting something a lot more potent than acid in the water in this stinking town," he mumbled. "What the hell? Go ahead...play it. I'm all ears, son."

Chapter Twenty-Four

Later that same afternoon, Skug delivered the photographs and the tapes in a large sealed envelope to Grampy. He found Grampy, as usual, sitting on his porch. Grampy did not appear well, but Skug said nothing.

He told him simply the envelope contained photographs and tape recordings. "Shall we keep digging, Grampy? We have still not located the newspaperman."

"Watch the newspaper tomorrow or the next day," he answered. "You will." Grampy thanked him for everything. "Your work is done. Heinz or Alexsandr will have the extra money promised for the photographs. Just tell them how many. Any documents other than the tapes?"

"None."

"Thank your father for me. And, again, thank you. I will listen to the tapes later. Superb work, Skug."

"She needs to remain unidentified."

"Mrs. Beecham? Why would she not want to be identified? She's apparently broadcast her story to anyone who would listen. It doesn't make sense."

"The other lady."

"What?"

"Another woman came forward," he replied.

"I didn't know there was another lady."

"She came to me. She gave no name. Even if you recognize her voice or anything, do not identify her."

"That's agreeable." Grampy excused himself, and went inside.

He phoned Richard and asked him to come as soon as possible to pick up the information. He went to his den.

Richard arrived about an hour later. Grampy was in his den listening to the tape from the mystery lady for the third time when Richard tapped on the door and entered.

Grampy motioned for him to be seated and be quiet. When the recording was finished, Grampy got up and turned off the tape player. He faced Richard. He had a shine to his old eyes and a wide smile. He had real color to his face; he was not pasty looking, for the first time in weeks. Richard had just caught the tail end of the recording.

"Richard...you're listening to an answer to an old man's prayers. Praise God." He wanted to say: This woman, whoever she is, was one of the kids we pulled from Milly's. In her own words, Richard she says: I

have a good life now...I want it to stay that way. But he realized it was
not yet revealed to Richard the complexities of the overall situation.

"She has a very pleasant voice, Grampy. Like she's at peace with
the world."

"Isn't it wonderful? God bless this child!"

"I wonder who she is?"

"According to Skug she went to great effort to hide her
identity...we'll respect that." He removed the tape from the machine,
and he handed it to Richard. From his desk, he took the photographs of
this mystery woman's arm.

"This will prove most useful, Richard."

"Photographs, tapes, plus your records...that's enough to build my
case, isn't it Grampy?" asked Richard.

"Considering you have to keep to no more than one-hundred and
sixty pages...you bet."

"I took the liberty of duplicating this one," he said. "Music to an old
man's ears, Richard. You have no idea how happy I am this day!"

"You look well."

"I'm not...but nothing is going to spoil this day!" He motioned for
Richard to follow him. "To the kitchen, Richard. Fresh coffee...just
brewed. Then I have to talk to you...some serious talking. I promise not
to complicate your life...only enhance it. Have you got plenty of time?"

"A date with Lalinduh this evening...until then, I'm free."

"Are you back in classes yet?"

"No. I dropped out for a semester, Grampy."

"Hmm. Good move. What I'm going to show you today will open
your eyes to a lot of things that may well reshape your future. You may
decide against going back to school. We'll see."

"Sounds enlightening, Grampy."

"Oh, it is, believe me!" he replied. They entered the kitchen, poured
themselves some coffee.

"To the porch, Grampy?"

"Of course. Lead the way. I'll be right behind you. How's
Lalinduh?"

"Wonderful girl, Grampy. She really is. She took a few vacation
days she had stacked up...she's still upset by what happened."

"Are you happy?"

"Very."

"Are you serious about her?"

"Very."

"Do you need some money?"

"Always."

They reached the porch. Grampy sat in his usual chair, and Richard sat on the top step and backed up against a post. He looked up at Grampy.

"There's a lot going on I don't know about, isn't there, Grampy?"

"Yes. A lot. But today, Richard, I'm showing you everything. It will be a burden, but you've got broad shoulders. I can't think of anyone else I could trust more."

"Can we talk about it now?"

"It starts right here," he said. He placed a bony hand on his chest. He tapped his breastbone with a bony finger. "I don't have much time left, Richard. It has come down to a matter of a few days. The ticker is going to literally explode soon. I'll die almost instantly. I've known for a long time now. I've been expecting it. I'm sorry I kept it from you. You had a right to know." He raised both hands to squelch any protest. "There's nothing anyone can do, Richard. I just hope I die with dignity. I don't want to fall down dead just anywhere you know."

Tears welled in Richard's eyes. He looked at Grampy, and spoke quietly, sorrowfully. "I knew you weren't well, Grampy. I didn't think it was this serious. There's nothing anyone can do? Are you sure? Surgery? Medicines?"

"Nothing. I'm a dead duck...just not dead yet. I'll probably wake up one morning, get a bad bellyache, and drink a cup of coffee...and fall over dead. The doctor says it will be quick."

"I'm sorry, Grampy...I can't be that casual about it." Tears streamed down his cheeks. He got up and gave Grampy an affectionate hug. He kissed the old man's brow. "I love you, Grampy."

"I know." Grampy embraced him. "Don't make a fuss. That kind of stuff always bothers me. I'm ready to go, Richard. I'm ready to meet my Maker." He weakly pushed Richard back. "You sit now...the best thing you can do for me is listen. I have a lot of things you have to hear."

"I just don't want to let go, Grampy. You're more like a father than a grandfather...do you know what I mean?" He choked back more tears.

"Let go, Richard. Accept the inevitable. But I'm not dead yet. Stay with me until the end...will you do that? I don't want to die alone."

"Sure, I'll stay with you, Grampy. You know I will."

"Can you work from here?"

"I can bring my computer, a few odds and ends. Of course I can."

"Set it up then. Can you trust Lalinduh?"

"After what we've been through? I think she'll be a most trustable ally, Grampy."

"Good...get her out here, too. This is going to be a job for young blood. You both have a bad taste for the powers; you have only seen the tip of the proverbial iceberg. I'm going to show you what they are really all about." He looked relieved now that the time had come to pass the torch. "It will be your fight now, Richard. You and Lalinduh and Ladonna and Bud's too. The best I can do is get you prepared for it."

"Are you up to it, Grampy?"

"Oh, yes," he answered. "But I will warn you ahead of time you will not like what I'm about to disclose. I hope you have a strong stomach." He looked fondly out toward the lake. "I'm sure going to miss this place. I willed it to you, you know."

"Let's not discuss such things, Grampy."

"We must," he insisted. "Later. You get hold of Lalinduh, get into town and get the stuff. I'll be fine. I'll wait for you right here."

"It'll be a couple of hours, Grampy."

"That's fine. If she can, I'd like for Lalinduh to stay a day or two." He smiled. "I have a good feeling about that girl." He studied Richard's face for a reaction. Richard grinned. "You go now...I'll have things ready when you get back."

Chapter Twenty-Five

Diary of Prof. Alexsandr Simon, cont'd:

Bud stopped by today. He is under a lot of pressure. He has given me two more days.

He said he is prepared to subpoena anyone and everyone who might have any knowledge of the raid on Milly's if I force his hand.

He claims to have conferred with the District Attorney and the consensus they reached was not good.

Bud indicated, with the right approach, they would get a conviction. He stated quite clearly he did not want to put everyone through the process; if I would simply give him the name, he would cover as many tracks as he could.

Little does he know I cannot give him that name, nor can I be forced to yield it.

We have agreed, Heinz and I, we will stall until Grampy comes up with something.

I think the world of Grampy, but I don't think he can pull this off. But, as long as there is a chance, I'm betting on him.

The Lewski tape is damaging, to say the least. Heinz, of course, may call it all the ravings of a madman. Bud wants Jacob Lewski, because it is a clear case. But the Milly's raid...it has always been a hobby for him.

My own thoughts on the matter are that Bud, as serious as he is, has no idea what the originals did.

It may take some kind of miracle to save Rachael, but, as always, when I pray tonight, I will ask God to take charge. I hate to say it, but I must defer the final judgment to Him. I cannot, in my deepest reaches of conscience, condemn Rachael for what happened between her and Milly.

But Bud was right in one thing...it is time to practice what I preach.

I have decided to sit down with Rachael tomorrow and tell her everything. I am going to ask Ladonna to sit in as well. We cannot let Ladonna walk blindly into Bud's ambush.

One thing we want to avoid is disclosing the disposition of the children. We, ourselves, set it up so few of us would ever know where they ended up. All we know, most of us, is they went to good families, whereabouts unknown.

I have begged Bud not to pry too deeply into this aspect, for the sake of the children. In this, I think he concurs. He is not a mean-spirited man, but he is a dedicated servant of the law.

Grampy is the Philosopher. I am the moralist. As much as I hate relativistic morality, I never dreamed I would be backed into such a corner.

I know what I should do...but I do not have the courage to do it.

There is no question in anyone's mind that Rachael killed the woman. What bothers us all is where one can draw the line between doing what is right and doing what is morally right. There is a difference.

On the one hand, it is hard to break the law in a lawless city. On the other hand, the Supreme law...God's Law...must prevail or civilization itself can crumble. I know we should all answer to the Supreme Authority.

My question, at this time, is whether or not we should wait until we are dead and gone to do so. Bud may not let us.

I value Rachael's opinion highly. I do not yet know what she will suggest.

We put this behind us years ago or so we thought. It will come as quite a shock to her.

Behind it all, I have one thing hanging, and Bud is not moving on this. I cannot get him to answer.

How did he narrow down his list of suspects to the women? Perhaps, if we could find out, it might help us break down his case.

Any time now, I expect him to come to the door with a warrant. He is running out of time...Renwall wants his day in the press.

I guess when it is all said we have fooled ourselves all these years. We acted on the assumption right things could come from wrong deeds.

We broke the law to bring lawlessness to an end. We broke the laws of the State to bring law to the city.

We were successful, to a certain extent. Now, that which we desired above all else has turned on us, to consume us.

In an odd sort of way, by our own demise, we have been very successful.

May God have mercy on our souls.

To be continued:

Prof.AlexsandrSimon, Ph.D.

Chapter Twenty-Six

Grampy had everything set out in his den when Richard returned; Lalinduh, he explained, would be a few minutes behind him. It took Richard just a few minutes to set up his computer equipment and get ready to go to work.

Grampy had several stacks of documents, which he had arranged on the floor. He explained to Richard they would start with the stack on his right and work toward the left.

When things were in right order, the computer ready to go, Grampy asked Richard to accompany him to the porch where they would wait for Lalinduh. They went to the porch, sat down. Then Grampy explained, in generalities, what he had in mind.

"First, I want to go over some legal papers with you, Richard. I will leave it up to you if you want Lalinduh to listen in. I don't know how serious you are about her, but if she is in your future it cannot hurt for her to understand where I'm leaving you. I'm leaving just about everything I have to you, Richard, the house, the furnishings, the skiff, and everything else. Do with it what you will. Keep it, sell it...no strings attached.

I'm leaving you considerable holdings in stocks and mutual funds. Years ago, when you were born, I set up a Trust Fund...when you turn thirty, you will begin receiving monthly checks from that fund. At age forty, you will be able to cash it out, if that is your wish. You are not wealthy, Richard. But you will have some kind of measurable comfort for the rest of your life if you manage the assets.

There are two life insurance policies which combined will put roughly one hundred thousand dollars into your hands within days after my death."

"I...I don't know what to say, Grampy," he stammered, somewhat embarrassed.

"Say nothing. Nobody lives forever. I have had a very comfortable retirement, Richard. I have had an interesting life. I wish as much for you. Manage what I am leaving you, and you will be able to do as much or more for your own children. I would have done as much for your father and mother, God rest their souls." Grampy looked past him, at his beloved lake. "I have listed names and people to help you set things in order when the time comes. There's will be a smooth transition. I have made all the arrangements necessary for my funeral and burial. Complete instructions have already been sent forward."

"You know this is tearing me up, don't you?" said Richard. Tears dripped from his eyes.

"Yes. I do." replied Grampy. "Accept the inevitable, Richard. I have. There is one thing I want you to do."

"What's that, Grampy?"

"I'm to be buried beside your parents. I want you to pick out the headstone...something simple, no fancy stuff. Nothing to excess. Plain, not obtrusive. Maybe one of those bronze things they stick flat on the ground...or something."

"Sure, Grampy. Something plain and simple."

"Here she comes now, Richard. You really like her, don't you?" He looked past him again, at the approaching car.

Richard stood and turned to go out to meet her. "I do, Grampy. I'm going to marry her one of these days."

"Richard?"

"Yes?"

"Take time to know her. Don't rush into anything, okay?"

"Oh, I will, Grampy." He descended the steps and walked out to greet her. Grampy watched but could not hear what they were saying. Lalinduh got out of the car and handed Richard a newspaper, and she carried a second one. They walked, side by side, to join Grampy on the porch. Lalinduh exchanged a few pleasantries, then handed Grampy the second paper.

"Front page," she said.

Grampy opened the paper. "Two Unidentified Men Die in Bizarre Shooting Accident."

"Two unidentified men were found dead in what authorities described as a bizarre shooting accident at an old rifle range about fifteen miles outside of Nohartinit," Richard read out loud. "The bodies were discovered when a local resident, who has not been identified, went out to the range for target practice."

"Yak...yak!" said Lalinduh, totally disgusted. "Pardon my French...do you believe that shit!"

"What a crock!" said Richard.

Lalinduh read some more. "Police Chief Gary Renwall, who personally investigated the scene, said there was absolutely no evidence of foul play, and he said there would be no more information released about the accident until positive identification of the victims could be made. Neither of the victims was from Nohartinit, Renwall said. He deferred further comment until after his department has been able to properly contact and notify the next of kin."

"Saturday's paper," observed Grampy. "The story had to be set up Friday night to make the Saturday edition."

"Before the fact," said Lalinduh. "Grampy...what's going on?"

"Whatever it is," Richard grumbled. "Renwall's right smack in the middle of it!"

"This doesn't seem to bother you, Grampy? Why not?" asked Lalinduh.

"I expected as much," he replied. He put the paper aside. "You'll never see another word of any of it in print."

"The powers, Grampy?" queried Richard.

"Oh, yes. You don't have a clue how deep their influence is. But your understanding will change...very soon." He looked at Lalinduh. "You look a little more peppy than you did the last time we talked," he said, with a dry smile. "I hope I am not imposing on you."

"Of course not," she said. "I'm not exactly sure what I'm doing here, but it is not an imposition. I took a few days off after our backwoods misadventure. I needed some rest."

She hugged Richard. She looked into his eyes. She saw love there. "What am I doing here, anyway?" she asked.

"Grampy? I'm not sure myself. Can you fill us in?"

"Make yourselves comfortable. I will give you some background, and then we'll go inside. This is going to take a while, so get some drinks, or whatever. I'll wait."

They went inside and came back with soft drinks. They opened one and gave it to Grampy. They settled in, and Grampy proceeded with his stories.

Chapter Twenty-Seven

Memo: To Police Chief Gary Renwall
From: Det. Sgt. Bud Elbudro
RE: Jacob Lewski/ Mildred (a.k.a. Milly) Lewski

Chief Renwall,
It is my opinion sufficient evidence exists to convict Jacob Lewski on the charges pending. I have been in routine consultation with the specialists at County Memorial, and the man is, in their collective opinions, mentally incompetent.

I recommend the matter be turned over to the District Attorney for disposition. In truth, the man will never get past a competency hearing, and we should, at this time, consider the case closed.

In light of recent events, I believe we can find an agreeable resolution to another problem. In this other matter, the murder of Mildred Lewski a.k.a. Milly we have inconclusive evidence to file anything that will hold up. It is my firm belief, based on the information I have gathered over many months...and the confession given by Jacob Lewski, everything about the Mildred Lewski murder points to a gentleman by the name of Ralph Whalen, a former newspaper reporter for our local paper. There has been no sign of the man for many years, and no one seems to have any idea of his current whereabouts.

I recommend, for expediency and for other reasons, we close this case as well.

It would be convenient, I think, to tag Whalen as the perp and write him off as deceased. We both know there is some element of truth in this proposal.

Your dirty little secrets are safe with me.
Bud Elbudro
PS:I resign my position, effectively immediately.

Bud made an extra copy. Bud folded one memo, and placed it in an envelope. He addressed it to Chief Renwall. He sealed it.

He put the second in another envelope, already stamped.

He included a handwritten note:

Dear friend:

Your worries and mine are behind us now. I, too, love kids.

Don't worry about Detrick. He's off the case. He has a passion for the ladies...and I have the photographs to prove it. Good luck.

Bud.

He addressed it to Prof. Alexsandr Simon.

"Enough bullshit and lies to last a lifetime," he sighed. "I hate politics more than I hate those motherfuckin' drug dealers." He got up from his desk, and left his office. He dropped the envelope off with the Desk Sergeant. "Give this to that asshole Renwall when he gets back,...and drop this one in outgoing mail, okay?"

"Sure Bud," said the Desk Sergeant. "But the mail is already gone for today."

"Tomorrow...next few days...fine. No rush."

"Okay, Bud...heading home?"

"You betcha!"

He put his shield on the desktop.

"I'm going back to a small town in Maryland, from whence I came."

He turned to leave and then hesitated. He turned back to the Desk Sergeant. "You got a lighter?"

"Sure." He handed Bud his cigarette lighter.

"One last thing before I go." He took a cassette tape out of his coat pocket, stripped the tape out, and he lit it, holding it high like a piece of melting string.

He returned the lighter to the stunned Desk Sergeant. "Have you got kids, Sergeant?"

"A boy and a girl. Ten and twelve."

"They may never know it, Sergeant, but I just did them a favor." He tossed him the empty cassette cartridge.

"Whatever you say, Bud. I'll be sure to tell 'em."

Chapter Twenty-Eight

"Okay, now," said Grampy as he picked up the second set of documents. "These you will see are in chronological order. They contain accounts from the local paper going back several decades. Like this recent murder in the rifle range, these articles touch on and yet totally evade many events that could not be squelched completely. You'll find heart attacks, car accidents, and various accounts of accidental deaths. These people were usually in the way, knew too much, or openly tried to use the system to fight the powers. What you won't see in here are desecrated or burned out churches, trashed homes, and ruined lives."

"How are we supposed to use these documents, Grampy? Most people would see only old newspaper clippings...some rather routine and boring at that."

"They are not for most people...read them, boring or not. Look for closure...they all touch on the events and they never show up again. They will give you a clear picture of the depth of corruption in this town. Nothing has changed in decades." He handed the stack to Lalinduh.

"Now, the good stuff." He picked up the next stack of documents. "Lalinduh...this part I do not think you are acquainted with. There is a story here, about a little girl whose life was so corrupted by the powers she was eventually possessed and had to be destroyed by the powers that created her. Richard has some of the details. It is this story that will help you more than any others to break down the corruption inside the system.

The story is fantastic enough if you can go public with it, thoroughly documented, it will cut a path right down the middle of City Hall. I warn you both...give it all you have. Dot every i, cross every t. Lalinduh, your research skills will be invaluable here. Richard, I'm going to recommend a very strict format. Document just about every sentence if you can.

Richard has my file on this case. We have come across two recorded statements and photographs to back up my file. On top of that...this is a new one for you, Richard...we have an hour-long tape from an eyewitness to surrounding events that will chill you to the bone. You'll find it in my desk drawer."

"Grampy?"

"Yes, Lalinduh?"

"I really don't have time for this kind of project."

"Yes, you do. I have made time for you...if you want it. Years ago, a man...a General by the name of Perkins...put up a lot of money to find the root causes of corruption, violence, and things that make people go sour. Richard is familiar with the project."

"It is worthwhile, Lalinduh. Highly credible," said Richard.

"You two will have shared access to roughly forty thousand dollars in cash for expenses within days. With that kind of money, you two can take over where others left off. Richard can guide you through it. Quit the library, and tell no one what you are doing.

In a private matter Richard and I settled earlier you shall have access to an additional hundred thousand coming forward in a short time. After what you saw at the old rifle range, I didn't think you would be hesitant to do something about the corruption in Nohartinit."

"Slow down," she insisted. "You're tossing hundred dollar bills around like confetti. " She looked to Richard for an explanation. "I'm overwhelmed. I came here to visit...and now this?"

"Listen, Lalinduh. Maybe this does overwhelm you. A lot of this stuff Grampy is talking about is way over our heads right now. It is a chance, Lalinduh...one of those rare opportunities in life that comes your way. It can be a turning point for you...for us; it will alter the course of the rest of our lives."

"For the better?" Her huge brown eyes flashed expectantly. "You want me to quit my job to do this?"

"I won't beg you to help me. I'm in this thing and I have been for a while now. But I can't think of anyone I would rather have working with me," Richard said.

"Here's what it comes down to, Lalinduh," explained Grampy. "You are both basically decent people. One of these days...I hope...you will each get married, maybe to each other, and have children of your own. What I'm offering is that one opportunity to improve their world, not your world. When you get done with these files, the tapes, you will see a side of Nohartinit you would rather pretend does not exist. But it does exist. And it is eating people alive.

Every day I sit on my porch, I look at my lake, and I thank God each evening for it. I see the sky...I see the clouds...I see the pines. And I ask God in my prayers to forgive my transgressions, for I did my best to make this dust spot of a town worthy of His blessings.

If you two plan to stay in Nohartinit and raise a family here, you have a huge responsibility to discern good, to preserve good. That means you may have to fight this lost cause every step of the way."

"I'm not the hero type, Grampy. I'm just a librarian," she protested. "You're expecting me to be something I am not...and cannot

213

be. After what I saw out in the boonies, I'm scared to death of the powers!"

Grampy went to his tape player. He put in a tape. "I want you to listen to this," he said. "You are about to hear the voice of an angel. I hope after you hear this, you will change your mind." He turned on the recording, fast-forwarded it, and then stopped it. "Listen to this voice...to the tone...to the peace covering what must have been a terrible and horrifying existence. You can hear the rest later if you want to."

I was unofficially adopted when I was ten years old...a year before that a series of events took place which changed my life forever. Nohartini...was a vile and corrupt place...full of saloons and brothels and evil people and human misery...I never knew my real parents. From what I know of them, they were as vile and corrupt as any of them. They sold me into prostitution when I was but four or five years old, and they subsequently disappeared altogether.

There were other children who had met the same fate as myself.

There was a special room in the brothel where they kept a teenage girl, maybe fourteen or so, locked up. She was known as Crazy Girl, and from time to time, I could hear her violent tantrums through the door of that special room. We were warned never to go into that room under threat of painful punishment if we disobeyed. One day, foolishly, I sneaked the key to the room and let myself in. I found the girl cowered in a corner, trying to hide a late-term pregnancy. She had her head slouched downward, as if staring at the floor to hide her shame.

Grampy stopped the tape when he saw Lalinduh's reaction to it.

"Oh, my God! I know that voice! Oh, my God!" Lalinduh put her hands to her face as if it might help her hide from the reality of what she had just heard. She had obviously put the voice to the face to the name. "There's no other voice like that in the world! She's one of the nicest people you'd ever want to know...oh, my God!"

"You must never reveal her identity, Lalinduh...never!" begged Grampy. "They'd kill her, Lalinduh...they'd kill her. She knows too much."

Richard tried in vain to calm her.

"They'd do that?" Lalinduh demanded an answer. "They'd do that, Grampy?"

"And never blink an eye, Lalinduh. You must never reveal her name. Never. And they'd take out her family if she has one."

"It took a lot of guts for her to come forward," added Richard. "I don't have a clue who this woman is. But I could never doubt her sincerity...not in a million years. She's not a hero, Lalinduh. Just plain folks like you and me. She just did the right thing."

"Richard?"

"Yes, Grampy?"

"Once you transcribe the tape, lock it up somewhere. If Lalinduh knows the voice, others do, too."

"And the photograph?"

"Damn! To save this woman, you may have to scrap the pictures. The scar is more of a target than evidence. That goes for Mister Beecham's picture, also."

"It will weaken the case, Grampy," Richard warned. " It will break it down a lot. Maybe we can re-record with voice distortion."

"Damn!" Grampy growled. "You'll have to make the call, Richard," he said.

"I won't do anything that will compromise this woman...she has kids...grandkids, for God's sake! And she's got a great husband! A good job!" Lalinduh said.

"You're in, then?" asked Richard. "This is the kind of stuff Grampy and others have been fighting for decades."

"This stuff is sick and offensive! Damn right I'm in." Lalinduh wiped tears from her face. "It makes me want to puke just thinking about it...but I'm in. Those sons-of-bitches...who do they think they are anyway? Show me what to do...scared to death or not...I'll help you bring them down." She was angry now, a side of her Richard had not seen before.

"Okay," said Grampy. "Calm down. I have a plan. The story is so fantastic, it will draw a lot of attention to Nohartinit. What you'll have to do is put it together, in the most careful and professional way you can...then circulate it...in Nohartinit, in Mayberight, send it to every newspaper in the state...send it to the Governor, Senators, every preacher and Priest in the county. You'll have enough money to launch a massive PR campaign. We old folks tried to fight them locally...now, you young folks have the chance we never had...to hit them with outside influence and force some kind of action using public opinion and public outrage."

"Everything we need can be found somewhere in these files," explained Richard.

"Alexsandr knows what I'm doing, Richard," explained Grampy. "He downloading his records and files to floppies, and he will deliver them in a day or two. He's donated one of his computers to back up your system. He will stay on in an advisory capacity until the project is done."

"Alexsandr?" queried Lalinduh. "I don't know anybody named Alexsandr. Who is he?"

"A retired Professor. He used to teach upstate," Richard said.

"He's spent most of his adult years fighting these suckers," Grampy said. "He's got his own records which also go back several decades."

"Okay. I'm in. Tell me what to do? Am I supposed to just pack up my things, quit my job, and start digging through old files?"

"That's it in a nutshell," said Richard. "Don't forget...give up your apartment, too."

"You will be working here," added Grampy.

"Nobody knows what's going on here," Richard assured her. "You'll be perfectly safe."

"I've talked to Alexsandr, and we'll make sure things stay safe," added Grampy. "We'll set up a private room for you, furnish it, any way you wish."

"You'll be free to come and go as you see fit," Richard explained. "You'll have spending money. No strings attached. Absolute freedom...just help us...all of us...get these guys once and for all."

"Make up a shopping list...try to organize your work. Anything you need just write it down...you'll get it," said Grampy.

"I don't know anything about this kind of stuff."

"You've helped hundreds of people with research, Lalinduh."

"More like a dozen or two," she said. "I think I've met every student to pass through the so-called University in the last few years. There are fewer all the time."

"You can do it," encouraged Richard. "I have a lot of faith in you, Lalinduh."

"So, you and I, huh?" Lalinduh said, flashing a big smile. She hugged him. "I like that idea."

"Until we get blown away...sick to death of each other...or get married...whichever comes first."

"And you, Grampy? You'll be working with us also?" she asked.

"Right up to the very end," he said.

Chapter Twenty-Nine

Richard and, this time, Lalinduh:

I may ramble again; so be it. I'm old. You have to tolerate my inconsistent ways, Richard, because you have my blood in you.

Lalinduh, you ought to put up with my ways because you love my grandson.

Richard, I want you to love Lalinduh with all your heart. Let love rule your life.

If Lalinduh returns that love in kind, you two will be able to endure anything this world may throw your way.

Tonight marks a turning pint...the time has arrived for us of the old ways to make way for those of the new ways.

I am happy because, for the first time in many years, hope has been rekindled.

You and Lalinduh are about to collide with the corruption of the powers and you are well prepared. But, more than that, I watched you two at work for a couple of hours this evening.

You work very well as a team. You seem ideally suited to the task that lies before you. Unless there is some radical change of events, you have a wild chance you can beat them!

Praise God! At last...at long last...through you two very able young people it looks like the full story of Nohartinit's nasty, brutish, and evil past will be revealed in crisp and biting detail.

Do not despair; you have a lot of backup and support. I firmly believe, especially through the rebirth of Monica Lewski, not only will the originals be understood for what they did, but also they may be judged impartially and fairly by coming generations.

I feel a sense of calm after all these years. I thank you both for this.

You joined the struggle with new enthusiasm and energy, something the effort has sorely needed for a long time now.

I tried my best to explain to you what the Monica Lewski rebirth was all about. You have a clear picture of the powers now, and this will serve you well.

You have concentrated your efforts right now on reconstructing the tragic life and premature death of this hapless girl, Monica Lewski.

You understand most of the reasons behind the raid on Milly's.

You understand, in some small way, the nature of the death of Milly under the club wielded by Rachael Simon. You have accepted, I think, the context of the times, and have no hard feelings toward the part you are playing in protecting Rachael.

I am clinging to the hope Bud Elbudro will back down...for the sake of the children.

I do so wish I had been there with Skug when he spoke to my angel. I would have hugged her, I think, and I would have probably drenched her with tears of joy.

I thank God for His bringing her to light, in answer to my prayers. Protect her.

I know my time is short, but I can rest in peace now, and I am ready.

I want you to make arrangements for Alexsandr, Heinz, and Rachael to hear the tape, so they too can enjoy the feelings I now have. I am sure they will feel, as I do, our raid was not in vain.

It is a good thing you do not have to take the law into your own hands. We, the old folks, set that stage for you. When you hit, remember to hit hard and do not back down. You should save your best punches for the ninth round.

You can take on this war with your computers. Oh, how beautiful it will be!

Once you are prepared, in a matter of minutes, you will be able to put Nohartinit under scrutiny through every high political office, every spiritual institution, and every legal channel in the state!

What an odd thing it will be! Decades of persistent effort will culminate in a matter of minutes through your work and bring down...or at least severely cripple...the evil powers that be!

A couple of days it will take you to rough in what you have to do. Get your brief about Monica to Heinz as soon as you can.

I love the twist...you...for whom we expended all past efforts...will be the ones to redeem us!

I suppose that's progress at its best...we old folks can pass the torch and you young people can take the handoff and do more, in a tiny fraction of the time, than we did in decades!

Truth will out, they say. Have we, in Nohartinit, run the full circle and it is time for truth to prevail? Is it time for the forces of good to prevail?

It is reserved to God alone to create life from lifelessness. Yet we have resurrected Monica Lewski and through her, dead as she is, wrongs will be righted, evil will fall under the weight of good.

I know, in my swollen heart, it will be so.

In our own way, we have done the impossible; we will have successfully changed the sum total of who she was...and we will prove, in time, that it is never too late for distributive justice, that it is never too late to accept the fact that one plus one does, in fact, equal one.

By that equation and through your work...in the name of the Father and the Son and the Holy Spirit I pray for the soul of that dear tortured child and for my own soul that we are both in God's time redeemed and forgiven in His eyes and in the eyes of man.

Final entry.

With all my love...to both of you,

Grampy

Richard Cox

BOOK THREE

.

Chapter Thirty

They buried Grampy unceremoniously, just the way he had wanted, in the cemetery outside of town, in a plot next to Richard's parents.

The cemetery was situated on a few rolling hills, and dated back a long time. It had, at some time in the past, been cleared of all but a few stout and sturdy pines, and had been planted, somewhat successfully, with evergreen bushes, which were trimmed now and then by local volunteers, mostly old women with nothing better to do. Every now and then someone would volunteer time to mow around the graves, but more often than not the graveyard looked more like a pasture than a cemetery.

For the most part, small headstones marked the graves, and they peeked out over high weeds like petrified stumps. More visible were the occasional large and often gaudy monuments that marked the spots where moderately successful townsfolk were laid to rest.

There were several graves marked with flags, where local citizen soldiers had been put down, but one had to hunt around clumps of weeds and high grasses to find them. Several wars were represented. Every few years, the Nohartinit chapter of the VFW collected money to buy new flags for the graves, but there had been no recent replacements. Most of the flags were faded and tattered and torn, and looked more like overgrown weeds with water soaked tissue paper stuck to them than some testimonial to service.

As Grampy wished, Richard placed the order for a simple bronze memorial, a plate that would lie flat on the ground and bear the inscription, in a simple unobtrusive way:

GRAMPY
b. 1926 d. 2000

It was a warm and sunny day; Richard and Lalinduh stood over the freshly turned grave, and pondered the future and paid homage to the past. The rising sun cast their shadows over the grave.

Four days had past, and the newness of the loss was still very much with them. Trampled weeds around the site were beginning to rise up. Lalinduh knelt over the grave and picked out the wilted or dead flowers that covered the plot. Richard stared blankly at the turned earth.

Images in his mind fought for control of his senses:

He remembered Grampy in his casket, a simple gray colored, cloth-covered thing with a white satin lining. He remembered the phony-looking smile the undertakers had forced upon his face. He remembered the poor makeup work they had done.

Grampy had been buried in a brown suit, white shirt, and a very simple dark blue tie. At his request, only a few close friends had attended the service, and it lasted only a few short minutes. Father Wyman had said a few words, and then it was done.

Alexsandr, Heinz, Lalinduh, and Rachael, helped Richard serve as pallbearers, and they were assisted by one of the funeral home's employees.

He remembered after the service and before they closed the casket, Alexsandr had placed an opened envelope in the casket, the contents of which were not revealed. He said it arrived the day after Grampy died, and he said he knew he would have wanted to see it. Richard had asked what it was about, and Alexsandr had replied, with calmness, "It is a note from a mutual friend...in behalf of some children."

He remembered Rachael gently gripping his arm and looking into his eyes, saying, "Richard...if you need anything, don't hesitate to call."

He remembered the simplicity of the service, as Grampy had requested. He remembered the funeral director in his freshly cleaned suit, telling him, in a flat and monotonous tone, "Everything was prearranged. We've taken care of everything,"

"Lalinduh? Let's go home now," Richard said, sorrowfully.

She carried the dead and wilted flowers with her, to dispose of them in a more appropriate setting. Side by side they followed a narrow dirt path that led out of the cemetery back to the car.

"He knew, didn't he?"

"They say just before a heart attack, one becomes overwhelmed by an eerie feeling of impending doom. I don't think he died that way. Oh, yes, he knew his time was up. He was just waiting for closure."

"Closure?"

"He had two things in his life which kept him going. First, there was Monica Lewski...you know that story now. And the attack on Milly's...the fate of the children...you know that story, too. He wasn't going to die until these two points in his life found resolution."

"The voice of an angel," she recalled. "He knew then, didn't he...when he heard that tape."

"He knew. She released him."

Richard stopped and hugged Lalinduh. He looked into her huge brown eyes. "I love you," he said. "Thanks for standing by me."

They walked on, side by side, holding hands.

"And when you described her life...as it is now...kids, grandkids, a wonderful husband, a good job...remember? You were angry. He was elated. I saw it in his eyes as you were speaking. Take my word for it...he died a very happy man."

Lalinduh stopped. She tugged on Richard's arm and motioned him toward two fairly fresh graves, side by side. She walked toward them, and motioned for him to follow. At graveside, she divided up the dead and wilted flowers, and laid a small bunch on each grave.

"I have a funny feeling we have met these guys," she said.

"Hmm," he whispered.

"Okay, let's go now. Our business here is done," she said.

A car pulled up next to their car as they resumed their walk. From it emerged two men in business suits, Alexsandr and Heinz. They each carried a bouquet of flowers. Alexsandr carried red roses. Heinz had a mix of flowers. They waited for them.

"We thought we could find you here. We stopped by the house but you were gone, obviously. We've come to pay our respects."

"Heinz...I didn't know you had it in you?" said Richard. "You never struck me as the sentimental type." He noticed Heinz had even shined his cane for the occasion.

"Well, I am," he replied. He twitched his moustache. Richard could see tears forming in his eyes.

"Are you heading home now?" asked Alexsandr.

"Yes. We have work to do," Richard said.

"You'll find a package inside the front door...and a Thank You note from Rachael."

"How is she?" asked Lalinduh, sincerely.

"Sad for your loss, somewhat relieved by recent turns of events...and more determined than ever to keep at it."

"I hope the Monica Lewski packet helped you, Heinz?" asked Lalinduh.

Heinz grinned, widely. "As fate would have it, we didn't need it. But...the whole packet is tucked away in a safe deposit box...just in case. Excellent work by the way. I don't know how you guys pulled it off, but I was damn near convinced this Red-Eyed Boogie woman really did exist!" He smiled, widely. "No doubt about it, that was unquestionably the best scam Grampy ever dreamed up in all the years I knew him! I could have danced a jig around the prosecution. You bet!"

"How'd you guys do that, anyway?" asked Alexsandr. "I've got to hand it to you...the pictures, the tapes...it all seemed so real. Remarkable. Absolutely incredible."

"Well, for that Monica Lewski masterpiece, I owe you one," said Heinz. "Brilliant...no doubt about it!"

Lalinduh looked back at the two fairly fresh graves. She looked at Heinz. "You never know, we might call you on that," she said. A dry smile creased her lips. "We just might uncover something that will bring you back to town."

"Hmm," said Heinz. "I hope not...I hate Nohartinit." He shook hands with both of them. "I'm returning to Mayberight this afternoon. I'm getting a bad feeling about Nohartinit...like some dark cloud is about to descend and never rise again. I'll be glad to get back home. If ever I can help you with anything, don't hesitate to call." He sniffed the flowers in his hand. "All the papers are in order, Richard. If you'll excuse me now, I have some business to discuss with an old friend. Good luck to you both."

"I have business to discuss as well," said Alexsandr. He excused himself.

"Hmm," said Richard quietly. "Grampy used to say any time the three of them got together, some kind of problem was sure to find them. I wonder what it will be this time?"

"They sure are an odd couple of guys," commented Lalinduh, as she opened the car's passenger side door and got in. She closed the door. "They didn't believe any of it, did they?"

"Would you, if it came at you cold?" replied Richard. He stood for a moment before getting in. He watched as Alexsandr and Heinz placed their flowers on Grampy's grave. For some reason, it caught him by surprise when they both kneeled in prayer, Alexsandr on both knees and Heinz partially supported by his cane. "Hmm," Richard mumbled as he got in and closed the door. He started the engine, put the transmission in gear. "Lalinduh? Have you read anything in the paper or heard anything about any kind of shakeup at the Police Department? Anything at all?"

"Nothing at all. Why?"

"There's something going on...I'm just not sure yet what it is."

"If it spells trouble, I'm sure it will catch up to us, Richard. Let's go home, okay?"

They drove back to the house.

As they entered, Richard picked up a small brownish shoebox that Alexsandr had placed there. On the top was taped a note from Rachael, thanking them for their help. On the inside were floppy discs, lots of them.

"Heinz is sending us some stuff, also," said Richard, as he carried the box into their workroom. "I don't know about how you feel,

Lalinduh...I feel like we can really make a difference and turn this city around. I'm sure glad we are not locked in by any kind of extremely tight deadline."

"Why me, Richard?" she asked. "Why did Grampy want me in on this...why not Ladonna...or James and Stephy?"

"He liked you, Lalinduh. But more than that, he trusted you. He felt like you were the one."

"The one?"

"He wanted a woman's perspective, Lalinduh...someone detached from everything, who could look at things without being biased by personal events." Richard smiled, and he kissed her. He looked into her huge brown eyes, and he swept back her hair. "You know what he told me, not long before he died?"

"Tell me," she replied.

"He said you reminded him of somebody he cared for very deeply."

"Did he say who?"

"Apparently Alexsandr had a daughter who died of polio many years ago. This was the first time I'd ever heard her mentioned by anyone. Apparently Grampy had become really attached to the girl."

"Hmm," she mumbled.

"He asked me one evening not long before he died if you were busy. I wasn't quite sure what he meant. We were sitting on the porch, enjoying the sunset over the lake. He had that faraway look in his eyes like he was out there fishing. Anyway, he asked me if you had anything planned over the next few months or years. Of course, I had no idea what your plans were.

I said you probably planned to go to work every day, pay your bills, just like everybody else does, and he just smiled.

Then he asked me if I thought you might like a paid change of pace for a couple of years."

"And you said?"

"Ask her."

"He never did...I got recruited," she answered. "But why me? Why would he set it up for me like this? I mean...I don't understand. I hardly knew him except through the library...until you and I got together, that is. Let's go sit outside."

She headed outside, to sit on the porch. Richard followed her out. They sat down on the steps, and she looked absently out across the lake. "I can understand his wanting you to have the best opportunities he could give you? But why me...in many ways, I was a perfect stranger. We seldom talked much. He hardly knew me."

"I guess what he's doing for you, he would have done for Alexsandr's daughter if she were still alive. I guess he sort of adopted you. He left Alexsandr's son, Jeffery, a pretty decent Trust Fund. He provided Rachael with five thousand dollars to use for kids, no strings attached. He gave a thousand dollars each to people he never knew but only knew about…Donald Bell, and Associate Pastor Grayborn. I don't know how Grampy accumulated his wealth, but he had a small fortune stashed away. I think he inherited a goodly sum when his parents died, and he built on that." Richard looked across the lake. Then he looked back at Lalinduh. "He didn't have anybody but me…and his closest friends, Lalinduh. He told me he wanted to do something for some good people who might otherwise never get a foothold."

"I just feel kind of strange about it all, you know? I've never had much of anything in my life except parents who loved me very much. I was their only child, but we were poor. I don't know anything about not having to struggle for everything. I guess I'm just uncomfortable, that's all."

"Well, I hate to add to your discomfort, Lalinduh, But Grampy wanted you to have this." He took out his wallet and slipped a card from it. He handed it to her.

"A credit card?" she said, as she examined it.

"Actually…a debit card…sort of like a checking account. Grampy put five thousand in an account for you…no strings attached. He wanted me to wait for a few days after the funeral before giving it to you…for propriety's sake. You just call the bank to activate it. Just follow their instructions."

She broke into tears. Then she apologized for it. "I'm just not used to people being like this," she sobbed. "This kind of stuff is not supposed to happen in real life."

"It happens…you just never see anything like it around Nohartinit," explained Richard.

"So unexpected," she replied.

"He liked you, Lalinduh. He liked you a lot. That's all there is to it." Richard gave her a hug and wiped away her tears. "Grampy put a lot of money into what he considered good causes…lots of it. He loved money for what he could do with it, and he hated it for how people misused it for evil purposes."

Richard stood. He looked down toward Lalinduh and extended his hand. "Enough gloom and doom…let's take a walk by the lake…get our feet wet. Grampy would want us to keep going…keep on living. Tell you what…I know a great spot for skinny dipping, back behind the rocky point."

"Is that an indecent proposal, young man?"

"Hmm...could be."

She stood, and they started down the steps.

"There's a nice little cozy spot..."

"I know the place," she interrupted, as she walked. She hunched her shoulders playfully. She seemed almost embarrassed. Her huge brown eyes flashed. "Oops! I guess you didn't need to hear that, did you?"

"Hmm," he joked. He took her hand in his, and they headed for the edge of the lake.

They stopped for a moment at the water's edge, gazed absently at the skiff. Then they moved on, walking slowly, hand in hand, toward the rocky point.

They had gone a few yards when Lalinduh suddenly stopped.

She shivered, and then it passed quickly.

She looked around cautiously.

"What is it?" asked Richard.

"I'm not sure...I just had the strangest feeling...like something's going on we should know about," she replied. "Do you feel anything?"

"Kind of a cold creepy sensation? Kind of like something wrapping around you, trying to pass right through you?"

"Something like that," she said. "I don't believe in ghosts...this was something a lot bigger than some lowly shiver or something. More like some kind of evil spirit or something. That dark cloud descending, Heinz spoke of?"

"I felt it earlier this morning."

"I don't know...an omen...maybe my nerves or something. It has been a rough few days."

The sun was high now, and a very gentle wind brushed gently across the surface of the lake.

It was shaping up to be one of those days that Grampy would have liked, a perfect day for fishing.

Chapter Thirty-One

The next day, Alexsandr woke to a sluggish feeling, and to the ringing of the bedside phone. He answered it. On the other end of the line, a gruff-sounding voice gave him some information, which brought him around quickly.

"Alexsandr, the powers are in a real bad mood," the voice said.

"Are you sure?" Alexsandr asked.

"Yes. Very sure," the voice said. "Something big. Real big."

"I'll see you in about an hour, then?" He did not relish the news. He, like Heinz, had sensed something was amiss in Nohartinit, some specter of ill will the likes of which he had not felt in years. He knew, in his heart, something terribly wrong was about to descend upon Nohartinit, and he did not like it. All he had left to do was find out what was going on and act or react to events as they unfolded.

Rachael was not in bed beside him. He got up quickly and called for her. She answered from the kitchen.

"Are you okay, Rachael?" he called as he quickly put on a red and blue plaid robe and started, barefooted, toward the kitchen.

"I'm fine, Alexsandr," she said, as he entered the kitchen. She was wearing a brightly colored flowered housedress and sandals. She greeted him with a warm, loving smile.

He breathed a sigh of relief. Then he poured himself a cup of coffee, and he sat at the table. "Do you feel it, Rachael?"

"Feel what, Alexsandr?"

"Something cold...something kind of moving around, surrounding everything? A evil spirit?"

"Alexsandr, you're rambling this morning...did you not sleep well?"

He got up from the table, walked to the window above the sink, and he looked out. "Gray skies...looks like a storm moving in. A mean one."

"Maybe the barometric pressure is affecting you, Alexsandr. How's your blood pressure these days?"

"No...no...that's not it." He returned to sit at the table.

"I'll have breakfast ready in just a few minutes. Maybe you're just tense...after Grampy's death and all."

"No...no." He thought to himself: Come on, Alexsandr...you know this feeling. Think! Think!

"Alexsandr?" Rachael had placed a hand on his shoulder, and he had not responded, as if he was in a trance.

He looked up. "Just a minute...just a minute," he begged. "Give me just a minute!"

"Alexsandr? You're making me nervous, Alexsandr! What is it?"

"Good God Almighty. Rachael? Listen...don't argue. Say nothing!" he begged. "I have to think. Can you get in the car...find Ladonna...she's probably working...get her, tell her boss I'm real sick or something...whatever it takes...and Jeffrey and Sarah...get out of town...go to Mayberight...for a couple of days." He got up to get dressed.

"Alexsandr?" Rachael said. "Are you okay?"

"Rachael I don't care if you have to drag them kicking and screaming...get them out of Nohartinit for a couple of days."

"What's happening, Alexsandr?" she demanded.

"The powers are in a real bad mood, Rachael. Something big...very big. Things are going to get rough in the next few days. I want you all out of danger. Mayberight...two days...out of town."

"Okay...okay," she said, defensively. "I'm going. I'm going. They're going to think I'm crazy, Alexsandr," she said, defensively. "They don't trust your instincts as much as I do."

"Better crazy than dead! This time, Rachael, it isn't instinct. I just got a call. Make up something...give them a reason to leave town. Good God Almighty! Get going, Rachael," he demanded, fiercely. "Wait! You'll need some money...do you have any money?"

"In my purse, Alexsandr."

"Go...go! Use the credit cards if you have to." He was ready to shove her out the door, but she was heading that way. She was confused but not frightened, and did as she was told. She knew better than to challenge him on his eccentric behavior. And, she knew, if he said Mayberight, it had better be Mayberight.

She could not fathom even a wild guess what had come over him, but she knew when he said the powers were in a real bad mood it would be best to be away from Nohartinit. She also knew if Alexsandr said use the credit cards, it was something very serious that was afoot!

They had not used the code real bad mood in years. In the by-gone days, the Originals used it among themselves; a bad mood meant the powers were going to take some kind of enforcement action...trash someone's house or place of business, work somebody over, torch a church. It meant be extremely cautious and alert to danger. A real bad mood meant someone was going to die.

For a brief moment, Rachael recalled the fundamentalist church the powers had burned to the ground years back. She remembered how the

Pastor and his wife were beaten to within inches of their lives and left to die in the churchyard.

"Meet me...call me...in two days at Grampy's. Take everybody to Mayberight...get a motel room. Get going and don't look back. Two days, Rachael. Not one minute sooner! Don't come back this way...not for any reason...until I tell you it is safe. I'll get hold of you through Heinz, if you can't get me at Grampy's."

She knew if he said two days it had better be two days. She hurriedly gathered clothing to take with her. Before she left, she kissed him good-bye.

"Has everyone been notified?"

"It is in the works right now," he replied.

"Why are they doing this, Alexsandr? What's going on?"

"I don't know."

After seeing Rachael safely off, he returned indoors to dress. He dressed quickly, and, as if in some confused state of mind, he roamed from room to room, as if chasing some imagined intruder. As he moved about, he mumbled to himself, time and time again: "Those crazy sons-of-bitches! Those crazy sons-of-bitches! What's their next move? Think, Alexsandr! Think!"

He was, in actuality, looking for his watch. He found it in the bathroom.

He then went into the basement to his computer room. He pulled up a file, and sat down to study it, mumbling: "Put it together, Alexsandr...come on, you can do it! You can do it!" About a half-hour passed.

"Alexsandr?" a voice called. "Alexsandr? Are you here, Alexsandr?" It was a deep and gruff-sounding voice, with a deep bass resonance to it.

"Down here...in the basement," he called back. He heard the heavy footsteps as the person came down the steps.

Alexsandr did not look back; as if he had eyes in back of his head, he greeted his visitor: "I didn't expect you so soon, Father...you feel it, too? Pull up a chair, Father...see if we can't figure this out."

Father Wyman pulled up a chair and sat next to Alexsandr. He was a huge man, big enough to be a professional football player, maybe a guard or a tackle. He had pitch-black hair, and dark eyes. He was wearing black slacks, a blue short-sleeved shirt. To look at him, no one would ever guess he was a preacher. He put a reassuring hand to Alexsandr's shoulder. "Try to relax," he said. "I got the word out."

Without looking at his visitor, Alexsandr explained he had sent Rachael for Ladonna, Jeffery, and Sarah.

"What did you tell Rachael?"

"Two days, no more and no less,...I sent them to Mayberight."

"I love these computers," Father Wyman said. "Too bad they can't save souls." He looked on. "Let's see what we've got, Alexsandr."

"First, we need to figure out their timeframe...then their operative moves."

"They put things into motion yesterday, about mid-day, Alexsandr. That gives us another twenty-four hours at the most."

Alexsandr typed in the information. "Are we looking at a skirmish or an all-out war, Father?"

"Lots of fancy black cars passing through town, Alexsandr. I think we're in for something rather substantial."

Alexsandr typed in the information.

"Is it in-fighting...or are they unified?"

"They are not rank and file, Alexsandr. I think they're carving up the town...for future reference."

"You do get around, don't you, Father?"

"That's my job, Alexsandr."

Alexsandr typed in the information. "Anything else?"

"They brought their Real Estate team with them, Alexsandr."

"Oh, man." Alexsandr groaned. The implications were discouraging. He typed in the information.

"Anything else?"

"No."

"I hope we did this right, Father...I hope this program works." He hesitated an instant, then he pushed the ENTER button. "This will take a few minutes," he said. "There's fresh coffee upstairs."

They got up and headed out of the room. Alexsandr stepped aside for Father Wyman to go out first. Then he followed him upstairs and into the kitchen.

"To the porch?" asked Father Wyman after he poured himself a cup of coffee.

"After you," replied Alexsandr.

Outside things were brewing for a nasty storm. The sky was darkening, the winds was starting to gust. The temperature was falling.

"Why now, Father?"

"To be honest, Alexsandr. I think it has a lot to do with the man you helped nab for the murder of the fellow downtown, the County Memorial case, Jacob Lewski. I understand he talked about some pretty heavy-duty stuff. They may feel threatened, maybe even vulnerable."

"How's he doing, anyway? Heinz was blocked when he tried to get through to him."

"You haven't heard? He's dead. Officially, he drank a bottle of bleach during an insane rage. We know, of course, he knew too much. His talking may have triggered all this, Alexsandr."

"Any other casualties?"

"No. They had a mysterious fire in the County Memorial records room. No one was hurt."

"I wish I had never heard the name of Jacob Lewski," mumbled Alexsandr. "Nothing but trouble...trouble...and more trouble."

"This is big, whatever it is."

"No clue what they're going to hit?"

"No clue." Father Wyman sipped his coffee. "Do you think he said enough to open up any kind of large-scale investigation, Alexsandr?"

"Whatever he said, I assure you, will not be on record anywhere. I know these guys. You know these guys. They're thorough and unscrupulous. I also know they won't take any chances. I can feel it, Father. I can feel their evil intentions."

"And...it is something big, Alexsandr. Really big."

"Do you think they're going to take it back?"

"I don't know. If they feel threatened, there's no telling what the next move will be." Father Wyman shifted his weight forward in the chair. "Is there anything going on I should know about, Alexsandr?"

"Maybe Jacob Lewski told enough stuff in front of enough people to make it impossible for them to cover it up."

"Alexsandr...don't stall me. Is there anything going on I should know about?" Father Wyman growled.

"Jacob Lewski named names, Father...they know the names of at least half-a-dozen of the originals that I know of. It is just a matter of time before they hunt us all down. Bud Elbudro put the pieces together. They will, too. This is the first time in all these years the names have come out. Do you know the implications?"

"By the time they figure out how many of us there are, how many connections we've made along the way, they may have no choice but take it back...their way."

"Jacob Lewski knew quite a bit...I heard the confession tape, Father. No telling what else he said."

Father Wyman sipped his coffee again. He put the cup aside. "You could be in real danger, Alexsandr...along with a lot of other people." He looked out toward the rumbling heavens. "Tell me this: Have you concentrated your records or anybody else's in a single location? Is there a central data bank, Alexsandr?"

"Yes. But it is a secure location."

"No, Alexsandr. You underestimate these people."

"They'll never find them, Father," Alexsandr said. "You didn't know about them, did you?"

"Nonetheless, you better warn your people. Tell them to stand by, be ready for just about anything."

"How far in is your guy, Father?"

"Far enough," he answered. "The man's got nerves of steel, Alexsandr, but he's going to have to bail pretty quick before he blows his cover. Things are heating up...fast. I've already made arrangements to get him out of town on quick notice. The old network is still intact."

"Well, let's check back with our program, Father. Maybe it will have something solid for us. My bones are telling me it is going to be a rough storm...I'll be aching for a week," Alexsandr complained.

They went back to the basement, returned to their seats in front of the computer screen.

"Hmm," said Father Wyman. "Looks like a bust, Alexsandr. There's nothing substantial here...just a few odd businesses not already in their pocket. They have no use for these places, Alexsandr. They're not even in good locations."

Alexsandr typed in a few lines, and he pressed ENTER. "Let's see if there is any kind of pattern."

"No commonalities. No, Alexsandr. This is small time stuff. They didn't bring in their Real Estate team to monkey around with small time stuff."

"Okay. Let's try this." He typed in a few more lines. He pressed ENTER.

"Hmm," said Father Wyman. "Every available parcel in town plus the small stuff wouldn't add up to a hill of beans."

"Okay, Father. Let's look at it." Alexsandr leaned back in his chair and swiveled to face his friend. "They've got the newspaper, grocery stores, the gas stations, the bars, the pawn shops, the drug traffic, most of the back side of Main, a big chunk of the bank, and they hold the notes on just about every house, car, truck, boat, or business in town. They own City Hall and half of the police force. There's nothing left? When you have that kind of hold, what more can there be? What are they after, Father?"

"Hmm," he answered. "That's a good point, Alexsandr; let's look at it from the opposite direction. We know what they have in Nohartinit. They've got their claws into everything except the chemical plant...and the people who work there...they've got power, Alexsandr." Father Wyman pondered the situation. "But...not control. That's what they want Alexsandr...they're fighting for control...of the people, Alexsandr. If the stuff gets out...the stuff Jacob Lewski talked about...people will be upset, even angry. Maybe they fear political repercussions. That's got to be it, Alexsandr. It is not about power...they have that...it is about control."

"They can't run the risk of the good guys winning...it could upset the whole power structure." Alexsandr was thinking about the +1 personalities and their desperate need for power...and control...at any cost.

"There's talk of the chemical plant expanding again...bringing in a lot more people...maybe enough to shift the balance; if enough bad publicity hit at the same time the new wave came in, it could have some huge political implications."

"Is that it, Father? Do you think they're going after the chemical plant?"

"They don't have enough money to get it, Alexsandr," he answered. "I mean they're big...granted...but not that big. They couldn't touch it. It has to be something else." Alexsandr gave it some thought.

"There's nothing important enough around Nohartinit to expend their efforts on. They've already gobbled up everything that's worth anything. Maybe they're moving into Mayberight."

"No," Alexsandr insisted. "They want Nohartinit. Why would they move into Mayberight? Think bigger than that, Father...we're assuming a peaceful legitimate takeover of the chemical plant. We both agree that they could not do. Ask yourself this, Father...suppose they wanted everything...every square inch of a whole city...dirt-cheap? How would they do it?"

"Unthinkable, Alexsandr."

"Why? Because we don't think on that scale...and we consider consequences...and we see people's lives at stake?"

"It just doesn't make sense, Alexsandr." Father Wyman insisted. "They wouldn't...they couldn't...get rid of the chemical plant if they had to. Besides that, what good would a city be without an economic base? They'd have control, sure...of a ghost town."

"Oh? Tell me, Father...what would happen to Nohartinit if all of a sudden the entire payroll at the chemical plant quit flowing?"

"The whole city...would...collapse, Alexsandr. In a matter of a few months."

"Who would call in the notes, Father? Who would pick up just about every piece of Real Estate in the entire city...for the proverbial song? Who could hang while every small business and working stiff slowly went belly up?"

"No, Alexsandr...I can't go there. The whole idea is preposterous and absurd." Father Wyman scratched his chin. He looked back at the computer screen. He looked back at Alexsandr. "Like I said...they'd have control of a ghost town. It doesn't make sense."

"The object here is control, Father...not common sense. Not economic sense. Control...power and control."

"You're telling me they would ruin the entire city just to get control of the remnants? Control for the sake of control?"

"Yes. That's exactly what I'm telling you, Father. You're looking at homes and people...families. Men and women and children. They're not. We just need to figure out how they're going to do it...and then figure out a way to stop them...if we can."

"My man says something really big is coming down, Alexsandr. Tomorrow, whatever it is, we'll know about it."

"That's the best he could give you?"

"That's it."

Alexsandr typed in a few more lines and pressed ENTER. "We don't have a lot of time, do we?"

"Not enough."

"We have to try."

"What are you looking for now, Alexsandr?" Father Wyman propped his chin in his massive hands, resting his elbows on his knees.

"I'm going to try to run a damage estimate in dollars; if something happened to the chemical plant, it might be possible to project the economic impact. If we run jobs times the average monthly income and cross that with the total economic picture, we can get an idea if the whole thing is feasible. They would not dare do anything to the plant if the impact could not collapse everything."

"You're groping, Alexsandr."

"Any better ideas? Maybe we can eliminate the plant as a possibility, if nothing else." He read a page, and then cancelled it. He typed in a few more lines.

"Now what are you looking for, Alexsandr?"

"I want to put some faces or names behind all this stuff, Father. We've never gotten close enough to these guys to even know who they are. We've been calling them the powers for decades now...and nobody knows who they are."

"Is that important, Alexsandr?"

"It just occurred to me I've hated these sons-of-bitches all these years and I don't even know who the hell they are! Think about it, Father...we know what they're capable of, we've witnessed atrocities, we've been chipping away at the graft and the corruption, but never once, not in all these years, have we had so much as a potshot at any one of them."

Outside thunder rumbled now, and rain began to fall. The pounding of the rain reverberated in the basement hallway.

"They're untouchable, Alexsandr. Think about it: It is like they're invisible. They exist, but nobody knows where they are, who they are, how they do what they do." Father Wyman sighed. He shook his head. "Frustrating, isn't it, Alexsandr? Even the black car guys are not the top dogs. It is entirely possible, Alexsandr, that not a living one of the truly powerful has ever laid eyes upon Nohartinit or even been within a thousand miles of this place."

"That would mean everything we've ever tried to do has been in vain, wouldn't it, Father?"

"Ah, Alexsandr," he answered somewhat sadly. "It often seems like that; I never seem to make any headway. The majority of people in Nohartinit have ruined souls. For every poor snook I pull off the streets, there are two or more to take his place. The numbers are expanding exponentially. We're past the point of no return. I just pray every day and go back on the streets. I never ask myself if the good guys are winning or losing...we lost, Alexsandr, a long time ago...I take it one day...and one person...at a time."

"Father...is that good enough?"

"I don't know, Alexsandr...but that's all I have to give. I dream that maybe someday enough people will wake up, break free of their illusions and change this city. Until that happens, I do what I can."

"Let's go back outside, Father. I'll let this thing run the numbers. I want to watch how this storm is developing. Maybe we'll have a flood and it will wash away the problems."

They went back for more coffee then went back to the porch. Father Wyman seated himself and sipped his coffee. He seemed to be reflecting on events, ignoring the onslaught altogether. Rain pounded heavily on the roof of the porch. "Did Heinz have much time to look things over?"

"Oh, yes," answered Alexsandr. "I trust his opinion, Father. He say there's nothing substantial, from a legal perspective, strong enough to warrant any kind of investigation. Nobody's pinpointed, there's no decent paper trail, nothing strong enough to even make it into a subcommittee. I think our legal route is closed. He says our only option is an appeal to the people on moral grounds; he laughed at the possibilities of that option. We've got to get names, Father...who the hell are these guys?"

"Hmm," answered Father Wyman. "Right now I feel like Noah must have felt...we may have no choice, Alexsandr, other than just sit here and watch Nohartinit float away." He sighed. "If the numbers don't look right and it isn't the plant, Alexsandr, what is it?"

"The bank, maybe?"

"They're going to rob their own bank?" Father Wyman chuckled. "They don't want any Feds snooping around, Alexsandr."

"Damn! I don't know." Alexsandr looked around, at the rain falling in sheets, at the trees bending with the wind, at the dark clouds taking complete control of the sky. "But...but," he stammered. "We can't just sit here."

"Why not, Alexsandr? I've given it a lot of thought lately. We can watch the storm. Look at it this way Alexsandr...do you think for one minute you can step off the porch, look up, mumble a few feeble words and make this storm back off? That's kind of what we're up against, Alexsandr. Forces and powers so far beyond the control of any of us, we can't do anything but roll with the flow, so to speak. It was a losing battle from the very beginning...we just didn't know it."

"So...what's your solution, Father? Sit here and do nothing?"

"Walk away from it, Alexsandr. Retire. You've done your part. Give it to the young people...let them handle it from now on...if they can." He sighed. "We're getting old, Alexsandr."

"What are you saying, Father?" Alexsandr moved to stand at the porch railing. He put his hands on the rail and hunched over. "Are you saying give up the fight?"

Father Wyman smiled; it was weak and resigned. There was a certain melancholy reverberation in his voice. "We have overlooked another possibility, Alexsandr. We're too old, too set in our ways to accept it. The good guys lost a long time ago, but we refused to believe it. After all these years...what progress have we made? Maybe nobody wants anything to change...maybe they're content to let Nohartinit rot from within. Maybe they like it just like it is, Alexsandr. Our cause is just as dead as their souls...and has been for decades."

Alexsandr listened, without comment.

"Do you think you could mobilize enough people to make any changes, Alexsandr?"

"I doubt it...nobody cares, do they?"

"Oh, a tiny few, Alexsandr. But times have changed. There's no sense of unity...no sense of shared purpose. Those are by-gone things, like you and me. The old church, the old faith, the old moral codes are dead, Alexsandr. What I see every day on the backside of Main is what there is. That's all there has ever been."

"Have you given up hope, Father?"

"For Nohartinit? Yes. We're done here. There's no love here." He frowned. "There's a time to get real, Alexsandr. We've met it. We should have seen it years ago." Father Wyman stood, walked to the porch railing, and he put his hands on the rail and hunched over. He looked absently into the storm. Misty remnants of blown rain blew against him. Then, calmly, he looked back at Alexsandr, his dark eyes shining. "Did it ever occur to you, Alexsandr...we are the ones living in the illusion...the dreamland...the new never-land? What you see out there is all you get, Alexsandr. Face it, old buddy...the good guys lost...a long, long time ago. We simply held onto the struggle because we could not live with the idea we lost our Holy War. We let the struggle justify and define our existence. It is time to move on. We don't fit in anywhere any more, Alexsandr. Read Proverbs 21:16, and think about it." Father Wyman extended a hand. "I better go now, Alexsandr. There's probably a drunk or an addict waiting for me somewhere on the backside of Main. You ought to give serious thought to joining Rachael as soon as possible. Leave town, Alexsandr."

Alexsandr clasped the huge hand. "You be careful." Then Father Wyman walked into the storm, and Alexsandr watched until he got into his car and drove away. Low-level thunder, extremely loud and threatening, shook the house. Alexsandr shook his head in disbelief, lowered his eyes toward the floor. In a moment he raised his eyes again, and looked blankly into nowhere. "Proverbs 21:16?" he mumbled. He remembered the many hours he had spent as a boy trying to memorize Proverbs. "Ah, yes, I'm sure it fits, Father." He went inside, and he picked up his Bible. He carried it to his bedroom, where he laid down upon his bed. He opened his Bible to Proverbs, and he read the passage quietly: "...the man that wandereth out of the way of understanding shall remain...in the congregation...of the dead." And to that he said, "Amen."

He put the Bible aside. Then he fluffed his pillow, laid his head back; he was determined to meditate, storm or no storm, come what may. He knew he would not rest easily, for he had a problem: By presence alone, the powers had a hold on him; he had fought them for so long, it had never occurred to him until now he had removed truth from his own equation. Now, he knew, with certainty, he and the others had won a few battles...but they had lost the war.

The thunder and the pounding rain reverberated through the house, rattling window panes and shaking the house, and it seemed to Alexsandr the storm was increasing in severity. The thunder seemed to be rolling, like a continuous roaring beast. "This storm's going to do some damage somewhere," he mumbled, as he closed his weary eyes.

If he had gone back to the porch, had he stared into the sheeting rain, had he listened to the thundering noise a little more closely he would have been drawn to the sounds of a mighty blast and explosion, and he would have seen a huge fireball boiling up hundreds of feet into the stormy sky...from the chemical plant. If he had watched a little longer he would have seen secondary explosions as they leaped from tanker car to tanker car, right through the middle of town; the tanker cars exploded one by one, taking out everything for hundreds of yards on either side of the tracks by concussion, by huge shards of steel plating streaking through the darkness like fireworks, and by rivers of fire...cars, homes, buildings, people...as if the train had supernaturally transformed in a matter of minutes into a huge groaning and bucking fire belching serpent hell-bent on a wild undiscriminating rampage.

It was only when the warning system was tripped at the fire station did Alexsandr realize something was wrong...terribly wrong. Wrapped in the pitch black and noises of the ferocious flailing storm, straining to hear against the blaring seemingly desperate wailing of the warning sirens, against the puny sounding sirens of fire trucks, ambulances, and police cars, against the earthquake-like trembling and groaning of the ground, Alexsandr struggled to comprehend what was happening. He got up to go outside and see for himself.

At the same time not far outside of town, standing akimbo on an overlook, silhouetted by the raging flames, Father Wyman looked down upon the spectacular inferno.

Had Alexsandr been at his side, he may have concurred with Father Wyman's terse assessment. Father Wyman's face was aglow with a certain satisfied feeling that reached deep inside. His eyesight was blurred by tears...of joy. He was drenched but seemingly oblivious to the rain that pelted him. It was a moment of bittersweet triumph for Father Wyman, one of those singular moments in a man's lifetime when his work comes to fruition. He saw not a disaster, but an opportunity to rebuild.

"I could feel it coming," he whispered. He got down on his knees and bowed his head to humble himself in the eyes of God. Then he summed it up, as he saw it: "I'm not saying it is...I'm not saying it is not, but it looks to me, Dear Lord, like Nohartinit's Judgment Day," he whispered. "Dear God...have mercy on their souls."

Epilogue

It was one of those days, toward the end of summer, when the sun tried to broil everything; even the wind off the lake was hot. Not a cloud was in the sky to block the sun, if only for a few minutes. Richard and Lalinduh, both wearing shorts and white tee shirts, sat quietly on the porch, drinking cold beers from large glass bottles. They had not had many, and neither was drunk. Just trying to cope with the heat for now, they waited patiently for sundown so they might take a leisurely stroll along the strand.

They had completed the Monica Lewski story, and had contacted a friend to write it. They connected him with the principals involved in the story. They hoped it would be in circulation soon. They decided it would be better late than never. People were looking for answers. No one knew what to expect.

For weeks now, they had been in constant contact with Alexsandr, by phone, fax, and e-mail; they were working closely with him to perfect the +1 scenario. The other material was in storage. Alexsandr and Heinz had convinced them it was fruitless; lacking names to attach to the crimes, it was useless.

Not far around a bend in the lake road, Alexsandr was building a cabin, and he would soon be their neighbor; it was far enough along now, he and Rachael and sometimes Ladonna spent occasional weekends there. Alexsandr was to have a neighbor, too: Father Wyman. Ladonna and David had gone their separate ways, and she was helping Alexsandr with the +1 scenario. Jeffery and Sarah had moved to Mayberight to open a computer store.

As they sipped their beers, they watched as a solitary silver-colored old Ford sedan wound its way around the perimeter of the lake. It was far enough away they could not identify the occupant, and they did not recognize the car. A thin trail of dust kicked up behind the car and floated off in the wind and heat waves.

In a few minutes, the car pulled up in front of the house. A man, wearing dark shorts, a light, sweat-drenched tee shirt, and grubby once-white tennis shoes with no socks got out of the car. He had a very expensive camera hung around his neck. He was sweating profusely.

He was a thin fellow, with bony-looking pale white legs. He had light hair, blue eyes, and a smile that seemed big enough to cut his face in half. He identified himself as Chester Wilkerson, freelance photographer.

243

They invited him to join them on the porch, and he accepted. Lalinduh went into the house to get him a beer.

"So, Mister Wilkerson," asked Richard. "What brings you out this way? As lakes go, this one is not especially scenic. Just a lake, you know. There's a nice little cove behind that rocky point, but that's about it."

"Oh, I'm not here to photograph the lake...I'm going into Nohartinit. I'm doing a photo study of the old chemical plant; a mutual friend passed along your name...you are Richard Politnitroff, aren't you?" He did not wait for an answer, but paused long enough to wipe sweat from his brow. "He thought you might have some background information for me...you being a writer and all?"

"A mutual friend?"

"Bud Elbudro...used to live around here...worked as a cop?"

"I know Bud...how is he these days?"

"Fine."

"His family?"

"Fine."

Lalinduh brought him the beer, and she seated herself beside Richard. Richard told her he was a friend of Bud's.

"How do you know Bud?" she asked.

"From time to time I do some photography work for him. Sometimes historical stuff. Sometimes crime stuff. Nice guy. He's working freelance these days, based in a small town called Buckysville in Maryland. He is trying to put together two books at the same time. One is a history book of some kind, and the other is a story about a cathouse murder. He gives me crime scene access, and I give him historical stuff. I make a lot of money with pictures of blood and guts...that's people for you."

"Why would Bud still be interested in a burned-out, God-forsaken place like Nohartinit?" asked Richard. "Why would a guy like you want to photograph the place? There's nothing left but bars, brothels, and crack houses. No decent person even goes through there any more if they can avoid it."

"No. Not the town...the chemical plant. Bud got wind of the tragedy a few weeks ago. The place blew up or something a couple of months ago?"

"The chemical plant?" replied Lalinduh. "There's nothing left but a burned out rusting shell, twisted concrete, and a string of blown apart-tanker cars that took out half the town. Nobody even bothered to clean up the mess."

"Well, you know Bud. He seems to think there's a story there." Mister Wilkerson smiled again. "Can you tell me what happened?" He sipped the beer cautiously.

"There's nothing to tell, really. By all accounts, during an especially heavy storm a few months back, lightning struck a critical storage area and ignited a chain of explosions. The explosions jumped to the tracks, blew up tanker cars on the railroad tracks. The explosions traveled right down the tracks, from one tanker car to the next. In a matter of a few hours, half the town was either burned up or blown to hell and back; dozens of people ended up dead or injured. Nohartinit blew up and what didn't blow up burned up, Mister Wilkerson. It was a major natural catastrophe. Some called it an act of God."

"You can see the craters where the tracks used to run, where the tanker cars exploded, Mister Wilkerson; you can see them from the highway," said Lalinduh. "Some of them are thirty feet deep."

"Nohartinit looks like the Air Force used it for bombing practice," added Richard. "There's nothing to see that hasn't made most of the papers for miles around."

"That's the official version of what happened?"

"Official version, Mister Wilkerson?" quizzed Richard. He sipped his beer. "Would you be implying there's more to it than that?"

"Oh no...no,no,no. Not me," he said, defensively. "You know how Bud is..."

"Tell me, Mister Wilkerson?" insisted Lalinduh. "He's got a different version, I suppose?"

"Can we keep it between the three of us?" He sipped his beer. "Bud said you could be trusted."

"We are trustworthy, Mister Wilkerson," replied Richard.

"Well, Bud seems to think it was sabotaged. He says there was a connection between some two-bit hood who stole a case of dynamite from a construction site and some powerful people who wanted the chemical plant gone. And he intends to prove it. He wants me to get photographic evidence. That's why I'm here. This isn't a sightseeing tour."

Richard chuckled. "Good luck, Mister Wilkerson. That's a splendid hypothesis, I guess."

"Listen," said Lalinduh somewhat impatiently. "People around here lost a lot of friends and family members in that explosion and fire. They've dispersed and most would not look kindly on anyone bringing that disaster back to the forefront. You tell Bud he ought to leave things alone, as you should, Mister Wilkerson."

Mister Wilkerson sensed his welcome had been exhausted. "One other thing. Bud said you were writing sort of a history of Nohartinit...he wants a copy when you're done. If you get me a pen I'll give you his address."

Lalinduh went inside and returned with an address book. "I'll write it," she said.

He gave them the address. "I've got to get going. I may need good light." He sat the beer on the porch, then changed his mind and decided to take it with him. "Thanks," he said.

"No problem," said Lalinduh. "Would you like one to chase it?"

"No. This will be just fine. Thank you, anyway." Mister Wilkerson headed back toward his car.

"Mister Wilkerson?" called Richard.

He turned to look back at them.

"If you're smart, you won't spend the night in that hellhole...Mayberight is about twenty miles on down the highway."

He waved good-bye, got in his car, and started the engine. He turned around, and headed back out the way he had come in.

"Strange little guy, isn't he?" said Lalinduh.

"Wait 'til Alexsandr hears this...he'll bust a gut," said Richard, as he tipped the bottle to his lips.

"Wouldn't that be a kick if Bud really was on to something?" said Lalinduh, casually. "Even so, it ought to be left alone."

"A nutty idea, even for Bud," said Richard. "Why in the hell would anyone sabotage the only decent place of employment Nohartinit ever had? It makes no sense, Lalinduh. No sense at all."

"I guess you're right, Richard. What's done is done...there's no going back." She wiped sweat from her forehead. She sipped her beer. "Boy...is this heat ever going to let up? I feel like I'm sitting in a convection oven."

"Give it a couple of hours...let's go swimming later, you want to?"

"Past the rocky point?"

"Sure. Why not? I know this cozy little place just on the other side of the rocky point..."

"I know the place," she interrupted, with a wide grin. "They say it is a great little spot for skinny dipping, Mister Politnitroff."

He smiled, and he nodded his approval. "Is that an indecent proposal, Mrs. Politnitroff?"

With that said, they finished their beers in silence; after that, they went indoors, holding hands lovingly, to get out of the heat for a while and take care of some personal...and intimate...business.

The End

About the author

Richard Cox, the third of four children, was born in Mobile, Alabama, in 1948, but grew up in and around Frederick, Maryland. He was educated in the public schools of Alabama, Maryland, and California. After four years in the Army from 1968 to 1971, he returned to school; he got his Bachelor's Degree in English from California State University at Sacramento and his Master's Degree in Education from Southwestern College, in Winfield, Kansas. He broke into print in the early 1970's, and, since then, he has authored dozens of articles and several books.

Mister Cox resides in the small town of Cedar Vale, Kansas. He works full time as both a freelance writer and substitute teacher.